ALL YOU NEED IS MYTH

Editing & Illustrations: Dave Randall

Research: Jade Sylvan

Cover Art: Landon Elmore

ALL YOU NEED IS MYTH

The Beatles and the Gods of Rock

STEVE WAGNER

Waterside Publishing

Printed in the United States of America

First Printing, 2019

ISBN-13: 978-1-941768-96-9 print edition
ISBN-13: 978-1-941768-97-6 eBook edition

 Waterside Publishing

2055 Oxford Ave
Cardiff, CA 92007
www.waterside.com

For Jack.

TABLE OF CONTENTS

FOREWORD

It is late at night. We are listening to music with friends. Our imaginations drift into the worlds of song stories. Gradually, our responses spill into conversation. The lyrics seem to be getting at something we have been thinking about. The phrases help us find words to express ourselves.

Most of us have had serious late-night discussions about the implications of some phrase that seemed enormously significant at the time. Those conversations really were important. The music of our lives is worthy of careful attention.

The 1960s represent an essential chapter in the story of rock music. That era represents a shift in the role of popular culture in the shared experience of the spiritual imagination. Those affected by the legacy of that decade have participated in cultural shifts fueled by the creative powers of songwriters. Poets have always been guides in times of radical change. One of the many gifts of the period was how popular music became significant literature.

Songs can be transformative. They affect a person's inner life and worldview in ways that can last a lifetime. It is worth our time to consider how and why the music of the sixties, especially the Beatles, has had such a lasting personal impact. The hits of that era became some of the best-known melodies on the planet. It seemed as if we were all united by some mysterious alchemy done in recording studios. The lyrics took on weightier topics than those that came before.

The words are now so familiar that we might have missed some wisdom hiding in plain sight. The mythic imagination is the power of metaphor to transmit greater meanings beyond an image or story. It is the use of fiction to get at profound truths. Taking a mythic perspective on pop music is an opportunity to explore hidden elements that influence our perspectives. A well-crafted ballad can put us in touch with unseen beauty. The brief stories deal with tough personal issues. The narratives touch on the same universal qualities as high art forms, like opera or drama.

Such condensed emotional expressions can speak to us in several ways at once. The practical aspects of our personalities appreciate the assistance for navigating life. The playful child-like energies find songs to be great fun. The quiet, spiritual side is grateful to have the experience of reflection.

It is crucial to have a new cultural revelation periodically, to restore our shared connection with transcendent energies. The emerging levels of awareness can break through in unexpected forms. Some compositions are so fresh that a new vitality emerges. The talents of the sixties' musical avant garde provided just such an opening. The impact of the song-weavers of that time, led by the Beatles, represents a significant event in contemporary religious history.

Noticing significant religious themes in pop music reminds us that the holy is not the private property of theologians. Yearning for connection with the sacred is spontaneous in people from all walks of life. Spirituality is not confined to houses of worship. It is as likely that a profound experience will come to those hearing a poignant ballad as to the faithful listening to a choir.

The ideas of Carl Jung demonstrated how inspiration does not always descend from the heavens. Illumination can also seep up from beneath. That is, archetypal energies can rise from the commonplace to become a powerful current for renewal.

Sometimes, popular culture goes through periods of remarkable spiritual renewal. A vanguard of a new consciousness is revealed in the music of the sixties. This parallels the rise of generations of seekers who chose the adventure of self-discovery. For those on a path, key phrases can provide hints for coping with various inner lessons. They provide opportunities to learn about our deeper selves. Directions to invisible portals can be conveyed by such poetics. A songbook can be a seen as a kind of mystery school.

Seekers are often looking for the meaning of life. Joseph Campbell thought what we really need is the experience of being alive. Music is a vital way to be immersed in an artistic expression of emotion. We are drawn directly into feeling something meaningful.

Some of the most memorable sixties lyrics have spiritual underpinnings. This aspect has strong appeal to those with any level of interest in the life of the soul. Music infused with archetypes represents a kind of wisdom literature. Great songwriters respond to the same timeless questions as the ancient sages. Reaching us by way of beloved tracks, the mythic imagination gives us profound guidance through everyday life.

One great human universal is that we all yearn for something beyond ourselves. For some, it is a calling. For others it is something religious. For many it is love. Those who have experienced childhood trauma might have a deep need to belong. Perhaps we all hope to be accepted. It might be that we just yearn to be acceptable. Is safe to say we all want to belong. Most people want to feel like their life is worthwhile. Popular music, especially writers given to philosophical moments, speak to these large concerns.

Art rich in symbolism can provide insight into wide range of emotional tasks. Mythic perspectives nourish something in us. We reconnect with universal patterns that move the human heart and soul. In some new way, we see the rich beauty of ordinary life. When we enter the world of the song, we are participants. We are the narrator yearning for acceptance and love.

We can even see ceremonial elements in our devotion. Going to hear a favorite performer in concert can be like a pilgrimage. Many fans count it as a major life event. It can be a momentous occasion to gather with thousands of kindred seekers.

As a psychologist, I tend to value any opportunity for self-discovery. It can be valuable to revisit key memories. Sometimes, the exploration enters dimensions we never noticed before. A useful contemplative exercise would be to ponder song you loved years ago. Noticing details not caught before might show how you have changed. You might be surprised what will surface for you. Looking ahead, the same lyrics may well be guides through upcoming challenges.

When we come back to the same story after a time, it will tell us new things. This unpredictable element keeps the encounter lively. It mirrors how we are all caught up in currents that are larger than ourselves. Even such obvious powers as the flow of history, family dynamics, and life-stage transitions take us to places we do not entirely choose. The more we can know about the impact of these and other forces, the better chance we have of making the best of our adventures.

Daydreaming during such a review is the unconscious at work, reminding you of the personal meanings and guidance the memories hold for you. The hidden dimension we enter by way of dreams and fantasies includes the sublime qualities of everyday reality. You could see pop music as the soundtrack for the movie of your life. These songs may represent the poetry of the inner world. The tunes we heard at formative ages helped us form an identity. They still help us sort out our emotional lives.

Music helps us mark the stages of the journey. For many people, adolescence was a challenging part of the journey. There are twists and turns of new emotional experiences. Popular hits often reflect teenage hopes and dreams. For many of us there was a time when the songs on the radio seemed to mirror the deepest concerns of our inner lives. Those brief compositions were layered with emotion. The feelings were important. They seemed to hold something larger than the sentiment expressed in the stanzas.

We have our setbacks at various points, especially in our youthful years. The first day in a new school is a gauntlet. Fitting into community can be difficult at any age. The first time at everything is hardest because we don't yet know what we're doing. Our first successes are often hard won. Failures can be devastating. Dramas with friends are highly charged. Rising to these challenges is the initiatory process of becoming who we are meant to be.

Early romance can be marked by intense highs and lows. The longing for love can feel overwhelming. Lost love can bring devastating pain. On reflection, it might feel like we lose ourselves. Maybe that is what some of the longing in the words is all about. We lost track of ourselves somewhere along the line. In the end, the drama might not be about the object of desire at all. A lot of it might be longing itself.

Music can help us express what we are going through. Listening can also be like having a supportive friend. The songs provide company, reminding us someone, somewhere, understands what we are feeling. The poetry consoled us when we were lonely. They encouraged us when we lost our nerve.

At certain stages in the journey, the records are like mentors. Wise guidance is essential during difficult transitions. Themes of struggle and endurance in musical stories can represent the process of claiming and developing inner strengths. In earlier times, the bards and mystics were often poets. Today, our most influential poets are often minstrels and balladeers.

The words work on a psychological level partly because they include mysterious qualities. Unexpected developments in the narratives remind us life is not always orderly. Rude events can launch us into something larger. As we listen, surprising leaps into the unexpected can seize the imagination. Gradually, we can learn to allow the uninvited to speak to us and stir personal revelation that shift how we look at our adventures.

Sometimes, the through-line of the narrative will turn. Maybe the tale starts with great sorrow, and then by the end it is lifting you up. Perhaps a note of keeping faith enters in, with a message about not giving up. This echoes the transformation described in the initiatory adventure Joseph Campbell called *The Hero's Journey*. The process begins with a call. Usually there is some major difficulty. Then a departure takes us into new learning. Finally, we return changed forever.

Art of all kinds allows us to glimpse what is going on inside ourselves. It helps with emotional learning and growth. Like high culture, popular music can shape us. For example, a balled can be a master class in the mysteries of romantic love. Falling in love can be the call. It is simultaneously a wonderful event and a wild ride. Hearing a well-rendered tale of heartbreak helps us get through romantic disappointment. Singing the blues makes us feel better. There's the implication that we are somehow going to make it through.

Favorite lines may even evoke courage to carry on in the face of devastating difficulties. At some point, we all reach bottom. This is the dark night of the soul when all seems lost. It can be a crisis of faith in the seeker's life. This is like a baptism from hell. If we survive this ultimate ordeal, we will likely be able to face anything else fate throws in our faces. We gain a depth of character by having seen the worst. It is tempting to wish awful things had not happened, but that would miss the lesson. In the end, the rough sections are the most valuable parts of the journey.

It is during troubles that we are transformed. The new confidence and skills that will serve us for the rest of life's journey are gained by way of the toughest challenges. The last stages of the initiatory journey are celebrated in songs of joy, triumph, and survival. There is a soundtrack for every part of the quest.

There are moments when poetic phrases express emotions that have not quite found their way into words yet. These can be as varied as confidence, grief, hope, or desire. It is helpful to get access to these feelings that have been lurking below consciousness. Songs can also help us glimpse our aspirations.

Like ancient uses of ritual and chanting, playing music can help us shift consciousness. We call it a change of mood, but it might be a larger breakthrough. Sometimes, an upbeat tune just helps us relax and not think about our troubles. A catchy track with a strong beat can conjure a party atmosphere. We can sing along and have a good time. This can recharge a bad day while softening the anxious need for control. Moving into a playful mood can open us to more of our resources, like creativity, and the wisdom of the body. Sharing favorite music helps bind us together. Significantly, being drawn into unity is also a key function of religion.

The rhyming narratives can provide archetypal frameworks for our projections. Sometimes, the brief dramas closely mirror our inner dynamics, giving us a chance to learn what is happening in our own hidden places. We are all part of the story. This is your journey. You have lived with these compositions. They are still in the part of your inner world where the treasures are kept.

This was and is the poetry of our time. It alludes to the source of our deepest yearnings. People say, "You can always remember a song you fell in love to." Maybe part of what we fell in love with was the song itself, and our own capacity to feel such things.

As you ponder the deeper significance of popular music, you may start seeing mythic patterns everywhere. It is not a fantasy. The clues were there all along.

Jonathan Young, PhD Psychologist
Founding Curator, *Joseph Campbell Archives*
Santa Barbara, California

NOTE FROM THE AUTHOR

Looking back on the chapters of my life, it seems they all were pointing me in the direction of this book. I grew up feeling sheltered in a religious community and saw how it united—and divided—good people who mostly desired a consistent moral framework with which to examine and plan their lives. I studied literature and comparative religion in college, then spent the rest of my twenties as a touring musician and singer with a rock band.

Throughout my thirties, I worked as a film critic and television host; and my forties were spent as director of a gallery specializing in rock photography, collectables, and original album cover art. All these experiences—playing and singing the music of the classic rock era; dissecting archetypal plot, character, and symbolism in film; and immersing myself in the imagery of rock history—were preparing me for a work that may bring to light a novel, and perhaps important, new approach to the golden years of rock & roll.

Ten years ago, I started to write the book about the Beatles that I've always wanted to read. I've long intuited that rock & roll inspires an often unspoken, but profound spiritual response in listeners and fans. This aspect of the story has been mostly overlooked in studies of the Beatles and their contemporaries. I sensed there were deeper elements underlying our love for, and resonance with, these artists, and this inspired a creative journey of discovery that has been the most illuminating of my life.

On a personal level, I hope this book will entertain you with a unique view of popular music; in a more universal sense I hope it may have a positive and healing effect on our collective ability to examine symbol and response, subjects that have become so polarizing and misunderstood in our current culture. Perhaps, by using love of music as a unifying principle, it can further the spiritual conversation and bring a deeper sense of empathy and understanding to topics that remain sadly unresolved in our greater discourse. Thank you for your interest in *All You Need is Myth* and the themes it explores. I hope it opens doors of perception for you as it did for me.

—Steve Wagner
San Francisco, California

Let knowledge grow from more to more,
but more of reverence in us dwell;
that mind and soul, according well,
may make one music as before.
-Alfred, Lord Tennyson

Preface

❧　❧　❧

More Popular Than Jesus

In March 1966, in a feature article titled "How Does a Beatle Live?" for the *London Evening Standard*, journalist Maureen Cleave quoted John Lennon saying the Beatles had become "more popular than Jesus." Though it caused some Christian apoplexy at the time (in the United States, at least), it's now cited as a harmlessly poignant observational comment on the strangely spiritual role of the rock star in the modern, media-sculpted cultural landscape.

The relative truth of John's statement, already becoming clear by 1966, is now hard to deny. Religion and modern pop culture have intermingled as the romantic couple whose relationship is an open secret. *Star Wars*, with its basic plot derived from Joseph Campbell's notion of monomythic narrative and heroic archetypes; *Star Trek*, with its humanistic guiding principles and embrace of diversity and social justice; the Marvel and DC universes, populated by super-humans often disguised by everyman alter-egos liberating the populace, lord over the box office of cinema and adorn the living room walls of legions of followers. For the massive fan bases of these and other sci-fi brands, Comic-Con is a Western world commercial Mecca, a sacred pilgrimage shared with countless like-minded true believers.

This we know and accept without much inquiry. While literary critique uncovers the mythic bedrock of our most beloved works of fiction and narrative poetry, the savior characters of print, television, and film remain our most reliable protagonists, and, as always, consciousness-expanding treasure maps to the idealistic pearls of our perfected selves. If our sacred texts have become dusty and yellowed by time and increasingly impenetrable to modern minds, we are still drawn en masse to Christ-like heroes and their stories of redemption and transcendence like ancient moths to ever-flickering mythic flames.

Still, we dance around the subject of religion in popular music like tongue-tied suitors, desperate to avoid embarrassment, clumsily pursuing it and yet all too willing to retreat to the safety of the conventional wisdom, which maintains that rock & roll, and for that matter the whole of secular art and media, is simply a grotesquery of our religious tendencies, a fun-house mirror rather than an actual object and catalyst of our evolving mythic experience. Rarer still is it that one steps back and views the phenomenon of the Beatles (or Dylan, or the Rolling Stones, etc.) from a truly detached perspective, applying structural and symbolic analysis to their story and art as one would to the underlying meaning of a film, novel, poem or, in our case here, the mythic narratives and characters that seem to consistently be found at the core of our spiritual pursuits.

The Beatles are uniquely exalted figures in Western culture. Contrasting with other stars of enormous magnitude like Frank Sinatra, Elvis Presley, or Michael Jackson, the Beatles have never experienced, or ever needed, a "come-back." Their renown has remained untarnished by time, their image as durable as stone. Unlike the case of politicians, sports figures, movie stars, and traditional celebrities, their fame and acceptance does not seem predicated on trends, whims, or terms, and is impervious to geography, language barrier, and generational bias. From the catalyzing moment when they appeared on *The Ed Sullivan Show,* and continuing now for the past half-century, the Beatles have been among the most popular human beings––the most popular *things*––on the planet Earth. Their images and music have become so engrained in popular culture that we use their names as personality paradigms and their songs to break down social barriers and unite multitudes. Not even the dissolution of the band itself or the deaths of two of its members have weakened their impact. Their story has inspired millions upon millions. They've been obsessed over, emulated, evoked, and, yes, worshipped. It is hard to imagine how anyone could honestly gauge or qualify the Beatles' unprecedented level of popularity, fan devotion, and cultural influence without referencing religion or using religious language.

But, *why*? If we step out of our media-saturated reality, take down the *Abbey Road* poster, turn off *A Hard Day's Night*, and pause *The Beatles: Rock Band*, isn't it odd, or at least a serious cultural poser, that a handful of twenty-something troubadours in the mid-part of the last century were, in effect, elevated to the status of gods during their own lifetimes, and that their apotheoses continued even as they stopped producing, aged, and died?

This phenomenon, as John so shrewdly alluded, can really only compare to quasi-historical religious figures of the past, such as Moses, Buddha, and, yes, Jesus. Of course, those characters were, and still are, believed to possess some sort of explicit metaphysical or divine inspiration and authority. Why have the Beatles, who only ever claimed to be artists, played such spiritual, mythic roles in our collective and personal lives?

To find an answer, we need to view the Beatles through a mythic lens. We need to consider the very nature of myth itself, and allow ourselves to ask the question: Is it possible that Jesus and the Beatles fulfill the same psychological need in their followers and respective cultures?

Merely asking this question is likely to rankle some; therefore, a more comprehensive description of my operating philosophy and goal is here required. First, I ask the reader for a dispassionate viewpoint and a willingness to understand I am not making any claims regarding the efficacy of specific religions, nor am I intimating that the Beatles or their iconic contemporaries are in any way supernatural agents, or even that they somehow engineered their careers with the objective of deification in mind.

My treatment of Christianity as mythology and not divine edict may elicit the most impassioned response from its adherents, however, this conversation would not be possible without this distinction. Even still, I don't suggest it dissuade the deeply held beliefs in the fundamental truth of Christian theology, nor for any belief system surrounding Moses, Mohammed, Buddha, Krishna or the saviors and prophets of any religion. As with all authors, I hope that my work is read and discussed by everyone with interest in the subject matter, and, acknowledging that I am incapable (and admittedly unqualified) of writing the ten-thousand-page study that would do proper justice to the nuances of each religion past and present, I have strived to draw from as many mythic wells as possible.

Examining the mythic aspects of Christianity is only possible if Christianity contains or is informed by mythic concepts in the first place. The fact that it *is* imbued with mythic narratives, employs archetypal symbols and characters, utilizes fictional devices, and draws in part from literary sources is understood and accepted by all but the most fundamentalist biblical scholars. To ignore this would be disingenuous to my subject and ultimately diminish the potential discussion for members of all faiths. There is a reason that Lennon said the Beatles were more popular than Jesus rather than saying they were more popular than Dionysus or Osiris. Christianity has been the Western Hemisphere's most followed religion for nearly two thousand years; we therefore cannot attempt debate on the nature of modern mythology without considering its influence any more than John could. Furthermore, if the Beatles do indeed suggest a new mythic phenomenon, it could only have established itself on the shoulders of our previous religious beliefs. Media theorist Marshall McLuhan once mused: "While people are engaged in creating a totally different world, they always form vivid images of the preceding world."[1]

That said, let us consider the relative truth of mythologist Joseph Campbell's observance that "mythology may be defined as other people's religions, and religion may be defined as a popular misunderstanding of mythology."[2] And yet, before we can adequately draw a distinction between "religion" and "myth," we need to answer, at least in the context of this book, the foundational question: What is myth?

The word "myth" is often used in modern culture to mean "lie," but that pejorative definition says more about how we view and treat our own mythology rather than the actual intention of myth. Modern misunderstanding is, to a large degree, a product of myth's various forms and multi-fold designations. In a historical context, nearly any true story containing a famous narrative connecting past and present is commonly understood as mythic. Baseball, for example, is a mythology unto itself, comprised of stories ranging from triumphant (Bobby Thompson's pennant-winning "shot heard round the world") to tragic (Roberto Clemente's death in a plane crash). Here, we will refer to this type as *Temporal Mythology*, meaningful within its own historic context but without the underlying features and structures to communicate the truths and mysteries of the human condition; though, as with most community endeavors, it will contain drama and noteworthy events that captivate the hearts and fire the imaginations and aspirations of its participants and followers. Baseball affects us on a temporal level; as it unfolds through history, we find meaning in it to the degree that we grant it credence.

World history is rife with events we understand as mythic, or to which we affix the term, if only because of their notoriety and/ or importance to our quality (good or bad) of life. D-Day is understood as mythic, for it changed the course of history, likewise the creation of the American Constitution, the Wright brothers' first flight at Kitty Hawk, the dismantling of the Berlin Wall. But historical import is not analogous with mythology in any classic sense of the term. We call these world events mythic perhaps because there is no better word to describe the enormity and depth of their influence. When historical narratives become intertwined with ongoing cultural identities, they become temporal mythologies.

Classical mythologies—Egyptian, Greek, Roman, et al.—bring us closer to the quintessence of myth, but even with those sterling examples we still find ourselves, in the here and now, separated from the archetypal heart of the matter. These mythologies, once believed to be true representations of reality and thus functioning as religion in the lives of believers, are now artifacts—epic poems and tales, "histories" of deities, celestial hierarchies, even the simple writing down of word-of-mouth legends—*created* by humans for often specific goals.

Homer's poetic synthesis of Greek folklore, Plutarch's "biography" of the dying-rising Roman god Romulus, and the Egyptian Book of the Dead are examples of mythic creations by authors with worldly objectives, however other-worldly the themes they explored.

Consider the Arthurian romances and Grail legends, which, along with the Christian traditions, likely comprise the Western world's most vividly symbolic and psychologically all-encompassing mythology. As with many ancient myths, they may have been at various times attempts to synthesize and record crucial historic events (temporal mythologies). However, over the centuries, many authors and poets have employed them as the basis for fictional works likely meant to bring cultural cohesion to the British and Gaelic peoples. That the authors employed archetypal characters, symbols, and narratives to achieve their goals is, to some degree, a means to an end. In any case, the mythic aspects of the stories—even if those concepts were the product of centuries of distillation into distinctly mythic forms with symbolic meaning—are still one step (at least) removed from the human unconscious where these symbols originally manifest, the resting place of what psychoanalyst and dream interpreter Carl Jung called "primordial images."[3] If there is a true *prisca theologia*, a singular vision that informs all religions, this psychic realm is where it both slumbers and awakens. We will refer to the archetypes and symbols of this psychological space—and the art and drama they inspire—as *Archetypal Mythology*.

This is illuminated by the very roots of the word "archetype." First brought into cultural consciousness by social anthropologist Sir James George Frazer in his book *The Golden Bough* and used as a demarcation to explore and explain human psychology by Jung, it derives from the Greek compound of *archē*, meaning "first principle," and *tupos*, meaning "impression." To clarify, the word archetype denotes both the creative source of symbolic forms and the tangible manifestations of those very symbols. Jung says, "The concept of the archetype, which is an indispensable correlate to the idea of the collective unconscious, indicates the existence of definite forms in the psyche which seem to be present always and everywhere...in the field of comparative religion they have been defined as 'categories of the imagination.' "[4]

When archetypal mythology comingles with temporal mythology, we have the potential for religion, or *Communal Mythology*. To quote literary theorist Northrup Frye: "Religion is applied mythology."[5] When significant numbers of people come to believe, for whatever reason, that an archetypal mythology is true in an historic or material sense, and then organize their lives around its tenets, prescriptions, and theology, it creates a communal mythology that is then frequently handed down from parent to child as a natural explanation of the temporal world. Often this phenomenon is initiated by revelation(s) experienced and recorded by the person who will become known as the founder of the faith. Muhammad's revelation of the angel Gabriel, thus creating Islam; Joseph Smith's revelation of the angel Moroni, thus creating Mormonism; and St. Paul's revelation of Jesus Christ, thus creating (or at least cohering and evangelizing) Christianity (which could more accurately be called "Paulism"), are examples of this method birthing what came to be widespread religions, or communal mythologies. Jung asserts, "Wherever we can observe a religion being born, we see how the doctrinal figures flow into the founder himself as revelations, in other words, as concretizations of his unconscious fantasy."[6]

Frye clarifies, "A purely individualized myth is an obsession, sometimes a psychosis. A purely socialized myth is an ideology, which sooner or later also becomes obsessive or psychotic. A myth that has either the direct current of transcendence or the alternating current of imagination rises clear of this grisly antithesis."[7] If that assessment is true, and I believe it is, then the Beatles certainly qualify as a mythic phenomenon, containing both the "current of transcendence" and the "alternating current of imagination."

Indeed, the Beatles have manifested all three levels of mythology: (1) a temporal mythology that is contained within the still unfolding historical record; (2) an archetypal mythology experienced through music, art, and narrative, communicated with aural and visual symbols, characters, and stories; and (3) a communal mythology that is reflected in their immense (global) fan base, whose reverence for the Beatles' music and message is now passed down through generations.

The Beatles' temporal mythology is beyond well-documented. It is one of the most studied social and cultural subjects in history. Hundreds of books focusing on every conceivable aspect of their lives and art have been written in the last fifty years. They have inspired an ever-growing intellectual dialogue and a grail-like search for exactly who did what and when, where and why. Their story is so culturally and historically intriguing it has spawned scores of rock & roll detectives, sleuthing musicologists searching for clues with the relentless zeal of Dead Sea Scroll fragment-hunters, discovering and then determining with scholarly aplomb how each factoid solves the mystery of every song, clarifies the meaning of every statement, captures and logs the relevance of every impression. It is an expansive and magical tale, a sprawling epic that carries in its limbs the evolving concerns of the modern world, activating its deepest emotions and informing its highest aspirations. This true story has held the rapt attention of the world for generations and continues to rivet us as it progresses.

The archetypal mythology of the Beatles springs from their artistic expression and generational narrative. Conveyed through song, film, and numerous other art forms, it is the world they created with the language of sound, visual imagery, and lyrical symbolism. The Beatles' songs function as modern aural archetypes, collectively experienced through poetic and musical idioms to produce an alternate, abstract reality—one in which creativity is the prime directive, positive intent is the approach, and love is the answer. And, crucially, the music and art created by the Beatles succeeds as remarkably direct communication with their audience and listeners (effortlessly crossing over age boundaries with songs for both children and the elderly), creating a primal bond that enabled a cultural awakening to unfold over eight revolutionary years, both transforming and mirroring a global shift in consciousness.

Their songs are, as the late Beatle publicist and raconteur Derek Taylor once suggested, "the proof that this story isn't a fiction."[8]

Indeed, their story is so significant and far-reaching in scope it would hardly be believed true if it weren't for the undeniable historical documentation. That the Beatles' music and art constitutes a body of work with psychological depth as influential as a Goethe, Carroll, or Joyce is certainly remarkable; that their historical narrative also manifested in a distinctly mythic form elevated their archetypal mythology into uncharted realms of cultural resonance and communal experience.

These two mythologies (the temporal and the archetypal) coalesce with the active participation of the collective to manifest the Beatles' communal mythology. Crystallized by the unprecedented mass experience and acceptance of their sound and message, the Beatles have become more than a historical phenomenon, and even more than the greatest musical icons of the modern age. The Beatles have come to embody a new savior archetype, one that emphasizes a group of individual "gods" working together to create, support, and transmit a profound spiritual reality. They are now a vibrant and seemingly permanent symbol of harmony, transformation, transcendence, and, most of all, love.

Elevated as much by our deep, collective need for mythology as a conduit for the expression of essential truths as by the historic and cultural forces that set their stage, the Beatles became the central symbol of creative enlightenment for their age, and they were the guides a generation followed through the greatest mystery initiation of the twentieth century. Moreover, if this was indeed the case, would it not follow that our most iconic rock stars are likely themselves re-imaginings of familiar mythic archetypes? Go to any college dorm room or suburban finished basement and you'll see small altars to the deities of our time: the prophetic Dylan, the devilish Stones, the shamanic Hendrix, and, of course, the transcendent Beatles. None of this is new or shocking; journalists and writers picked up on these strong alignments almost instantly, and even fans have an instinctive understanding of the mythical resonances of their most beloved artists. We refer to our favorite albums as "the bible" or "the holy grail," and the concert as "church." Rock & roll "saves" us. Some even say rock & roll can save your soul.

Rock & roll, in mythic terms, is the real article. I base this statement on thousands of years of observable phenomena, for while the "truth" of any given mythology (or religion) can only be speculated upon and interpreted subjectively, the *fact* of mythology can be, and has been, studied and codified. As reflected in the research and theories of many of the world's leading scholars in the fields of literature, religious studies, psychology, and world history, it is clear that mythology continually reinvents itself to be relevant for each new era, language, and culture. Moreover, when applying this rubric to the age of mass media and communication, it becomes equally apparent that mythology has powerfully manifested in the great story of rock & roll, and that the same psychic impulses and mythic symbols and structures are at play within this milieu as they have always been in the past.

In his influential 1949 book *The Hero with a Thousand Faces*, Campbell states, "For when scrutinizing in terms not of what it is but of how it functions, of how it has served mankind in the past, of how it may serve today, mythology shows itself to be as amenable as life itself to the obsessions and requirements of the individual, the race, the age."[9] He explains that for religions, philosophies, and the arts, "throughout the inhabited world, in all times and under every circumstance, the myths of man have flourished."[10]

I propose that the Beatles and the iconic stars of the classic rock era function as modern forms of ubiquitous mythic archetypes. While focusing primarily on the savior mythology of the Beatles, I also align the historic chronicle of the '60s musical renaissance with key mythic themes and archetypes such as the Child, the Goddess, the Devil, the Prophet, and the Holy Spirit, among others. By identifying equivalent narratives and symbolism from classical (Egyptian, Greco-Roman, Judeo-Christian, Persian, Eastern) mythologies, I seek to illuminate ancient philosophic concepts such as death and rebirth, resolution of duality, visions of paradise, rites of initiation, sound and harmony, and the cosmic relationship between the physical and spiritual realms, to show how the rock pantheon also reflects these ideas.

(I anticipate cries of "parallelomania," a practice understood in biblical criticism and comparative religion as assessing similarities and analogies between mythic traditions that are in some measure inaccurate. I don't doubt that in cases my logic may be faulty, however, the fact that mythology is inherently open to interpretation, even within the parameters of agreed-upon definitions, leaves a study such as this, at least to some degree, subjective. To those who feel I am "reaching" here, my response is simply that I didn't have to reach very far.)

I feel that we have been witnessing, in our new age of mass media and global communication, a decisive shift in our ability to both manifest and experience mythology, and therefore that our practice of religion itself is morphing along with our gods. It is my hope this book will inspire a fresh and focused post-modern conversation on these topics, or at the least serve as an entertaining Trojan horse that will slip the casual reader past the gates of dogma and inside the truly inspiring world of mythology, past and present.

Finally, it should be added, in September 2009, Britain's *Telegraph* newspaper reported that more than forty years after John Lennon "invoked the ire" of Christians by claiming the Beatles were more popular than Jesus, "he has been proven right by an analysis of search terms on the Google search engine." The article claimed that "in the last four weeks more computer users have typed in the search word 'Beatles' on the Google website than 'Jesus.' "[11] Perhaps it is just a coincidence that the following spring the Catholic Church officially forgave the Beatles for their boasts concerning Jesus, and also their "dissolute" lifestyles in the 1960s. In a front-page article, the Vatican's official newspaper *L'Osservatore Romano* noted that "listening to their songs, all of this seems distant and meaningless. Their beautiful melodies, which changed forever pop music and still give us emotions, live on like precious jewels." Editor-in-chief Giovanni Maria Vian also commented that he "loves the Beatles," and that "in reality, it wasn't that scandalous, because the fascination with Jesus was so great that it attracted these new heroes of the time."[12]

Exactly. This book contains my thoughts and observations on that very idea.

The [mythic] cycle is now to be carried forward, therefore, not by the gods, who have become invisible, but by the heroes, more or less human in character, through whom the world destiny is realized.
–Joseph Campbell

ROLL OVER, JEHOVAH

❧ ❧ ❧

Mythology in the Twentieth Century

Since the early twentieth century, Western culture has longed for a new mythological framework with which to once again understand the forces, not of nature around us, but of our humanity within. In the 1960s, we collectively re-created that context through rock & roll, unconsciously re-imagining familiar archetypes and narratives for the age of television and mass media. Though they were wearing modern clothes (and playing guitars), the innate characteristics of our "Rock Gods" remained true to timeless and steadfast forms, as did the human impulses and psychology that, in centuries past, congealed to create the great religions.

Therefore, it is important to note at the outset that the mythos of the Beatles and rock & roll did not form in a vacuum; it was a product of the same forces that have always informed and fueled humanity's spiritual needs but birthed this time in a radically new context of mass communications. And, though it appears at first glance to be a wholly new phenomenon, on closer inspection it becomes clear that the rock mythology shares much with previous traditions while also marking a distinct evolution in their expression. What follows is a brief look at historical context through examination of a few twentieth century mythologies from around the world that will set the stage for understanding the coming explosion of rock & roll into a modern mythic conception.

In many ways a product of evolving communication technology, the rock mythology resulted from an organic process that began

1

with Guttenberg's invention of the printing press and quickened under an avalanche of scientific advances, a process that gradually scaled back the mountains of our previous belief systems. Like DNA, myth is self-replicating, but mutates in a new environment. When fresh scientific, cultural, or spiritual information comes to light that pulls the glowing chariot out from under the old god, there instantly arises from its ashes a nascent god, ready to carry the suffering, love, passion, and image of its creators again into those realms perhaps too grand, profound, and eternal for the human animal to enter alone.

Our ability to communicate with one another, indeed the very type and reach of our communication, is intrinsic to our distinct creations of mythology. We often see the bedrock of belief moisten and sprout a novel—or in most cases augmented—mythology when a culture undergoes a significant shift in its experience of basic communication, be it the absorption of a different language or the shock of collision with dissimilar religious traditions. When travelers, migrants, or conquerors enter a new culture, bringing with them stories and myths which drastically contrast with those of their new home, oftentimes the myths will marry, producing a child who displays aspects of both, but who also possesses individuality and uniqueness.

Myth is astoundingly mercurial, as we see in the phenomenon of the Cargo Cults in Papua New Guinea, wherein previously isolated societies on once-remote islands in Melanesia came into contact with the technologically advanced West. For millennia (50,000 years according to some anthropologists),[1] these Oceanic peoples had adhered to primitive (in the strict, non-judgmental sense) myths: creation stories accounting for the land and sea, sun and moon, and man and woman; and belief in a host of benevolent and malevolent spirits that inhabit animals, plants and, sometimes, humans. Western explorers, missionaries, and militaries began visiting the archipelago at the turn of the twentieth century (with heightened frequency during the WWII years), and an amazing mythic hybrid blossomed that survives to this day, with scores of followers who worship deities known as "John Frum" (John from America?), "Tom Navy" (Tom from the Navy?), and, in one tribe, England's Prince Phillip. Members of these cults, having no concept of modern technology and goods, believe that the manufactured items introduced by their visitors were created by ancestral spirits, and they await the second coming of their messiah (John Frum et al.), who they believe will bear the bounty of miraculous "cargo" and the resurrected dead of their people.

Legend has it that the ghost of John Frum appeared to tribal leaders in or about the 1930s and urged them to remain true to the beliefs of their ancestors and resist the pressure of Christian missionaries and Western colonialists. Even still, these cults appropriated many of the symbols associated with their new influences, such as using crosses as grave markers, digging airplane "landing strips" in the jungle, attempting to fashion radios with straw and coconut husks, and the wearing of Western military garb to entice the return of John Frum.[2] One tribe, the Urapmin, adopted (as late as the 1970s) what seem to be elements from Baptist Christianity, such as glossolalia (speaking in tongues), group hysteria, end-of-the-world prophesying, and a new-found belief in original sin.[3]

Historians have noted the similarities of the Cargo Cults with the beliefs and practices of the early Christians (who shared many similar socio-political challenges and apocalyptic expectations). Anthropologists tend to classify both as *millenarian movements*, i.e. collective belief in a coming final societal upheaval and transformation in which the corrupted power structure is overturned and control returned to the oppressed community. We also see this phenomenon in the Native American "Ghost Dance" movement of the late nineteenth century, wherein those oppressed peoples suffered extreme cultural crisis in the wake of Manifest Destiny and the onslaught of industry.[4]

Also, in the 1930s, as the Cargo Cults were developing in Melanesia, Rastafarianism emerged in Jamaica. Another millenarian movement deeming that the end of the world is nigh, the Rastafarians came to believe that Haile Selassie I, after his coronation as emperor of Ethiopia, had fulfilled prophecy foretold in the Bible and was the second coming of Christ. Selassie, a global figure (and *Time* magazine's "Person of the Year" in 1935), explicitly denied his divinity.[5] Still, his refutations did not change the beliefs of his flock or slow the growth of the Rastafari religion, which today numbers over one million followers.[6] Even Selassie's death in 1975 was widely disbelieved within the ranks of the Rasta faithful, and many consider it to have been prophesied anyway in the apocalyptic book of 2 Esdras, a text not currently recognized as orthodox by most Christian sects but still included in many modern Bibles.[7]

Like the Cargo Cults, the Rastafari faith focuses on the idea that the influence of Western secular society, which they refer to as "Babylon," is an existential threat to their native customs and worldview and signifies the impending end of time. Also like the Cargo Cults, they envision a return of their messiah, who will restore power that has been eroded by colonialism, and specifically to those of their race who have been displaced from the continent of Africa, particularly Ethiopia, which they believe was promised to them by God in holy scripture.[8]

Though the similarities between these belief systems are apparent, what is interesting for our purpose here is the difference in response to their cultural crises and the elements that produced the distinctions in their mythologies. While both were impoverished island cultures grappling with a quickly-changing world forcing a rapid evolution of thought, the Cargo Cults responded with mass hysteria spurred by hallucinatory visions, while the Rastafarians answered by searching their sacred texts for signs and prophecy that would elucidate this temporal challenge in spiritual terms. Put simply, the Rastas had a long tradition of Judeo-Christian mythology with which to consult, while the Melanesian islanders had only their imaginations and dreams. Jung clarifies, "Primitive mentality differs from the civilized chiefly in that the conscious mind is far less developed in scope and intensity ... the primitive does not think *consciously* ... thoughts *appear*. [He] cannot assert that he thinks; it is rather that 'something thinks in him.'"[9]

Essentially, the novel Cargo Cult and Rastafari belief systems were informed and sculpted by their existing levels of contact and communication with the outside world. Native Jamaicans were well aware of their African heritage, identifying with Ethiopian culture and religion that had been a hotbed of Christian activity and belief dating back nearly two thousand years to the founding of the Coptic Church of Alexandria, one of the oldest Christian churches in the world. Though somewhat isolated, the Rastas saw themselves as part of a long religious tradition, and their new mythology drew from this deep well of established, i.e. written, communication. On the other hand, the Cargo Cults, in their extreme isolation—further complicated by near-total illiteracy and the hundreds of distinct languages spoken by the New Guinea natives—created their new mythologies through the same intuitive means they had always employed to understand and explain their circumstance.

Now consider the mythic phenomenon surrounding Eva Perón (née Duarte) in Argentina in the 1940s and '50s. Born into relative poverty in rural Argentina, Eva moved to Buenos Aires as a teen and spent the next decade pursuing a career as a stage, radio, and film actress. She married Colonel Juan Perón in 1945, and the following year he was elected president of Argentina. Eva quickly became a powerful force in the Perónist government, speaking out in support of labor rights, founding and running the Eva Perón Foundation (a charity dedicated to improving the plight of the impoverished), and creating and presiding over the Female Perónist Party, the first women's political party in the history of Argentina. She became an international figure in 1947 when she embarked on her "Rainbow Tour" of Europe, meeting with luminaries, royalty, and heads-of-state, including Francisco Franco, Charles de Gaulle, and Pope Pious XII.

In 1952, following her husband's second inauguration, Eva was given the title, "Spiritual Leader of the Nation." She died soon after of cancer at the age of thirty-three, and was afforded a state funeral, the likes of which were previously reserved only for presidents. The *Chicago Tribune* reported: "The impact of the meteoric rise of the former unknown actress to the pinnacle of power here as the political associate as well as the wife of the president has been surpassed by the devotion of the thousands of poor men, women, and children who braved rains and chill winds for 12 to 18 hours to stand in lines so they might get a last glimpse of their benefactress… Twenty foot high portraits of Mrs. Perón have been placed on pedestals in six principle plazas and three parks. Beneath each is a shrine where people halt to pray for the peaceful repose of her soul… Roman Catholic requiem masses are being said daily for Mrs. Perón. Masses were also celebrated daily for nine months while she was ill."[10]

This scant biography does inadequate justice to the extraordinary mythic effect Eva Perón (affectionately known by the Spanish diminutive "Evita" for her identification with the poor, i.e. "little people") had on the Argentine populace, who regarded her, figuratively if not literally, as a saint. Biographer Robert D. Crassweller, author of *Perón and the Enigmas of Argentina*, compared her to the Christian saint Ignacious, writing that she was like a "one-woman Jesuit Order… As her public crusades and her private adorations took on a narrowing intensity after 1946, they simultaneously veered toward the transcendental."[11] Her final message to the people of Argentina clearly reflected an understanding of the mythic character they needed her to be: "If I die it does not matter. I will continue to be with my people and with Perón from the land and from the sky."[10]

The psychological basis for the veneration of Eva Perón can be tacitly explained by the fact that the masculine is traditionally understood to represent physical power while the feminine is seen as a symbol of spiritual depth. That the Peróns governed, at least in the eyes of the people, as a duo would likely bolster this perception; if Juan was seen as a "strong man," it is natural that his counterpart would be thought of as a "wise woman." But this demarcation only goes so far in explaining the religious aspects of her influence, which were distinctly Roman Catholic in nature.

The mythic ascendance of "Santa Evita" was a product of both government propaganda and the pre-existing spiritual beliefs of the Argentine people, and her sainthood was effectively sold to the masses through media that was rapidly modernizing. Juan Perón's proto-fascist regime, true to form, employed concentrated, large-scale advertising techniques to elevate its leaders to god-like status, and when Eva proved to be a useful symbol and messenger, the government used this apparatus to create a mythic persona for her, one based on charity, solidarity, empathy, and emotional reassurance for the common people—in short, the very qualities we associate with the mother's role in parenting. For Argentines steeped in Catholicism, this naturally translated into identification, if mostly unconscious, of Evita with Mary, Mother of Christ.

However, not everyone in Argentina was enamored with Mrs. Perón. Political enemies and members of South America's burgeoning socialist movement were intensely opposed to Perónism and sought to overthrow their government, or at the least besmirch Eva's elevated status. Along with political accusations of fascist and Nazi, she was (erroneously) alleged to have been a former prostitute and suspected of having slept her way to power with many men, including Juan Perón. Ironically, the attempt to smear her reputation had the effect of deepening Eva's mythic import by aligning her with another compelling Christian female archetype, Mary Magdalene.[12]

This book is certainly not the first to draw attention to Eva Perón's conflation with the Virgin Mary and the Magdalene, or her persona signifying both mother and sex goddess; indeed, many have suggested this was a conscious inference encouraged and staged by the Peróns themselves.[13] But it was really the emergent media that created the foundation for the depth and breadth of her modernization of classic goddess archetypes. Already moderately well known in Argentina prior to meeting Juan Perón, when Eva became first lady, she became a major celebrity. Her previous work in theatre and radio brought ease in front of audiences and experience as an orator, and her career as a film actress helped her develop an "on-screen" persona and intuitive sense of media performance as an art. And the media were certainly enamored with her; the Rainbow Tour made global headlines, and she was featured, alone, on the cover of *Time* magazine in 1947. To be sure, her mythology grew to enormous proportions, first in Argentina and increasingly around the world, and these potent Christian elements in no small part fueled her rise to international fame and, to this day, define the very essence of the mythic Evita.

Eva Perón's media celebrity is an illuminating precursor to that of the Beatles and the rock mythology. Their shared reliance on developing communication technology and its broadening reach reveals the powerful manner by which the cult of modern celebrity affects the human unconscious. Rastafarianism and the Cargo Cults shed light on our current subject, in that their creation of myth through revelation and the realignment of previous religious belief are also mirrored in the rock mythology. Perhaps more than anything, these examples from New Guinea, Jamaica, and Argentina illuminate the role that communication capability plays in our modern experience and creation of mythic content.

They also show that myth is alive, always. Contrary to the popular misconception that mythology is merely an ancient endeavor or that religions stopped occurring after the establishment of Christianity, Islam, or Mormonism, we see in these examples that myth is ever-ready to emerge when the conditions are prime. Indeed, all three of these mythologies remain in force and reverberate in modern culture to this day: Evita's legacy through the highly-popular Broadway musical and Hollywood film; Rastafarianism through the global reach of reggae music and customs; and the notion of Cargo Cults as a theme of the annual New Age desert bacchanalia Burning Man.

To summarize, the Cargo Cults created a communal mythology to answer an earthly crisis, while the Rastafarians appropriated their communal mythology to explain their own challenge. The Argentines reacted to archetypal symbolism communicated through a media figure, and this reaction was based upon their established communal mythology. Whether or not the mythic elements inherent in the Evita character were the result of political propaganda (and to some degree they likely were) is moot. The relevant question might be: is it possible that we in our modern secular culture are similarly susceptible to the impulse to create a re-imagined archetypal framework in response to our collision with cultural upheaval, mass media, and celebrity?

The Beatles' phenomenon suggests that this is indeed the case. With them, we witness a great leap forward in the evolution of myth: in response to a mostly *existential* crisis, and through unprecedented mass communication and media, the expression of *archetypal* mythology created a *temporal* mythology from which emerged a new form of *communal* mythology. In this modern landscape, the popular will (and purchasing power) of the collective became directly integral to the very creation it worshipped. And, as with our previous examples, the mythology of rock and the Beatles particularly conveyed pre-existing religious symbolism, this time, though, not through conscious augmentation, but as an unconscious reaction to its fading relevance, and a needed psychological replacement of it.

By the time of the Beatles, the Christian mythos and the belief it had inspired for nearly two millennia had already been in various states of decline for decades. Members of intelligentsias had long questioned its origins (as members of intelligentsias are wont to do), and Darwin and his theories had only served to give them more cause for skepticism or outright disbelief. The mid-century discoveries of the Dead Sea Scrolls and Nag Hammadi texts brought scholarly debate in theological circles to a frenzied pitch, and as books, journals, and finally radio and recorded media brought literature and ideas once reserved solely for the erudite to a wider and wider audience, these questions eventually found their way from the abbeys and university halls to the pubs and parlors.

As early as 1937, Jung observed that the Christ image was appearing less and less frequently in the dreams of his patients.

Jung, who identified himself as a Christian (albeit a very mystical one), nonetheless intuited the inevitable. Christianity, as with all mythologies, would become less effectual with the advance of time and eventually run its course. He stated, "The Christian religion seems to have fulfilled its great biological purpose, in so far as we are able to judge ... [It] has lost its significance, therefore, to a yet undetermined extent."[14] Jung felt Christianity's profundity would influence, inform, and pave the way for the next mythic era, and he believed that the Christian mythos was still valid conceptually, if not culturally: "Not only do I leave the door open for the Christian message, but I consider it of central importance for Western man. It needs, however, to be seen in a new light, in accordance with the changes wrought by the contemporary spirit."[15]

Jung was one of numerous twentieth century social theorists, including Karl Marx, Emile Durkheim, and Max Weber, who predicted that an ever-increasing secularism would rise alongside the evolving modernization of society. The focus on the spiritual ramifications of this, at least in intellectual circles, had been initiated in the late nineteenth century, with German philosopher Frederick Nietzsche's existential cry of pain, "God is dead!" A core theme in many of his works, Nietzsche wrote eloquently on the topic in his philosophical novel *Thus Spake Zarathustra*, written in 1885 and published in 1891. Often misinterpreted as a nihilistic worldview, Nietzsche's famous edict proved to be prescient social commentary, inspiring debate and thought that became, by the time of the Beatles, impossible for even the Church to ignore.

In 1961, French theologian Gabriel Vahanian published the controversial book *The Death of God*, launching a radical movement within the very core of the clergy. He declared, "The Christian concept of man has been devalued. It offers no point of contact to modern man, because his self-understanding is completely divergent from the Christian concept. Emphatically, it is not simply a question of the loss of the sacramental dimension manifest in the classical Christian image of man. Nor is it a question of the loss of the sacral dimension so indelibly characteristic of past stages of

Western culture. The loss is incomparably greater and deeper. It has affected man's outlook on life, his *raison d'etre*, and his view of reality."[16]

Time magazine did a cover story on the Death of God movement in 1965, where they summarized, "Vahanian believes that the church's concept of God today is...an idol that is no longer relevant to secular culture and has been either neutralized by overexposure or rejected entirely. Thus, he declares, God is dead, and will remain so until the church becomes secular enough in structure and thought to proclaim Him anew in ways that will fulfill the cultural needs of the times...The death-of-God theologians do not argue merely that Christianity's traditional 'image' of the Creator is obsolete. They say that it is no longer possible to think about or believe in a transcendent God who acts in human history, and that Christianity will have to survive, if at all, without Him."[17]

While Vahanian invoked the God is Dead "crisis" largely in terms of its relation to the future survival of Christianity in particular, Nietzsche felt that it signaled an evolutionary calling to become an entirely evolved human being, which he called the *Overman*, or more commonly, the Superman. Moreover, he surmised that the vestiges of Christian dogma and ritual would run counter to and delay the individuation needed for one to make the leap into this advanced state of self-mastery. Jung also considered the process of individuation necessary for a person to become self-realized, however he emphasized the importance of balance and harmony over the power of the individual will.

In his book *Revolution in the Head: The Beatles' Records and the Sixties*, Ian MacDonald concludes, "Far from appearing out of thin air in the sixties as many conservatives now like to believe, the decade's mass-transition from sacred to secular represented a climactic stage in the historical rise of science. Over the recent centuries, the Christian glue which once cemented Western society had been progressively weakened by the shocks of scientific discovery...socially liberating, post-war influences conspired with a cocktail of scientific innovations too potent to resist."[18]

As the Christ image slowly dissipated from the dreams of the twentieth century, the savior archetype itself seemed to be hibernating in the West, waiting for the day it could attach to a new host, take a new name, and reflect a new world in the collective imagination. The influence of the "Jesus as Savior" mythos in Western culture was monumental, but, inevitably, as time brings ever-unfolding new realties to bloom on planet Earth, even the seemingly invincible Christian god (as were all other gods before him) would need to cede some sacred ground to the dreams and reflections of modern men and women. And now that they were leaving the churches, these modern men and women were finding a multitude of competing technologies whose prime directive was to capture their attention and imagination with compelling story, song, and spectacle.

In addition to shaking up the religious foundations of the West, by the 1960s science had taken a technological turn sharply in the direction of communications, entertainment, and media. If the advance of literacy took the first few decades of the twentieth century by storm, no one could have been prepared for the blitzkrieg of information that would accompany film, radio, and television by its midpoint. The sudden widespread promulgation of homogeneous images and sounds as entertainment affected the '60s culture by simultaneously imprinting the consciousnesses of a great number of people. These images and sounds then became a part of the shared experience of anyone who witnessed them, and during that decade—when there were still only three television networks and most AM radio stations chirped the same Top-40 list of songs—these collective experiences quickly became important foundations of a modern common reality.

To put this in historic context, for millennia human beings had mostly communicated on a one-to-one basis. After the invention of the printing press, humanity slowly but surely moved toward a "one-to-many" mode of communication. This method of interaction reached its zenith in the era of the "Simultaneous Collective Imprint"—the 1960s and early '70s—when the American culture of television and mass media realized an apex of widely disseminated uniform images and sounds. By the late '70s, we were already entering the next phase of our communication evolution, the era of "many-to-many," now commonly called the information age. The '60s generation had grown up primed for simultaneous collective imprinting from the evolving media, and along with the societal mirror offered by television and radio came a culture-wide blurring of the line separating that fantasy from reality. After all, if everyone experiences the *same* fantasy at the *same* time, what's the difference between that and what we call reality?

This was the world that the '60s generation inhabited, and it was drastically different from that of their parents. During World War II, a large percentage of adult males (read, most of the working population) were overseas fighting Hitler or Tojo, leaving able-bodied women behind to take up many of the necessary labor positions left open by the shortage of men. When the war ended, the men rushed home to their wives and met them in bed, causing a sudden and unprecedented population surge. Upon starting households, the men and women of the 1940s and '50s resumed their traditional gender roles and settled in to create the ideal nuclear family in the wake of the bomb and the Holocaust.

Economic prosperity from the end of the war through the late '50s continued to encourage couples to have children, while the GI Bill, which guaranteed an education to returning soldiers, enabled record numbers of men to graduate high school and attend college. The "American Dream" was more attainable than ever before and was indeed being achieved in record numbers. In 1954, annual births first topped four million and did not drop below that figure until 1965, by which time four out of ten Americans were under the age of twenty.[19]

It was at this time, when forty percent of the population had never known a world without television and sixty percent still remembered rationed butter and the threat of Nazism, that the phenomenon dubbed the Generation Gap became fully apparent. The "Baby Boomers" had been born into a prosperous, postwar culture in a world that was suddenly and rapidly globalizing as never before. The phenomena of television and radio, imprinting images and sounds as shared human experience, were for them the very foundations of reality, while for their parents, merely remarkable inventions. (*What won't they think of next?*)

Just as this unique youth culture was swelling to its greatest proportion, a tragedy struck that deeply affected the Western world: the assassination of President John F. Kennedy on November 22, 1963. America was frozen with grief and loss, its denizens unable to understand or even respond to the madness they had all witnessed. Having long been an idealistic, strong, and confident young adult in the world family, America was now more abused child, psyche-scarred and frightened after witnessing the murder—the fratricide, no less—of its loving and protective father. The modern American story had suddenly taken a sharp and tragic detour, the protagonist and hero eliminated from the plot in the first act of the play, the arc of the tale now uncertain and a happy ending all but abandoned.

John F. Kennedy's bright smile, sonorous voice, movie-star hair, effortless charisma, heroic past, legendary family, and apparent destiny to occupy the highest office had become the proud, prevailing self-image of the American people. The ease with which the term "Camelot" came to be forever associated with the Kennedy family is exemplary of the mythic status of the man who reflected the collective American ideal more than any previous political or cultural leader, even more through his unique and affecting personality than his position and accomplishments. This stature was cemented by his assassination, for like the fabled king of the of the Arthurian legends, JFK was not the hero ultimately destined to deliver the grail, and with his demise so was America, at least for the time being, stifled in her quest for the holy cup—or for deliverance from the mounting anxiety of the atomic age.

Some, no doubt, sought solace in the arms of established religion, while for many, and especially the youth, this was simply no longer an adequate or fulfilling route to spiritual consolation. The modern, globalizing, technological world left little room for the clear-cut rights and wrongs of the baby boomers' parents, much less the Christianity that backed them up. Consciously or not, in the wake of Kennedy's death, the children and teens of the early '60s were existentially adrift and searching for some new incarnation to which they could attach a modern metaphysical framework.

In England, according to MacDonald, Beatlemania hit hard for "a society in which churchgoing was falling in inverse relationship to the rise in television ownership."[20] Beginning in early 1963, British Beatlemania served as a harbinger of American Beatlemania, with the added weight of England being viewed as a mother country to the United States and the origins of her language and culture. When the Beatles descended from the clouds and touched down at, appropriately, John F. Kennedy Airport in New York on February 7, 1964, the youth of America were wide awake in anticipation of these new saviors from overseas.

The audience applauds, not so much in recognition of the
individual onstage, but in recognition of one another.
—Buckminster Fuller

WE'LL FOLLOW THE SUN

❖ ❖ ❖

Meet the Mythic Beatles

When the Beatles appeared on *The Ed Sullivan Show* on February 9, 1964, an emergent mass collective became self-aware as it witnessed them through the medium of television. The event both unified and defined the children of the baby boom and ultimately led to the world-wide acceptance of the Beatles' sound and message. Though there were numerous historic turns prior and crucial events since that have chiseled this temporal mythology into its full-bodied form, there is no evolutionary line of demarcation more significant to the story and more exemplary of its impact. When American television introduced the Beatles to an unprecedented youth culture, a new covenant was sung into existence, answered and sealed with a scream of ecstatic recognition and release.

The effect was immediately palpable, so much so that the Beatles' appearance on *Ed Sullivan* has become one of the few cultural events that truly defined a generation, a "Where were you when…" moment that is arguably the only positive occurrence that has reached such a commonly agreed-upon status. The sudden emergence of the Beatles into American consciousness affected the inner reality and outer appearance of Western culture more specifically and immediately than any other event in history, including the beginning or end of a world war, the curing of a major disease, and the landing of a man on the moon. Not even the advent of the atomic age could produce an explosion powerful enough to transform the collective consciousness of a society the instant it occurred. While the maximum impacts of these reality-shifting events have unfolded slowly and consistently with time, one thing seems beyond debate: even to those who dislike the Beatles or decry their influence, the world certainly hasn't sounded or looked the same since the moment that awkward television impresario ceded the biggest stage in America to the four lads from Liverpool.

Significantly, for both the music and television mediums, the Beatles' triumphant appearance on *Ed Sullivan* was a crucial turning point. This single event allowed the impact of these two inchoate industries to manifest in a way which has never been matched in poignancy or salience, before or since. The decisive success of the show, as has been sensibly theorized in countless tomes, rags, and blogs, owed to numerous cultural, industrial, technological, and musical synchronicities that coordinated to create that indelible moment, which ultimately gave rise to a communal mythology that persists to this day.

The Beatles' commercial, creative, and critical dominance of twentieth (and now twenty-first) century popular music is simply staggering. In terms of sheer numbers, they are the best-selling musical artists of all time, also charting more number one singles and albums than any other artist, and it is worth mentioning that their strongest competition on the charts was often themselves. It is entirely reasonable to suggest that many of their widely acknowledged standards would have risen to the top had there not already been one of their songs in the number one slot.

Fueled by the creative collaboration of John Lennon and Paul McCartney, the most successful songwriters in history (32 number one singles for Paul, 26 for John—23 of which were written together), the Beatles spent the highest number of weeks at number one in the albums chart—174 in the UK and 132 in the US. As well, in testament to their extraordinary commercial durability, only the Beatles have charted a number one single or album in the American Top-40 in six consecutive decades. These distinctions are even more significant when one considers the remarkably short span of the group's recording career, approximately eight years total.

The Beatles' overall record sales and chart dominance in 1964 alone was, and remains, astonishing. Through the months of January, February and March, they accounted for sixty percent of all record sales in the US, charting nineteen hits in the Top-40 and thirty in the Top-100. Famously, during the week of April 4, 1964, they held the top five positions on the Billboard singles chart, and the following week occupied fourteen in the Top-100, crushing the previous record held by Elvis Presley (of nine concurrent singles during the week of December 19, 1956).[1] The Beatles' fifteen separate American releases in 1964 (nine singles and six albums) each sold one million or more copies, representing a total of more than twenty-five million record sales by the Beatles in 1964 in the US alone, and an estimated ninety million globally. Add to this the six Top-40 hits Lennon-McCartney composed for other performers, including a US and UK number one for Peter and Gordon ("A World Without Love"), and the immense commercial impact of Beatlemania comes into deeper focus.[2] But, as we well know, 1964 was just the beginning of a run of commercial dominance that has continued essentially unabated for now over fifty years.

It is important to note that at the time of this book's composition, the Beatles are still one of the hottest properties in world show business. An amazing run of successes in numerous mediums over the last several decades has shown them flexing their on-going commercial muscle. The following examples would each be a career pinnacle for nearly any other artist:

In November 1995, *The Beatles Anthology*, a ten-plus hour documentary on the band's saga, debuted to critical acclaim on ITV in the UK and ABC in the US; an accompanying double album, *Beatles Anthology 1*, was released concurrently and sold 450,000 copies in its first 24 hours, the largest one-day sales for any album or single in history. Over the next several years Apple released two more platinum *Anthology* double albums and *The Beatles Anthology* book, which topped the *New York Times* best-seller list.

Then, in November 2000 (a full thirty years after the Beatles' dissolution), their album *1*, a compilation of their number one singles, sold a record thirteen million copies in four weeks and topped the album charts in an estimated twenty-eight countries.[3] By the end of the 2000s, sales had topped thirty-one million, making it the biggest selling album of the decade.

Love, the Cirque de Soleil theatrical production featuring music, dance and acrobatics, debuted to rave reviews in 2006, and has continued playing at The Mirage in Las Vegas (in a venue specially built for the show) to sold out crowds into its second decade. Based on George and Giles Martin's re-produced music of the Beatles, *Love* also spawned a soundtrack album that quickly reached platinum status and won two Grammy awards—Best Compilation Soundtrack and Best Surround Sound Album.

In September 2009, just as *The Beatles Rock Band* video game from Harmonix introduced the group to a new generation of kids, the Beatles' re-mastered catalogue debuted, shattering sales records around the world and placing eighteen albums simultaneously on the Billboard chart (including five in the Top-10, and nine in the Top-20), leading to sales of 2.25 million albums in the first five days of release.[4]

One year later, in November 2010, through what was reported to be the most lucrative deal in the history of digital music,[5] the Beatles' entire catalogue was made available for online streaming by iTunes, resulting in 50 million plays within the first 48 hours.[6] By the end of the first week, iTunes claimed sales of 450,000 albums and more than 2 million songs.[7]

It has always been difficult to quantify the total sales resulting from Beatle-related product due to the many different media they have continuously navigated. A comprehensive study would also take into account hundreds of books, with two best-selling biographies in the new millennium alone, *The Beatles* (Bob Spitz, 2005) and *Can't Buy Me Love* (Jonathan Gould, 2008); feature films such as Iain Softley's *Backbeat* (1994), Julie Taymor's *Across the Universe* (2007), and Danny Boyle's *Yesterday* (2019); and a large number of documentaries, including Michael Epstein's *LennoNYC*, Martin Scorsese's *George Harrison: Living in the Material World*, and Ron Howard's *Eight Days a Week*. Suffice to say, factoring in these and numerous other ancillary products, releases, and re-releases (*Live at the BBC; Let it Be—Naked; Beatles Live at the Hollywood Bowl*), along with their aforementioned achievements, the Beatles have been the top-selling musical artists of the new millennium, decades after their final recording.

This is an amazing feat for any artist or musician, and yet it has become so familiar to see the Beatles at the "top of the charts" that the sheer predictability of their continuing accomplishments makes them seem almost insignificant. In other words, the Beatles have been so omnipresent (in our ears, in our eyes, and in our media) for so long that we are often simply too close to the phenomenon to see the unique imprint on history it is still in the process of carving. But the fact remains: by the end of that first *Ed Sullivan* show in February 1964, the Beatles had become the biggest attraction on Earth, and have essentially remained so decades after the band as an entity ceased to exist and two of its members have died.

This is in no way normal. Show business has always churned through new stars, styles, and fads, the press/media is a vicious "build them up and tear them down" machine, and the pop music market is notoriously fickle. Even the very biggest stars, the ones who are relevant (at least in commercial terms) for any longer than a few years, invariably have their time in the sun when they navigate the charts and adorn magazine covers, and then spend the rest of their years in the public eye as acts of nostalgia. Though they may continue to do very good business, and/or enjoy wide respect for having been innovative in their time and an influence on the modern market, success is nearly always limited to an artist's prime years of radio/television/video play and media infatuation. The few exceptions to this are stars such as Frank Sinatra, Elvis Presley, and Michael Jackson, whose cult of personality enabled them to play to sell-out crowds while they were alive, make records and films basically at will and when health allowed, and continue to attract media attention beyond their years as icons of youth. In even rarer cases, such as with the Rolling Stones, the high degree of popularity in their later years owes much to, and is somewhat dependent on, their against-the-odds longevity and is mostly generated by public appearances. As a live attraction, the Stones remain enormously popular decades into their career, and yet, comparatively speaking, have not generated substantial record sales beyond their "classic period." The Beatles, by contrast, haven't played a concert since August 1966, and their entire recording career lasted only 8 years, as opposed to 23 years for Elvis, 44 for Michael, 56 and counting for the Stones, and 60 for Frank.

Ironically, the Beatles were not even expected to remain popular beyond their initial splash, however noteworthy it was and strange that may seem in retrospect. Despite the immense hype of their arrival in New York in February 1964, or perhaps because of it, the American press was ready to cajole, tease, and dismiss the group, who they saw as merely another fad, like the Hula Hoop or the twist. They were in no way anticipating what transpired: the Beatles were composed, literate, clever, self-aware, unaffected, and in control—a four-faced entity that effortlessly deflected the barbs and bestowed insight and humor in response. Most of all, they were authentic, dispensing with traditional show-biz responses that emphasized gratefulness for their opportunity in the limelight in favor of self-effacing irony and brutal honesty. (As time went on, the genuineness offered by the Beatles in their interviews and press conferences became increasingly emboldened, as when they spoke out in protest of the burgeoning Viet Nam war and their stated refusal to perform in racially segregated venues.)[8]

By the end of that first televised press conference, the Beatles had triumphed over the toughest audience in America—the New York press corps—and two nights later they won over the rest of America when they debuted on *The Ed Sullivan Show*, watched by an estimated seventy-six million people, a full forty percent of the

United States populace (equivalent of 150 million in 2019). The national media—caught unaware but more than happy to jump on the gravy train—shined the planet's brightest spotlight on the Beatles and focused its full attention on the ensuing Beatlemania, with headline after headline attesting to the seemingly divine, almost alien, nature of the phenomenon: "'Beatles Descend on New York; Teen-agers Frantic;"[9] "Girls Go Bug-Eyed as Beatles Perform;"[10] "2,900-Voice Chorus Joins the Beatles—Audience Shrieks and Bays and Ululates."[11]

From the beginning, Beatlemania was described in terms of a religious experience. A week *before* the Beatles landed in New York, *Newsweek* magazine commented on the smash success of "I Want to Hold Your Hand," declaring, "The news sounded like an account of Old Testament retribution for all of the rock & roll that America had sent to Britain."[12] Three weeks later they stated, "[The Beatles] are a band of evangelists. And their gospel is fun ... their audiences respond in a way that makes an old-time revival meeting seem like a wake." The fans are called "the faithful."[13]

Time magazine reported that the Beatles "progress through scenes that might have been whimsically imagined by Dante."[14] *The New York Times Magazine* asserted, "To see a Beatle is joy, to touch one paradise on earth,"[15] deepening the discussion several weeks later with "rock and roll is a throwback, or tribal activism ... it is probably no coincidence that the Beatles, who provoke the most violent response among teenagers, resemble in manner the witch doctors who put their spell on hundreds of shuffling and stamping natives."[16] *Senior Scholastic* magazine claimed (scolded?), "In its fundamental sense, Beatlemania is a form of (primitive) idol worship ... There are even forms of graven images, such as Beatle wigs, pins, rings, sweatshirts, dolls, etc., to help the Beatlemaniacs along. In fact, Beatlemania has become a pseudo-religion."[17]

In an article for *The Saturday Evening Post*, Beatles press agent Derek Taylor is quoted describing Beatlemania as a literally rapturous experience: "It's as if they have founded a new religion." In his description of the band's recent tour down under, Taylor elaborated,

"In Australia, for example, each time we'd arrive at an airport, it was as if de Gaulle had landed, or better yet, the Messiah … it's as if some savior had arrived and all these people were happy and relieved, as if things somehow were going to be better now … the only thing left for the Beatles is to go on a healing tour."[18]

Upon the arrival of Beatlemania, the Beatles *were* immediately seen as potential healers. On their tours, they were continuously confronted by the physically afflicted, who begged for the touch of grace from what they believed, or hoped, to be a divine source. As Lennon described (in nomenclature reflecting the insensitivity of the time), "It seemed that we were just surrounded by cripples and blind people all the time, and when we would go through corridors, they would all be touching us[19] … They'd push them at you like you're Christ or something, or as there's some aura around you that will rub off on them … it got horrifying … like we were supposed to cure them."[20]

The messianic descriptions of Beatlemania in the press of the time provide a certainly-hyped but still somewhat objective perspective on the phenomenon, however there may be even more insight found in the subjective experience of those affected directly. When considering the descriptions from influential writers, poets, and musicians, the culture-shaping aspects and budding mythic impact come into deeper focus. Bob Dylan, who was already making waves as a groundbreaking songwriter and prophetic voice, saw in the Beatles the future of both musical and cultural evolution: "They were doing things nobody was doing. Their chords were outrageous, just outrageous, and their harmonies made it all valid … it was obvious to me that they had staying power. I knew they were pointing the direction that music had to go … in my head, the Beatles were *it*. It seemed to me a definite line was being drawn. This was something that never happened before."[21]

Leonard Cohen, the Canadian poet and songwriter who would rival Dylan in literary depth and critical favor, drew attention to the spiritual aspects at play: "[The Beatles] are speaking an elegy. They are dealing with some essence and handling it in a state of grace.

Music has a sacred function, and that sacred function is uniting Man, and honoring ancestors, and placing oneself in a reverent attitude toward the future. It has made things holy. They are the great public manifestation of those ideas that were being worked out by poets, and writers, and dreamers."[22]

Leonard Bernstein, the maestro of American classical music and composer of *West Side Story*, recognized instantly the Beatles' musical import and mythic quality: "I fell in love with Beatles' music (and simultaneously, of course, with their four faces-cum-personae) along with my children....Together we saw it, the Vision, in our inevitably different ways (I was 46!), but we saw the same Vision, and heard the same Dawn-Bird, Elephant-Trump, Fanfare of the Future....Saints John and Paul were, and made, and aureoled and beautified and eternalized the concept that shall always be known, remembered, and deeply loved as The Beatles. ...And yet, the two were merely something, the four were It."[23]

Two writers whose names are synonymous with music journalism, Lester Bangs and Greil Marcus, had similar revelatory experiences when they first became aware of the Beatles. Bangs recalls: "I can remember the first time I ever heard the Beatles as distinctly as, I suppose, everyone else in the Western world. Walking home from school, I stopped off at the local record store to check on the latest jazz, and there they were, spinning around and engulfing that shop with warm swelling waves of something powerfully attractive yet not quite comprehended, not yet. I wasn't much of a rock fan at the time, but there was some unmistakable stunning blare to that record that set it completely apart from what had come before...something that connected to broader concepts and idioms than any previous rock, like a muezzin's cry almost, and I stood in awe and thought, 'The Beatles in the sky.' "[24]

Marcus remembers: "There had been an item in the paper that day about a British rock & roll group that were to appear on the *Ed Sullivan Show* that night: The Beatles (a photo, too—were those wigs or what?). I was curious—I didn't know they had rock & roll in England—so I went down to a commons room where there was a TV set, expecting an argument from whoever was there about which channel to watch...Four hundred people sat transfixed as the Beatles sang "I Want to Hold Your Hand," and when the song was over the crowd exploded. People looked at the faces (and the hair) of John, Paul, George, and Ringo and said Yes (who could have predicted that a few extra inches of hair would suddenly seem so right, so necessary?); they heard the Beatles' sound and said Yes to that, too. What was going on? And where did all these people come from? Excitement wasn't in the air; it *was* the air."[25]

It is true there had been over-excited reactions to pop-culture heroes before. The word "mania" was first linked to the intense audience response inspired by Hungarian classical composer and pianist Franz Liszt. In 1844, critic Heinrich Heine marveled at the feverishness of what he termed "Lisztomania" in a review of Liszt's recent performances in Paris: "How convulsively his mere appearance affected them! How boisterous was the applause which rang to meet him! What acclaim it was! A veritable insanity, one unheard of in the annals of furore!"[26]

Since the dawn of the recording era we have witnessed numerous "fan-quakes" (Rudy Vallee, Frank Sinatra, Elvis Presley, Michael Jackson, Madonna, Nirvana, Eminem), but the Beatles represented something more creatively innovative and culturally potent than even their massive heart-throb status suggested. In retrospect, we can see that from the time of their triumphant appearance on *Ed Sullivan*, the Beatles swiftly conquered the entire domain of mass media—records, radio, television, film, newspapers, magazines, cartoons, books—and the media quickly became addicted to their consistent, dependable entertainment content. Their status as a generational phenomenon wasn't based solely on their musical output or fashion being in vogue, though that certainly was the case. The Beatles were so ubiquitous they became essentially indistinguishable from mass media itself. The two were in a sense one and the same, rising alongside one another, evolving in tandem, an ideal synthesis of form (media) and content (Beatles). The icons that came before the Beatles lacked the impact of the electronic media in full transmission, and those that came after could never be qualified as such culturally pioneering, commercially ground-breaking, media *creators.*

Concurrent with the Beatles' emergence into Western consciousness, Marshall McLuhan wrote two timely books, *The Gutenberg Galaxy: The Making of Typographic Man* (1962) and *Understanding Media: The Extensions of Man* (1964), that posited the increasingly cohesive role mass media would play in our communal mythologies. Several themes introduced in these works form the core of McLuhan's media theories: (1) the idea of mass media producing a new "Global Village;" (2) the recognition of new medias as a new languages; (3) the crucial role of the artist in navigating media landscapes; and (4) the concept of electric media facilitating the extension of human sensory experience, potentially providing a direct and outward mode of expression for what Jung had termed the collective human unconscious.

McLuhan, who is credited with predicting the internet and social media thirty years in advance,[27, 28] emphasized the resurgence of myth that would naturally blossom within the electronic media, and how it would manifest through the marriage of artistic expression and the active participation of the audience (whether or not the audience was consciously aware of its creative role in the process). He surmised that "the audience, as ground, shapes and controls the work of art,"[29] and that this symbiotic relationship would result in a "consciousness of the unconscious."[30] In *The Gutenberg Galaxy*, he writes: "The electric puts the mythic or collective dimension of human experience fully into the conscious wake-a-day world."[31] This view aligns with Jung's contention of a universal consciousness that fundamentally employs archetypal symbols to create reality. Jung believed that there is both a driving force, provided by instinctual energy, and attracting force, motivated by transcendental goals, behind the creation of a mythic symbol.[32] He felt archetypes "shape matter (nature) as well as mind (psyche)."[33]

The relationship between artist/communicator and audience/receptor becomes super-charged when communicating through sound and music, due to the fact of *entrainment*, a universal physical and biological occurrence wherein one system's rhythmic process becomes synchronized by or with the frequency of another system. This phenomenon was first identified by Dutch physicist and astronomer Christiaan Huygens in 1665, soon after he invented the pendulum clock. Huygens observed that two of these clocks, when mounted on a common wall or support, would eventually synchronize with each other, producing what is called *coupled oscillations*. Entrainment is now understood as fundamental to theories in many scientific fields, including physics, neuroscience, engineering, meteorology, linguistics, and social psychology.

Music, by creating a vibrational field, produces an environment wherein humans entrain with one another both physically and socially, fostering a true sense of emotional empathy between artist and listener, performer and audience, and audience member and audience member. Communicated through the immense reach of the electronic media, music—the Beatles' being of course the most pervasive—established a *cultural* entrainment that provided the ideal conditions for the expression and reception of archetypal mythology. In the era of the Simultaneous Collective Imprint—when the widespread transmission of images and sounds impressed the psyches of a great number of people at once—this push-pull relationship between a highly-focused mass consciousness and new musical prophets such as the Beatles profoundly affected the evolution of religious ritual and marked a significant leap forward in our ability to both create and experience mythology.

One may still ponder how this contemporary expression of and response to archetypal mythology (even if that was universally understood to be the dynamic) could be somehow defined as communal mythology, i.e. religion. After all, beyond our tendency to characterize the concert hall as a new church or the television as a modern tribal fire, the Beatles and the concomitant rock mythology didn't foster what, on the surface, looked like the religious ritual behavior of our recent past. Brick and mortar temples were not constructed to unite like-minded believers, the tenets of a belief system were not handed down from parent to child as factual explanations of temporal reality, moral prescriptions and eschatological expectations were not taught as social and spiritual dictums. How could rock & roll be said to have become actual religion if the reaction to it did not produce these or similar commonly understood definitions and results? The answer may be as simple as it is (admittedly) hard to qualify: Our methods and modes of ritual worship were, just as with our expression and experience of archetypal mythology, restructured by the advances of mass media and sound/image technology.

Consider the core paradigms of Romanian historian and philosopher Mircea Eliade, whose 1961 book *The Sacred and the Profane* influenced the understanding and interpretation of religious experience and ritual. Eliade posited that the divisions of *sacred and profane time and space* configure the experience of mythic reality sought in spiritual practice. Accordingly, we order our religious rites to take place in sacred spaces (churches, temples, family abodes, historic locales, etc.) at sacred times (annual festivals, religious holidays, weekly church services, daily prayer rituals, etc.) because this separation from the "profane" reality of our everyday lives offers a sense of timelessness, or, more to Eliade's point, a communion with the primeval time that birthed the mythology. He writes: "Just as the church constitutes a break in the plane in the profane space of a modern city, the service celebrated inside it marks a break in profane temporal duration. It is no longer today's present time that is experienced.... [It's] a *mythical* time, that is, a primordial time."[34]

The sacred and profane dichotomy was originally explored by French philosopher Emile Durkheim in his 1912 magnum opus *The Elementary Forms of the Religious Life*: "[The] division of the world into two domains, the one containing all that is sacred, the other all that is profane, is the distinctive trait of religious thought. ... But by sacred things one must not understand simply those personal beings which are called gods or spirits; a rock, a tree, a spring, a pebble, a piece of wood, a house, in a word, anything can be sacred."[35] Considered the father of modern sociology, Durkheim felt that religion provides the fundamental framework for the moral dimension that imbues a common cultural identity: "The totality of beliefs and sentiments common to the average members of a society forms a determinate system with a life of its own. It can be termed the collective or common consciousness."[36] Durkheim spoke from a sociological rather than psychological perspective, however, his view shares an important point of intersection with Jung's theory of a collective unconscious that springs from an archetypal source. For Durkheim it was a top-down process, one in which "society, fashioning us in its image, fills us with religious, political, and moral beliefs that control our actions,"[37] while for Jung it manifested from the bottom-up: "We shall probably get nearest to the truth if we think of the conscious and personal psyche as resting upon the broad basis of an inherited and universal psychic disposition which is as such unconscious, and that our personal psyche bears the same relation to the collective psyche as the individual to society."[38]

The nexus may be found in Jungian psychologist Joseph Henderson's concept of a psychological space existing between the overt machinations of society and the collective unconscious. Henderson, a former patient of Jung's in 1929 and founder of the Jung Institute of San Francisco, in his 1961 academic paper titled "The Cultural Unconscious," suggested a realm of "historical memory that lies between the collective unconscious and the manifest pattern of the culture. It may include both these modalities, conscious and unconscious, but it has some kind of identity arising from the archetypes of the collective unconscious, which assists in the formation of myth and ritual and also promotes the development in individuals."[39]

In the 1960s, the partitions between sacred and the profane time and space, individual and collective consciousness, even, perhaps, the archetypal unconscious and the budding cultural consciousness coalescing around the Beatles and their contemporaries, were redefined by the electronic media and ease of access to recorded sound. No longer was it imperative to practice "religious" ritual in a special place at a special moment to experience sacred time and space; the youth of the '60s could find spiritual solace anytime they turned on their radio or put a record on the player. For them, the sacred could manifest literally anywhere they could access the music—in a bedroom, in a car, in a theatre, on a street-corner, on a beach. Eliade's contention that "Man becomes aware of the Sacred because it manifests itself, shows itself, as ... a reality that does not belong to our world, in objects that are an integral part of the our natural 'profane' world,"[40] was perhaps even more prescient than it was astute. At a time when the artist was in many ways superseding the role of the preacher, and moving, as McLuhan suggested, "from the ivory tower to the control tower of society,"[41] the musically entrained youth of the '60's could experience the sacred whenever and wherever, from a radio, a record player, a jukebox, a television set, a guitar.

Author Tom Wolfe remembers witnessing firsthand the immediacy of such a major cultural shift. He aligns (as many did) the energy associated with the arrival of the Beatles with youth: "I was there at Kennedy Airport when the Beatles arrived. I'll never forget the sight of hundreds of boys, high-school students, running down a hallway at the international arrivals building with their combs out, converting their duck-tail hairdos into bangs. They'd just seen the Beatles. They were packed on this balcony watching the Beatles arrive. They saw these haircuts, and they started combing their hair forward, so it would fall over their foreheads like the Beatles. I will never forget that scene. That was symbolic of a big change; the last semblance of adult control of music *vanished* at that moment."[42]

It was a logical association to make. The new mindset was exuberant, vibrant, and sexual, and of course the Beatles and their initial fans were quite young (indeed, the *Associated Press* declared 1964 "The Year of the Kid"). As the world would find out, however, the revolution extended far beyond rousing the literal youth. The Beatles were in fact a completely new artistic and entertainment hybrid. As an artistic collective that composed their own music, wrote their own lyrics, performed their own songs, produced their own sound (the influence of George Martin still largely off the radar for the vast majority of fans), and insisted on remaining true to their authentic selves (eschewing, from their earliest mainstream success, the impulse to present themselves as traditional entertainers), the Beatles defined the sphere of influence the musical artist would assume in the new media landscape. Though they remained primarily musicians, the group quickly became prominent and influential in numerous additional creative realms: film, literature, fashion, hairstyles, pop art, music video, and, eventually, various expressions of social and political activism.

This amalgamation of art forms was not just a novel concept in the '60s. This specific brand of all-encompassing entertainment had literally never been seen before, or if it had, no technology had existed alongside it that could broadcast and preserve its influence across space and time, allowing a wide range of people to collectively share the experience. If a self-contained group of singer-performer-composer-writers had never existed before, the novelty and power of something so new would obviously turn heads. Still, though, why did *this* specific new vibration and visage capture the spirits of people across the world so furtively and so rapidly? The affected youth combing his hair forward the day after the *Ed Sullivan Show* couldn't know that this rock & roll group he'd seen the night before on television would transform the world over the next several years in untold ways, and yet *his* world had been transformed by what he saw and heard.

In order to unravel this mystery and determine how and why it has so deeply affected our individual lives and collective experience, we will explore the archetypal symbolism communicated by the Beatles that aligns them with the saviors of mythology. First, we turn to their narrative, a "passion play" that both inspired and exemplified the collective spiritual journey of the musically-entrained '60s youth. As we dive these mythic depths, let us reflect on McLuhan's words: "Psychic communal integration, made possible at last by the electronic media, could create the universality of consciousness foreseen by Dante when he predicted that men would continue as no more than broken fragments until they were unified into an inclusive consciousness.... This is a new interpretation of the mystical body of Christ; and Christ, after all, is the ultimate extension of man."[43]

Where there is the greatest love, there are always miracles.
—Willa Cather

SGT. PEPPER'S MAGICAL MYSTERY SCHOOL

❧ ❧ ❧

The Mythic Resurrection of the Beatles

The story of Jesus Christ has been commonly referred to in the Western world as "The Greatest Story Ever Told," but in fact, the narrative of Jesus is one of many regarding a "dying and rising" god, or *savior*. To understand how the Beatles' narrative aligns with the stories of resurrected saviors, it is helpful to consider the concept of the *monomyth*, Joseph Campbell's notion of a core plot that exists within many myths in many cultures and time-periods. In his book *The Hero with a Thousand Faces*, Campbell identifies a "Hero's Journey" story arc that pinpoints strong commonalities, not just among the tales of the ancients, but also as a prevalent narrative that can be found in our modern literature, film, theatre, and television drama. He expresses the hero's journey as sort of a three-act play—Departure-Initiation-Return—that contains within its essential structure numerous consistent characters and plot-points.

We know the story well: the hero (1) departs his or her community for an unknown realm, (2) is initiated while obtaining a boon (usually knowledge or treasure), and (3) returns with it for the benefit of the community. The character of the savior follows the arc of the hero's journey by *departing* the world of the living, becoming *initiated* in the mysterious realm of death, and then miraculously *returning* to life, bringing with him the ultimate boon——revelations about freedom from mortality. It is important to note that elements may be presented in varying orders from myth to myth, with the over-all structure of hero's journey remaining constant—in other words, the specific turns of plot might be unique, but the beginning, middle, and end of the stories are universal to a remarkable degree.

Campbell based his thesis in part on Jung's concept of universal psychological archetypes that underlie characters and narratives in dreams; he then refracted these concepts through the lens of comparative religion. The monomythic story arc he identified can be found in fairy tales *Cinderella* and *Jack and the Beanstalk*; literary classics, from the prototypal *Epic of Gilgamesh*, *The Odyssey*, and *Le Morte d'Arthur*, to novels *Moby Dick*, *The Adventures of Huckleberry Finn*, and *Lord of the Rings*; and modern films, including *The Wizard of Oz*, *Jaws*, and *Avatar*, among countless others.

Most famously, the hero's journey as defined by Campbell became the creative template for George Lucas's *Star Wars*, which inspired the most successful film franchise in the history of cinema. Lucas has long acknowledged his debt: "I've tried to take the ideas that seem to cut across the most cultures. . . . I think that's one of the things that I really got from Joe Campbell—what he was trying to do is find the common threads through the various mythology. . . . I wanted to try to explain in a different way the religions that have already existed. . . . I'm telling an old myth in a new way."[1]

Luke Skywalker aside, the mythic drama of the savior, one of the most universal and enduring examples of the hero's journey, is perhaps best known in the narrative of Jesus Christ, as told from several perspectives in the four Gospels—Mark, Matthew, Luke, and John—and the book Acts of the Apostles. Because these five books contain often unique (and sometimes conflicting) accounts of the various occurrences in the story of their subject, the complete arc of the Jesus narrative is often obscured in favor of focus on the specific episodes that, when combined, bring a comprehensive impression of the full life of Jesus Christ.

The savior archetype was especially prevalent in religious cults known as the Mystery Schools (or Religions) of antiquity. Evolving from the resurrection myths of the Sumerian Inanna (Ishtar, Astarte) and Egyptian Osiris, many of the Hellenistic mystery traditions in Ancient Greece and Rome, whose influences would be some of the major factors in the development of Christianity as a religion distinct from Judaism, involve a god, or man, or god-as-man, who enters the underworld and returns (Dionysus, Zalmoxis, Romulus, and Adonis being examples).[2]

The Mysteries were two-fold in design and practice. Each tradition featured an (exoteric) "Outer Mystery" that offered allegorical myths for the greater public, and an (esoteric) "Inner Mystery," which consisted of secret teachings and rituals for initiates seeking the mystical truths underlying the more simplified doctrines contained in the outer mystery. Western scholars are often reluctant to classify the early Christian sects as Semitic variants of the mystery schools, however the similarities in their stories, and the time-period in which they emerged, is quite telling. Further, Mark makes implicit reference to the secretive interior of the Christian faith: "Then Jesus said, 'Whoever has ears to hear, let them hear.' When he was alone, the Twelve and the others around him asked him about the parables. He told them, 'The secret of the kingdom of God has been given to you. But to those on the outside everything is said in parables.' "[3]

Savior dramas, or "passion plays," were the core myths taught in the mystery schools, and they often adhered to a common plot—Death-Transfiguration-Resurrection-Ascension—corresponding to the arc of the hero's journey: Departure-Initiation-Return. It is this transformation that aligns the Jesus story with the other resurrection myths, and of which the Beatles unwittingly communicated a modern allegory through personal narrative and archetypal symbolism in the 1960s.

Though the resurrection and ascension of Jesus are primary underpinnings of Christian theology, they are rarely emphasized (sometimes not even included) in popular cinematic versions of the story. Hollywood prefers to focus on antagonistic "good versus evil" conflicts, and usually opts to emphasize Jesus's struggles with adversaries, variously personified as Judas (*Jesus Christ Superstar*), Satan (*The Last Temptation of Christ*), and even non-believers, i.e., the Jews (*The Passion of the Christ*). While this approach may resonate on the vigilante-and-violence-obsessed American big screen, the more fantastic features of the story—the miracles, transfiguration, resurrection, and ascension—are highlighted in the churches, where they're viewed as proof of the divinity of a historical Jesus, inspiring the bedrock beliefs of the Christian faith.

Our focus here begins where Hollywood usually ends the story, with the death of the savior. In the Christian writings, the passion of Jesus Christ concerns his arrest by the priestly class, the Sanhedrin, and his trials before the Jewish high court and the Roman governor, Pontius Pilate. The charge against him was his purported claim to be the Messiah. Though he was found not guilty by Pilate, the people (the court of popular opinion) condemned him and he was sentenced to death by crucifixion.

The Beatles' passion play began, similarly enough, when John Lennon compared the Beatles to Jesus Christ. His infamous quote to the *London Evening Standard* in March 1966, which caused no reaction in Great Britain, was re-printed five months later in August in the American teen magazine *Datebook*, where it caused Christian outrage, public protests, and the burning of Beatle albums, photographs, and books: "Christianity will go. It will vanish and shrink. I needn't argue about that; I'm right and I'll be proved right. We're more popular than Jesus now. I don't know which will go first—rock & roll or Christianity."[4]

John's perceived claim of divinity, for all the rage it caused, was not a crime punishable by law. Instead, he was tried in the media and his character was vilified by the public and the harshest judges of his day—fundamentalist Christians. Soon he would sing, "Christ you know it ain't easy, you know how hard it can be. The way things are going, they're gonna crucify me."

Both Jesus and the Beatles, in their respective myths, experienced a years-long period of ministry/touring and works/songs (performing one "miracle" after another), during which they were consistently met with praise and adoration. In both cases, they increasingly spoke out against social injustice and leveled critique at the ruling class, which eventually culminated in their respective confrontations with authorities. It's noteworthy that in their February 1965 *Playboy* magazine interview (well over a year before the *Datebook* controversy) the Beatles were not only sharply critical of religion in general, but also claimed to be agnostics. John was, typically, the most outspoken: "[It's] the hypocritical side of it, which I can't stand."

If the *Playboy* content wasn't red-enough meat (likely because its interviews were considered serious, adult conversations), the comments appearing in *Datebook* gave Beatles detractors the opportunity to use the excuse of protecting the impressionable minds of American youth. Lennon was thereafter subject to trial by press conference, broadcast to an expansive viewing audience many million times larger than the witnesses Jesus faced at Pilate's palace. The media inquired, to paraphrase, "Are you saying you are God?" and "Will you apologize for whatever it was you said?" John began his "apology" with a sly retort, which, like Jesus's reply to Pilate ("You have said so"),[5] both deflected the question and illuminated the deeper issue at play: "I suppose if I had said television was more popular than Jesus, I might have got away with it." He reportedly wept afterward.

After Jesus died on the cross, Pilate handed his body over to Joseph of Arimathea, who laid Jesus in the tomb Joseph had prepared for his own eventual burial. After the Beatles quit touring, they "disappeared" for a short time to pursue personal projects, soon ensconcing themselves in the Abbey Road studio with producer George Martin.

Joseph of Arimathea is described in the various gospel accounts as a counselor, a rich man, a member of the Sanhedrin, and, most pointedly, a *disciple* of Jesus. Though he enjoyed a higher status, was wealthy and a member in good standing with the ruling class, he was a *believer*, and he accepted and served the cause of his upstart savior.

The importance of George Martin in the musical journey of the Beatles cannot be overstated. Martin took the raw talent and creativity of the band and counseled, developed, arranged, and produced them. He was a well-respected and successful member of the musical establishment who believed in them and humbly and steadfastly dedicated himself to their artistic growth and creative evolution.

In these respective stories, Joseph of Arimathea and George Martin represent the same monomythic archetype—the *wise old man*. A crucial ally to the hero, the wise old man is a father-figure and mentor, dispensing wisdom and offering guiding support by virtue of his maturity, experience, sound judgment, and higher social standing. This stock character is well known to audiences of literature and film, where he has been memorably presented as Obi-Wan-Kenobi (*Star Wars*), Gandalf (*Lord of the Rings*), and Professor Dumbledore (*Harry Potter*), just to name a few.

Martin's relationship to the Beatles was revealing. No other archetype from the rock pantheon can claim such a direct and crucial connection to a symbolic father. (The word "Abbey," incidentally, is derived from the Aramaic word *abba*, or "father.") Both George Martin and Joseph of Arimathea are, in these contexts, allegories for God in that just as humanity is seen to be guided by His wisdom, grace, inspiration, and love, the hero is guided by the wise old man. For the Beatles, as for Jesus, this relationship became more charged as the time of transformation approached.

The "death" of the Beatles was represented by the band's retreat from the stage after their August 29, 1966 performance at San Francisco's Candlestick Park. For the '60s generation, this was the equivalent of an end, or metaphoric death, of the group. They *stopped appearing live.* The Beatles as a live entity, and perhaps as a crucial part of the unfolding history of a generation, was seemingly over. A pop band's continuing production and ongoing cultural relevance without live performance had never occurred before. The lack of an official announcement only added to the unsettling fear amongst the faithful that the Beatles were now...gone.

But the story wasn't over. The Beatles had entered the transfiguration stage of the drama, mirrored in nature by the pupae stage of the caterpillar's metamorphosis into butterfly. This phase was marked by the most transitional album of the band's career, *Revolver*. The album's title alone was layered with implications that inferred the Beatles, as they had been, were over. It was time to become something more, something new. Even the abandoned working title, "Abracadabra," suggested that something magical was taking place. The songs on *Revolver* spun from one Beatle to the next, accentuating each and unveiling more and more layers of depth to their individual, elemental personalities—John, the innovator; Paul, the classicist; George, the spiritualist; Ringo, the emollient. The album in its entirety was an alchemical mixture announcing a revolution and evolution in the Beatles' sound and direction.

The Transfiguration of Christ concerns a Biblical event in which Jesus goes to the top of a mountain, is bathed in radiant light, and visited by two prophets, Moses and Elijah.[6] Though in scripture this episode takes place shortly before the arrest and passion, it has, since the early days of Christianity, been equally associated with the elusive time between the crucifixion and resurrection. Second century church father Origen wrote a theological treatise making this connection explicit, and henceforth the traditional church has considered the transfiguration a foreglimpse of the resurrected body of Christ, and a demonstration of the transformation Jesus would make during his journey into the underworld.[7]

Revolver was released in August 1966, the same month as the Beatles' final run of concerts. It joined two other seminal works released earlier that year by Bob Dylan and Brian Wilson (with the Beach Boys), *Blonde on Blonde* and *Pet Sounds*, respectively. All three albums were striking expansions of production process and a deepening of subject matter in popular music, marked a creative zenith in the careers of their creators, and were influenced by hallucinogenic drugs. Given that many scholars now deduce that psychotropic compounds were likely used in the mystery school cults, ingested during religious rituals in which the initiate enacted the transformational drama of the savior, it is intriguing that psilocybin (magic mushrooms) and LSD began to be used in earnest by the counter-culture in 1966 at the time of *Revolver, Blonde on Blonde,* and *Pet Sounds.*

The last song on *Revolver,* "Tomorrow Never Knows," is a poignant climax to this transformational album. Lennon was inspired by his reading of *The Psychedelic Experience* by Timothy Leary, Richard Alpert, and Ralph Metzner, which was itself inspired by *The Tibetan Book of the Dead,* a casual translation of a book titled more accurately, *Liberation Through Hearing During the Intermediate State*—in other words, a Buddhist guidebook for the transfiguration stage between death and rebirth through *sound.* Here, John found the words and, along with his band-mates, music to infer the timely psychedelic transformation of the '60s generation, the soul's journey through a liminal bardo death-state, and the end of the Beatles as a "live" entity.

Regarding the next phase of the drama, resurrection, Christianity's quintessential doctrine centers on the assertion that Jesus was raised from the dead by God. Afterwards, Jesus appears in the flesh, or not, depending on the narrator. Oddly, while the letters of St. Paul refer to a resurrected Christ, they never mention an empty tomb or describe any post-death physical appearances beyond revelations like those Paul claimed he and other early Christians were experiencing. On the other hand, versions in the Gospels and Acts do depict earthly appearances by the risen Christ. Perhaps the most well-known of these post-mortem cameos is the story of "Doubting Thomas," in which Jesus proves his identity by showing the skeptical disciple his pierced hands. While this story makes the point that Christ's body has literally been physically resurrected, there are several other accounts that present a not-entirely-corporeal Jesus, one who walks through walls,[8] disappears upon recognition,[9] appears differently to different people,[10] and cannot be touched physically.[11]

It was in a similarly vibratory realm of sound and story where the Beatles would resurrect with far more permanence and impact than their physical performances could ever inspire. Utilizing the recording studio as an instrument of musical language, *Sgt. Pepper's Lonely Hearts Club Band* was a concept album that revolutionized ideas about the potential of recorded music. The album's "concept," of course, was the Beatles' imagining themselves as a mythical band, while marking the first time a group of their stature represented themselves solely in the form of vibration, i.e. recorded sound and not in live appearance. The motif of rebirth was under-scored by the *Sgt. Pepper* album cover, on which the "new" Beatles, costumed in fluorescent uniforms, stood alongside wax figures of their former personification dressed in the mono-chromatic black suits of their touring years. All at once, they were reborn into the realm of mythic allegory. The Beatles were no longer *a* band—they were the very concept of "Band." They had become mythic creators, and their sound, image, and message increasingly expanded to define the youthful spirituality of their time.

The implications of resurrection for both Jesus and the Beatles heralded new eras in their respective cultures. If the early Christians and priests of the apostolic age saw in the resurrection of Christ an evolutionary leap in their conception of spirit, *Sgt. Pepper,* by redefining the future of music and further establishing the Beatles as a *mythic* phenomenon, performed the same function for the youth culture of the Western world. Accordingly, *Time* magazine greeted the album with a cover story titled: "The Beatles—Their New Incarnation."

The album was a turning point in the history of popular music and a zeitgeist for the youth of the '60s, immediately becoming the omnipresent sonic backdrop to the time we now refer to as the "Summer of Love." Contemporary reviews of *Sgt. Pepper* were nearly unanimous in ecstatic praise. *The Times'* theatre critic Kenneth Tynan described it as a "decisive moment in the history of Western civilization,"[12] while their music critic William Mann proclaimed it a "historic departure in the progress of music—any music."[13] *Newsweek's* Jack Kroll called it a "masterpiece," famously comparing "A Day in the Life" to T.S. Eliot's *The Wasteland.*[14] In *The New Yorker,* editor William Shawn hailed *Sgt. Pepper* as a "musical *event*," and further surmised that "the Beatles have done more to brighten the world in recent years than almost anything else in the arts."[15]

Sgt. Pepper was a watershed commercial success, spending twenty-seven and fifteen weeks at the top of the charts in the UK and US respectively, and winning four Grammy awards, including "Record of the Year" (the first rock album to win that category). When the dust settled, *Sgt. Pepper* was the top-selling album of the '60s, and to date has sold well over thirty million copies globally, making it one of the world's all-time best-selling records. Music historian Elijah Wald accurately summarizes that from *Sgt. Pepper* onward, Beatles' albums were "treated as musical novels, designed for individual contemplation in their entirety." Acknowledging the influence of the electronic media, he writes, "It was the age of Marshall McLuhan, and the medium was the message; musicians who had big ideas made big records."[16]

Then, on June 25, 1967, less than a month after *Sgt. Pepper* had entrained the youth of the West, the Beatles performed and recorded "All You Need is Love" as part of *Our World*, the first ever global satellite broadcast, seen by approximately 400 million people in twenty-six countries. With this performance, they played out the resolution and final act in the mythic resurrection drama, ascension––transcending the crude world to become one with all humanity. With this vibrational expansion, the Beatles' image and sound literally rose above the earth as they explicitly aligned themselves with the message of love.

The books Mark, Luke, and Acts describe the Ascension of Jesus, where he is taken up to heaven in a cloud in full view of his now eleven (since Judas has exited the story) disciples; he then (according to Mark) took a seat at the right hand of God. Known in Christian theology as *divinization*, the process of realizing divine essence is, in many syncretistic resurrection/ascension myths, achieved by some form of love: Osiris was killed and dismembered, and then resurrected through the love of his wife, Isis; Orpheus traveled into the underworld to resurrect his mortal lover, Eurydice, through the power of music and love; Dionysus braved the underworld to resurrect his beloved mortal mother, Semele; Demeter's daughter Persephone was abducted by Hades, the god of the underworld, and allowed to resurrect for half the year through her mother's love; and Jesus died, spent three days in the under-world, and was resurrected through God's love for humanity. In the New Testament, love is intrinsic in both the process of God-into-man: "For God so loved the world that he gave his only begotten son..."[17] and man-into-God: "Whoever does not love does not know God, because God is love."[18]

Universal love is essentially transcendence of the illusion of individual separation and recognition of the sameness of the self and something else (and by extension, everything else) that exists. If we can recognize the sameness in what we perceive to be oppo-sites, then we can see love as pervasive and omnipresent. In mythol-ogy, this universal love resolves duality—be it between heaven and earth, male and female, matter and spirit, or any number of polar-ized concepts—through harmony. As we shall see, the resolution of duality and the power of love are not just central tenets of the resurrection myths, they are also keys to understanding the elusive meaning and method of myth itself.

Duality is the manifestation of two opposing and interdepen-dent forces, entities, or concepts. It is also how we know anything exists. The first thing an artist learns is that both shadow and light are needed to create form. This is as true of our own emotions and inner lives as it is of the physical world: creation/destruction, empa-thy/judgment, joy/sorrow, etc. We see this inherent principle in the logic of computer programming—binary code works because it is modeled from our experience of existence, which is reducible to ones and zeroes. Yes and no.

If duality is the basis of our experience of the manifest uni-verse, it is logical that the un-manifest (the Godhead, Great Spirit, Brahman, et al.) would be imagined as something either singular and whole, or so fluid and multifaceted that it can contain two opposites—and really, all opposites—at once. The supreme dei-ties in nearly all religious belief systems are non-dual in nature, remaining wholly conceptual in human consciousness in that they are beyond all forms. They encompass *all*.

The Beatles' first single after they transcended with "All You Need Is Love" was a clever chart-topper, "Hello, Goodbye," that played with the problems of opposites: "You say yes, I say no, you say stop, and I say go, go, go ..." The flip side, "I Am the Walrus," opened with a declaration of oneness: "I am he as you are he as you are me and we are all together." But it was the band's 1968 post-resurrection narrative that expressed the resolution of duality as the natural denouement to their hero's journey.

The visual presentation of their next album would illustrate this notion. Created by Richard Hamilton, the British conceptual artist who coined the term "Pop Art," the cover of the self-titled *The Beatles*—their only official album cover that doesn't feature an image of the four Beatles—was an exercise in minimalism. In stark contrast to the vibrant hues of *Sgt. Pepper* and *Magical Mystery Tour*, the entire sleeve was pure white. The letters spelling out the title were only legible because they were slightly embossed; fans read the words "The Beatles" not in ink, but in the interplay of light and shadow.

Beyond its marketing innovation, this completely white album cover is a powerful mythic symbol. White is the color used to represent heaven—it is both everything and nothing, empty and all-encompassing. Like the Circle and the Mandala, it is a symbol for wholeness, purity, and bliss. White transcends color because it contains all colors, a spectrum of opposites in perfect balance. This concept was also punctuated through the music—never had an album contained so many opposing styles and approaches. With this incredibly diverse collection of songs, the Beatles seemed to possess the ability to balance and include any musical duality imaginable. Also, appropriately, this pure "White Album" contained not one, but *two* records, and was the only double album of their career.

The band's two primary social endeavors at the time of the White Album further evinced a dual spiritual/material focus. In February 1968, the Beatles made the pilgrimage to India to study transcendental meditation with the Maharishi Mahesh Yogi. The ensuing publicity and effect on their creative output exposed the West to Eastern spirituality, practice, and perspective. This voyage also marked George Harrison's enhanced role as a creative force in the Beatles, both culturally and musically. His increasingly sophisticated compositions broadened the band's artistic personality, while his spiritual pursuits—which inspired their journey to India—deepened the content of their archetypal mythology.

Upon their return, the Beatles announced their intention to deal with the demands of the temporal realm in a revolutionary manner. They launched Apple Corps, which included two record labels (Apple and her spoken-word sister Zapple), a film company, a clothing boutique, and several other divisions tending to various creative endeavors. The company's progressive business model was intended to help the band deal with material demands through a spiritual mode, and with great idealism they attempted to use their fame, wealth, and grace to develop budding artists in numerous fields. Though ultimately doomed as a failed business model, Apple (which would still administer the Beatles' catalog and legacy to enormous profits in the ensuing decades) in its conception was seen by fans as an admirable and brave attempt to give back to the world, strengthening the group's image as counterculture philanthropists.

Of course, the apple is one of popular culture's most indelible duality symbols, associated with the fruit of the Tree of Knowledge in the Garden of Eden story, even though a type of fruit is never specified in Genesis. Adam and Eve's fall from grace functions as an allegory for the human being's relationship to a dualistic, manifest world. Eden represents a harmonious state of being before duality; when the two lovers bite into the fruit they gain knowledge of the opposites—good and evil—and enter a realm of polarity.

Often masked at the time by the inclusive nature of their music and the seeming similitude of their members, there had always been duality at the core of the Beatles: John Lennon and Paul McCartney. Fans and writers have described the complimentary balance of the two partners through countless pairs of opposites: light/dark, soft/rough, bitter/sweet, etc. It could be argued that the most accurate combination is the one whose resolution through art was so sublimely suggested by Keats: Beauty and Truth.

In an existential sense, and one that speaks to their uncanny ability to both push the artistic envelope and yet always remain in perfect step with the tastes of their time, McCartney and Lennon suggested the concepts of Past and Future, respectively. Like the Roman god Janus, they faced both backward and forward—Paul wistfully looking back, celebrating and romanticizing the past; and John fearlessly gazing ahead, visioning and braving the future. Consider the songs they're most identified with individually: "Yesterday" and "Imagine." MacDonald contends that "the Beatles' ability to be two contradictory things at once—comfortably safe and exhilaratingly strange—has been displayed by no other pop act. A by-product of the creative tension between the group's two domi-nant personalities, this effect increased as Lennon and McCartney grew apart as writers."[19]

The two composers' most remarkable (one notable and one notorious) songs of 1968, "Hey Jude" and "Revolution #9," were extreme opposites. Presented as an empathetic sing-a-long for the ages, "Hey Jude" was the Beatles' most dominant Billboard chart hit, resting at number one in the US for nine consecutive weeks. It is still one of the most widely played songs in the world, and indeed was the tune with which Sir Paul closed the opening ceremonies of the 2012 Olympics in London. "Hey Jude" expresses the sentiment of "All You Need is Love" as a melodic invitation, imploring listen-ers to join together in song as it suggests that our ultimate healing is to be found in the acceptance of life and our harmony with one another.

Conversely, the turbulent sound collage of "Revolution #9" por-trayed social order in turmoil and creative vision in flames. Initially, it was savagely attacked by critics and fans who pointed to it as proof that John was losing the thread completely, but it is now, by the very virtue of its audacious and artistically daring inclusion on the White

Album—making it undoubtedly the most widely experienced piece of experimental *musique concrete* in the history of recorded music—reluctantly understood to be among the most unique and haunting artistic statements in the Beatle canon. With the benefit of time one could argue that it accomplished exactly what John hoped it would; it remains one of the most infamous recordings in history, and from a group that, due to their unmatched popularity alone, represented the very height of commerciality.

In 1968, McCartney furthered the Beatles' redeemer narrative, and once again lifted the bar for commercial success, while Lennon redefined and transformed the mythos and boldly proclaimed that *art comes first*. But by the time they finished recording the White Album, their partnership could not have been more artistically—and, by most accounts, personally—at odds. They were still somehow in balance but were so distanced from one another that it was becoming inevitable they would spin off-kilter. Besides, John was about to transcend the band and merge with a new artistic and life partner altogether.

Each of us is always looking for his other half, and when one meets
with his other half the pair are lost in an amazement of love and
friendship and intimacy, and one will not be out of the other's sight.
—Plato

THE BALLAD OF YIN AND YANG

❧ ❧ ❧

The Mythic Union of John & Yoko

Everything we experience in our material world is realized and created through a dance with its opposite. In myth, the notion of duality is often represented by male/female couplings. In Hinduism, there are god/goddess consorts, where each major male deity has a female partner or counterpart. The female aspects can be understood as the physical manifestations of the abstract concepts associated with the male god. For instance, Brahma is creation and Saraswati is music, art, and language; Vishnu is sustenance and Lakshmi is wealth, health, and prosperity; Shiva is destruction and Kali is the warrior and death.

When John Lennon left the Beatles to partner with Yoko Ono, the pair merged male and female energies, commercial and experimental artforms, and Western and Eastern cultures. Ono's concept of "life as art" brought to the partnership—and to Lennon's creative process—the abstract (masculine/art) expressed as the physical (feminine/life). No longer was John content to simply drop acid and sing about love, now it was his and his wife's mission to help love manifest in the world.

Never had John or any of the rock gods so intentionally wielded their own mythology. John and Yoko were intensely aware of the power their unprecedented fame had bestowed upon them and used that influence with more directed attention than any of their contemporaries. Assuming incomparable notoriety as an adult (she was thirty-three when she met John), farseeing Yoko provided a perspective on the potential of John's (and now her) opportunity that was perhaps unavailable to a man who had it all by the age of twenty-two. He admitted as much: "I learned everything from her. ... It is a teacher-pupil relationship. ... I'm the famous one, the one who's supposed to know everything, but she's my teacher."[1] John may have had the insight that he was "more popular than Jesus," but Yoko understood the implications and responsibilities of that reality.

In fact, their romance was consummated at the very time John was experiencing the feeling that he was indeed the second coming of Jesus Christ. As told by Pete Shotton, John's closest childhood friend who worked as his personal assistant, the two were sitting in John's home "after a bit of LSD" when John suddenly exclaimed, "Pete, I think I'm Jesus Christ... I'm back again ... I've got to tell the world who I am." The next day, at a band meeting, he gathered the other Beatles. "I've something very important to tell you all," he said. "I am Jesus Christ. I have come back again. This is my thing." John's fellow Beatles remained silent until someone suggested they adjourn for lunch, where the matter was dropped. Back at home later that evening, John told Pete he "fancied having a woman around." He said, "I think I'll give Yoko a ring. I'd like to get to know her a bit better and now's a good time."[2, 3]

Although it is tempting to dismiss John's revelation as the result of a drug-induced, inflated ego, his "messiah complex" must be understood through the lens of his unique experience, that of perhaps the most famous person in the world. By 1968, his unparalleled fan base had long been looking to him for answers to social, political, and even existential questions. He would be named "Man of the Decade" by both *Time* magazine and BBC-TV the following year, and the year after that offered the role of Jesus in Andrew Lloyd Weber and Tim Rice's rock musical *Jesus Christ Superstar*.[4] John's identification with Jesus wasn't simply his folly; it was submerged within the Beatles' mythic narrative and, though not an overt belief of his followers, the recognition was implicit in the generational status he had assumed and fueled through the tacit support of his massive cultural following.

Yoko's alignment with John distilled his messianic confusion into a distinct, powerful ideology and subsequent rise to action. Now, John's fame as a Beatle, heretofore his primary understanding of his cultural role, would become merely a process mechanism and subservient to the ideals of the pair's connection and Yoko's artistic impulse. Their efforts would be based on their love as an activator for the goal of world peace, and for the next two years, to varying degrees of success, the couple attempted just that. If John was looking for a way to utilize his renown for a high-minded moral cause, with the objective of delivering transcendence to "his people" (which is, after all, a primary function of the savior archetype), he certainly found the right partner and muse. John clarifies, "We met, we had to decide what our common goal was; we had one thing in common … we were in love … What goes with love, we thought, was peace."[5]

The two shared a natural symbiosis in their philosophies concerning the potential of art as a cultural and political tool, and their efforts were characterized through the alchemy of their previous endeavors. Yoko's background as a creative colleague of the iconoclastic Fluxus group brought a radical interdisciplinary approach to art with the goal of inciting mass participation in events and "happenings" to affect social change, while John's capacity as a locus of global media enabled them to utilize McLuhanesque approaches to a wide range of communication mediums. With their financial mobility and prime position in the media spotlight, rock star John and conceptual artist Yoko endeavored to spread their message of peace through a barrage of complimentary "intermedia" activities: records, films, concerts, interviews, publicity stunts, billboards, television appearances, radio spots, mail campaigns, and conceptual art events.

McLuhan had already signaled where we might naturally expect to see this evolved cultural expression and rapport first manifest:

"We live in the first age when change occurs sufficiently rapidly to make such pattern recognition possible for society at large ... this awareness has always been reflected first by the artist, who has the power—and courage—of the seer to read the language of the outer world and relate it to the inner world."[6] As early as 1951, he observed: "The business of art is no longer the communication of thoughts or feelings which are to be conceptually ordered, but a direct participation in an experience. The whole tendency of modern communication is towards participation in a process."[7]

The couple's first joint happening, the Acorn Event on June 15, 1968, evidenced the advantage of John and Yoko's celebrity to amplify their message—it drew international attention even while receiving a critical drubbing. At St. Michael's Cathedral in Coventry, which had been severely bombed by the Luftwaffe in 1940 (the charred remains of the church preserved as an anti-war symbol), the couple planted two acorns "for peace" as part of the National Sculpture Exhibit. Though church officials refused to allow their celebration to take place on the hallowed church grounds alongside the work of leading British sculptors Henry Moore and Barbara Hepworth, they were allowed to conduct their peace rite at an adjacent property, which was symbolically situated along an East-West axis.[8] Describing their work as "living sculpture," they titled it "Yoko by John, John by Yoko – This is what happens when two clouds meet." A year later, in a related action that also received wide media coverage, they sent acorns to heads of state in numerous countries with the hope these world leaders would join their movement by planting the acorns in support of peace.

Two weeks after the Acorn Event, at the Robert Frazer Gallery in London, John staged his first art exhibit: "You Are Here." He dedicated it to Yoko and, for the first time publicly, affirmed his love for her. At the opening ceremony, in an action reminiscent of a Fluxus marketing technique, the couple released 365 white helium balloons as John drolly announced, "I declare these balloons high." Printed on each balloon were the inscriptions "You are here" and

"Write to John Lennon, c/o The Robert Frazer Gallery, 69 Duke Street, London, W1." Inside the gallery, charity collection boxes arranged on the floor led to a large round canvas with the phrase "you are here" John had hand-written in tiny letters at the center.[9] Those viewing the canvas were secretly filmed from behind a partition, and their reactions were, as John later explained to television host David Frost, "the whole point of the show—that was the art, that was the happening."[10]

Over the next eighteen months the couple would continue to mount their peace campaign through a variety of events and performances designed to engage both media attention and mass participation. Inspired by a notion found in Antoine de Saint-Exupéry's *The Little Prince* ("One sees rightly only with the heart, the essential is invisible to the eyes."), they began advocating for peace from inside a bag, an exploit they termed "bagism." At a press conference in Vienna (the "City of Love"), they claimed that this was an act of "total communication," and that their dialog would hence be unmarred by any visual prejudice or preconception based on appearance. The absurdity of the "Bag Event" was not lost on the couple; John addressed the alternately amused and bemused media, saying, "If the least we can do is give somebody a laugh, we're willing to be the world's clowns, because we think it's a bit serious at the moment and a bit intellectual. That's the least we can do, because everybody is talking about peace, but nobody does anything about it in a peaceful way."[11]

Far more serious was the "War is Over!" campaign, which launched with John's first live music performance in Britain since the Beatles' final show there nearly four years prior. In December 1969, John and Yoko appeared at the UNICEF "Peace for Christmas" event at London's Lyceum Ballroom with an ensemble of famous musicians (George Harrison, Eric Clapton, Billy Preston, and Keith Moon, among others) they dubbed the "Plastic Ono Supergroup."[12] The concert coincided with a global peace initiative by John and Yoko centering on postcards, leaflets, newspaper ads, posters, and, most notably, billboards in twelve major cities around the world, all sporting the phrase "WAR IS OVER! IF YOU WANT IT" and, in smaller type below, "Happy Christmas from John and Yoko." The billboards featured bold black letters on a stark white background, and many were translated into the native language.[13] John clarified the message, once again stressing the need for active participation: "All we have to do is remember that we've all got the power. That's why we said, 'war is over if you want it.' Don't believe that jazz that there's nothing you can do, 'just turn on and drop out, man.' You've got to turn on and drop *in*."[14]

From John and Yoko's perspective, even their marriage and honeymoon provided an opportunity to proselytize for peace. While they managed to get married away from the invasive press with a secret wedding on March 20, 1969 in Gibraltar, they both knew this would be impossible to accomplish with their honeymoon, so they decided to simply incorporate their nuptials into their campaign. After the wedding, Yoko teased the press, "We're going to stage many happenings and events together and this marriage was one of them."[15] John, in a statement that implied the media/art viewpoints of McLuhan and pop artist Andy Warhol, further clarified their plans in a radio interview: "We're holding a Bed-In for Peace, and we're selling peace like we're selling soap, and everybody's got to be aware that they can have peace if they want it and as soon as they want to do something about it!"[16]

McLuhan believed that "the ads of our time are the richest and most faithful reflections that any society ever made of its entire range of activities,"[17] while Warhol radically applied this concept to his art, introducing at a New York exhibit in 1962 a series of works that redefined our idea of what art had become, or could be, in the age of mass media. His *100 Soup Cans, 100 Coke Bottles, 100 Dollar Bills,* and *Marilyn Diptych* incorporated themes of consumerism, advertising, and celebrity culture, and reflected the motif of mass-production through serial imagery and silkscreen print-making. Warhol's work was controversial, but as the decade unfolded increasingly influential, marking a distinct evolution in both the form and content of twentieth century fine art. John and Yoko advanced these notions one step further by transforming their public lives into celebrity advertisements selling a conceptual product: Peace.

The boldest of these publicity stunts were their "Bed-Ins for Peace," the first held at the Amsterdam Hilton Hotel a mere five days after their wedding. Inviting the world press into their honeymoon suite for interviews and photographs ten hours a day over the course of a full week, the couple endeavored to promote world peace, protest violence and war, and both endorse and demonstrate McLuhan's media theories in action.

Two months later, at the Queen Elizabeth Fairmont Hotel in Montreal, the couple held their second and final bed-in, and this time, in addition to the press, the two were joined by similarly iconoclastic media figures, including Timothy Leary, Allen Ginsburg, Dick Gregory, and Tommy Smothers. A month later, in an interview with Rolling Stone magazine, Yoko explained that while the bed-ins may have been high-profile events, the goal of peace was an on-going concern requiring diligent effort: "People take war for granted; they are conditioned to accept it. So, you've got to change their thinking. Like TV soap commercials, you have to keep pounding away with the message all the time. It's a full-scale campaign."[18]

Though the press largely treated the bed-ins as a "put on" or a transparent attention grab by the newlyweds, John and Yoko in many ways accomplished their goal of spreading their message, most notably in the song they produced in Montreal with the help of their celebrity guests. John composed "Give Peace a Chance" after he had repeated the phrase in response to numerous interview questions, and it was hastily recorded using just four room mics and a four-track recorder. Released as a single in July 1969, it quickly became the anthem of the anti-war movement protesting America's involvement in the Viet Nam conflict. On November 15, 1969, at a demonstration billed as the "Moratorium to End the War in Viet Nam," 250,000 people marched in Washington DC and were led in a mass sing-a-long by folk-protest singer Pete Seeger, who cried out phrases such as "Are you listening, Nixon?" and "Are you listening, Pentagon?" interspersed among the chanted choruses of "All we are say-ing ... is give peace a chance."

John and Yoko also introduced an element that had been notably absent in the Beatles' mythic narrative: erotic love and the sacred sex act. The two were very daring in sharing their sexuality with the public from the beginning of their public relationship, announcing themselves to the world as "Two Virgins" with a nude album cover. It's now almost hard to imagine a time when it was shocking for celebrities to pose for nude photos, but in 1968 the album caused outrage, and was sold inside a brown paper bag.

Unfinished Music No. 1: Two Virgins, released in November 1968, was recorded by the couple at John's home studio the night they consummated their relationship, and though the cover was highly controversial (EMI refused to distribute the album because of the image), it was a bold statement signaling the direction John and Yoko would take and the lengths they were prepared to go as they embraced their mythic roles. Stamped on the brown wrapper hiding their nudity was a verse from the book of Genesis: "And they were both naked, the man and his wife, and were not ashamed."[19] The pair would expose their bodies and bedroom to the public on numerous other occasions, including a 1969 short film entitled *Self Portrait*, which consisted of an extended shot of John's partially-erect penis, and *Bag One*, a series of erotic lithographs by John depicting various sexual acts between him and his new wife.

Two Virgins was the first of three albums the couple would release that contained random experimental pieces communicating the intimate details of their relationship. *Unfinished Music No. 2: Life with the Lions* featured on one side their improvised performance at Cambridge University (John accompanying Yoko's freestyle vocal wailings with guitar feedback), and, on the other, several pieces that chronicled their hospital experience as they suffered the miscarriage of their child. "Baby's Heartbeat" consisted of the palpitations of the infant's heart in Yoko's womb prior to his untimely passing.

The Wedding Album returned to the more familiar subject matter of the John and Yoko's love and commitment to peace. The double LP was released in an elaborate box containing photos and drawings, a reproduction of their marriage certificate, a Mylar bag stamped with the word "bagism," a booklet of press clippings concerning the couple, and even a picture of a slice of their wedding cake. The discs featured interviews with John and Yoko describing their peace campaign, random conversation from the Amsterdam bed-in, some acoustic blues by John, and a song about peace by Yoko, "Grow Your Hair."

Unsurprisingly, the three albums failed to generate fan support and barely managed to chart, John's Beatle celebrity likely the only reason why even minimal sales were achieved. Still, their relationship was quickly incorporated into the music and mythos of the Beatles. The song "The Ballad of John and Yoko," written by John between the two bed-ins and released as a Beatles single in May 1969, chronicled their romance and peace campaign, and featured memorable lines such as "The news people said, say what you doin' in bed? I said we're only trying to get us some peace," and the infamous "Christ, you know it ain't easy…" chorus, which caused it to be banned from many radio stations. Even so, the song was a top-ten hit in the US, and the Beatles' final number one single in the UK.

Melody Maker, a rock magazine that naturally held John and the Beatles in high regard, was compelled to criticize the antics of the couple in a story titled: "John Lennon—Genius or Just a Bore?"[20] Looking back years later, *Rolling Stone* writer Robert Christgau praised the couple for their synthesis of "East vs. West" and "Duchamp vs. Berry" polarities, but acknowledged that John and Yoko brought out each other's less-desirable features as well, a "rather naïve, self-absorbed fecundity, undercut with sly humor, artless play elements and a tendency to erupt in anger and pain."[21] John and Yoko indeed alienated many, yet it is difficult to name another high-profile couple who embraced their sexuality so unashamedly and to such a public degree; not even surrealist painter Salvador Dali and his wife Gala, who explored sexual territory in numerous fine art forms, allowed themselves to be seen so nakedly, or sought to illuminate through such brazen personal example. For analogs to John and Yoko's relationship, one must look to symbolism and narratives in archetypal mythology.

In the imagery of Tantric Buddhism, the *yab-yum* is a common symbol depicting the male deity sitting in a lotus position in sexual congress with his female partner on his lap. The concept of sexual polarity is a central tenet of Tantric philosophy, though its meaning goes far beyond the sex act itself and is more accurately understood as the balancing of male and female energies within one's own body.[22] Buddhist theologian Rita Gross clarifies this distinction, writing, "The yab-yum is always said to be an image in which the partners are in sexual union ... this image, nevertheless, is not literally about sex, as in sexual intercourse. It is about non-duality."[23]

This concept is represented in Eastern philosophies as the *yin-yang*, the Daoist duality symbol which depicts the male yang—representing light, action, and the spirit—interlocking with the female yin—representing darkness, passivity, and the body. A similar symbol in Hinduism, the *Sri Yantra*, shows the two poles of duality—the heaven-facing, white (like light, spiritual) male triangles and the earth-facing, red (like blood, physical) female triangles—which interlock to create existence.

The divine union of masculine and feminine is also expressed in the concept of *hieros gamos*, which derives from the Greek expression for "sacred marriage." In many ancient cultures, this described fertility rituals wherein participants representing their societal deities would engage in sexual intercourse designed to influence the fecundity of the land,[24] though in broader terms it encompasses both the spiritual and physical healing available through the sacred sex act. The implication is that the merger of "twin souls," i.e. soulmates, unites the male and female aspects of the life force and hence couples the realms of heaven and earth.

The Egyptian deities Osiris and Isis are a mythic representation of hieros gamos; as both brother and sister, and husband and wife, they symbolize twin souls in sacred union. The Old Testament romance and concomitant Arabian legends of King Solomon and the queen of Sheba (reflected in the lovers from the "metaphorically" erotic Song of Songs in the Old Testament) perform this function in Judaic mythology, as does the divine union of Shiva and Shakti in Hinduism and Zeus and Hera in ancient Greek conception. Jung contends that hieros gamos is emphasized in the "representation of Christ and the Church as bridegroom and bride and the alchemical conjunction of sun and moon."[25] Known as *maithuna* in Tantric philosophy and practice, this divinely inspired sexual congress produces *kriyā*, i.e. the essential energy cleansing of body and soul that reverberates throughout the earth and cosmos.[26]

The sanctified connections described in these myths are allegories for the metaphysical meaning of love, transcending the physical act of sex and encompassing the balance of spiritual energy. John and Yoko could be compared to these and many more sexual/ spiritual couples, but given the Beatles' (and John's, in particular) role as a savior, and the misunderstanding or outright vilification of Yoko, the most resonant for modern Western culture is likely that of Jesus Christ and Mary Magdalene.

It's been a popular view for the past several decades that Mary Magdalene was at one time viewed as Jesus's wife or lover, and then demonized by the patriarchal Church, who labeled her a sinner, hysteric, and/or a prostitute. In fact, apocryphal scriptures talk of this contentious relationship at the very birth of the movement. In Gnostic texts, St. Peter (whose legend has him going on to lead the Church on earth and, later, guard the gates of heaven as a transcended being) is especially resentful of Mary's presence. In the *Gospel of Thomas*, he pleads with Jesus, "Let Mary go away from us, for women are not worthy of life,"[27] and in *Pistis Sophia* complains, "My Lord, we will not endure this woman, for she taketh the opportunity from us and hath let none of us speak, but she discourseth many times."[28] In the *Gospel of Philip*, the rest of the (male) disciples also display resentment, distain, and jealousy toward the "apostle to the apostles" whom Jesus kisses "on the mouth." They ask Jesus directly, "Why do you love her more than all of us?"[29] One can only imagine a confused and jealous Paul, George, and Ringo asking the same question as John made it clear that Yoko had become his primary—really, his only—intimate collaborator.

No individual gospel gives a full beginning-to-end account of the resurrection story, but all agree on two occurrences: the stone in front of the tomb was found moved, and the first witnesses to the empty tomb were women, including Mary Magdalene. In all four gospels, Mary was present at the crucifixion and death of Jesus; she was also (according to Mark, Matthew, and John) sent by the risen Christ (or an angel) to deliver the news to Peter and the other disciples.[30, 31, 32] The implication of the movement of the stone is literal: matter can be moved by spirit. The significance of the women at the tomb, and Mary Magdalene particularly, concerns the resolution of duality and its role in divinization, i.e. becoming one with God. Often, female characters in male-centered monomyths represent the "Other," a character who is essentially different from the hero/savior. These others "complete" the transformation of the saviors through the harmonizing of fundamental opposites. They also symbolize love.

As with Mary Magdalene to Jesus, Yoko was by John's side when he died, and though the news of his passing was delivered through the media, the responsibility fell to her to help guide the world through the tragedy. The day following the murder, she released a statement: "John loved and prayed for the human race. Please remember that he had deep faith and concern for life and, though he has now joined the greater force, he is still with us here."[33] Yoko then announced there would be no funeral, and asked fans to remember John with ten minutes of silent prayer at 2:00 p.m. on Sunday, December 14, 1980. Millions of people around the world complied with her request (a reported 225,000 converged in Central Park in New York), and countless radio stations across the globe also went quiet for those somber ten minutes, most coming back on the air with John's utopian anthem, "Imagine."[34]

A month after John's passing, on January 18, 1981, Yoko published a piece in the *New York Times* and *Washington Post* titled "In Gratitude," where she reflected on the healing power of love, and the dualism that she and John sought to resolve in their relationship: "If all of us loved and cared for one person each. That is all it takes. Love breeds love. ... John and I believed we were one mind taking two bodies at this time." This sentiment (so suggestive of hieros gamos) echoed a December 1968 interview the couple gave on the Dutch television program *Rood Wit Blauw* (Red White Blue), where Yoko offered, "I almost think that we are just one body, but just for convenience we are taking two bodies. ... To have a dialogue you have to have two bodies."[35]

John marked his love affair with Yoko as the moment "when things began to change. That's when I started to free myself from the Beatles."[36] John's inevitable transcendence away from the group terrified fans afraid of losing the vision they had of their savior, but the vitriol the couple endured had roots deeper than simply the loss of a beloved musical partnership. The public's reaction to Yoko exposed still prevalent sexism and racism in Britain and America; her gender and race being easy targets in a male-dominated culture that still associated Japan with the Axis powers and World War II. She was the perfect "Other." The two were taunted and jeered at by the press, and Yoko was widely blamed for the break-up of the Beatles. The disrespect ranged from the merely insensitive ("Jap Girl Named in Lennon Divorce Suit"[37]) to overt insults ("John Rennon's Excrusive Gloupie: On the load to briss with the Yoko nobody Onos."[38]). As late as 1988, *People* magazine inferred that the widowed Ono (on the cover no less) was a witch who had manipulated and misled John, with the headline: "Under Yoko's Spell."[39]

But it wasn't just the press, fans excoriated her as well. Yoko recalls, "When John and I were first together he got lots of threatening letters: 'That Oriental will slit your throat while you're sleeping.' The Western hero had been seized by an Eastern demon."[40] In an interview with Larry King in 1999, she discussed the probable reasons why many did not accept her at the time: "I'm not British, I'm not even, well, the white race. I'm from the Third World, as far as they're concerned … and then I was a woman. So, I think it was a very convenient scapegoat."[41]

The Beatles themselves, sans John of course, also had problems with Yoko, to put it mildly. Much has been written about her presence in the studio breaking years of creative protocol that implicitly did not include wives and girlfriends. Richard DiLello, the "House Hippy" at Apple who wrote *The Longest Cocktail Party*, an insider's view of the Beatles' waning years, felt that Yoko was mistrusted as much for her creative and personal attributes as for her perceived negative effect on John and the music of the Beatles: "There was a lot going against Yoko Ono when she walked into the goldfish bowl. She was overeducated, spoke several languages, was highly proficient in the culinary arts and [was] a writer of verse and creator of sculpture. She was well-versed in history and a survivor of the New York avant-garde scrap race. She was also an older woman and Japanese. Somehow, she managed to carry it all with ease, as she did her hair, as part of the terrain."[42]

In the new millennium, with the hindsight of several decades, Paul McCartney (who may have been the Beatle most disappointed, if not outraged, by John's choice of Yoko as a creative partner) has acknowledged that the group was already unraveling when Yoko came into their lives, and he credits her with spurring John onto significant musical accomplishments. He readily admits that the Beatles were "threatened" by Yoko when she became a fixture in the recording studio, however "the band was breaking up and I think she attracted John so much to another way of life that he then went on to, very successfully, add a sort of second part to his career, writing things like 'Imagine' and 'Give Peace a Chance.' I don't think he would have done that without Yoko."[43]

What is often misconstrued when considering Yoko's effect on the Beatles demise is that she was no interloper; John wanted her there, in fact he demanded not only that she join him in the creative process, but also that the other Beatles acquiesce to this new creative approach, at least with *his* music. As Beatles biographer Bob Spitz notes, "Yoko's appearance in the studio functioned as a declaration of war. John knew the bombshell he'd drop by pulling such an aggressive stunt, and he seemed perfectly willing to light the fuse."[44] While likely an accurate assessment, it is also true that Yoko's adjoining with John allowed him to establish his independence from the other three Beatles, and thereby underline his primary creative position.

In their very public personal relationship, John and Yoko modeled a novel type of equality and mutual respect for the popular culture of the '60s and '70s. The two were equals— they represented a relationship ideal that had existed only as an abstraction to most people until they saw it modeled in real life. They worked together, created together, and seemed to be in a perpetual, cyclical state of mutual inspiration. Their union was supportive, self-contained, and self-sustaining, and allowed them (or perhaps forced them) to renounce the intrusion of the outside world almost entirely. They were like the Hindu gods Shiva and Parvati, married ascetics making love and practicing yoga in their house in the clouds.

This notion was reflected in the last of their media publicity stunts, though, as with the others, there was an underlying issue they sought to address. On April Fools' Day in 1973, the couple announced the formation of their own conceptual nation state: Nutopia. At a press conference in New York, in a satirical response to John's ongoing battle to remain in the US while facing deportation, they shared the "official" declaration for their new nation: "We announce the birth of a conceptual country, NUTOPIA. Citizenship of the country can be obtained by declaration of your awareness of NUTOPIA. NUTOPIA has no land, no boundaries, no passports, only people. NUTOPIA has no laws other than cosmic. All people of NUTOPIA are ambassadors of the country. As two ambassadors of NUTOPIA, we ask for diplomatic immunity and recognition in the United Nations of our country and its people." The flag of Nutopia was, characteristically, one color—white.[45]

The autonomous intensity of John and Yoko's relationship was evident from the start, but it became even more undeniable after their failed separation, a year-and-change-long "Lost Weekend" during which John stumbled through LA with high profile drinking buddies Harry Nilsson, Keith Moon, and Ringo Starr. The couple reconnected in 1974 at an Elton John concert at which John was a guest performer. Back at home together in New York, they set up an enclosed, all-encompassing domestic life.

Remarkably for the 1970s, they switched gender roles. Yoko went to work every day managing their finances and various art and activism projects, while John stayed home and learned to bake bread, proudly referring to himself as a "house husband." They became the image of a romantic couple in perfect balance, synthesis, and harmony. They never seemed to tire of one another; in fact, they seemed to dive deeper into the depths of their two- (and eventually, three-) person universe, reveling in its completeness.

Their astronomical fame served to liberate rather than shackle them. Because John and Yoko had dedicated themselves to serve a higher cause (and existed in the material world in a generally fulfilled, self-sufficient, connected symbiosis), the normal egoic pitfalls of fame were mostly avoided. Instead, they could selflessly use their celebrity, art, bodies, and love as vessels for greater understanding. They seemed to effortlessly embody the maxim: "All you need is love."

All's well that ends well, still the fine's the crown;
Whate'er the course, the end is the renown.
–William Shakespeare

The Long and Winding Myth

❧ ❧ ❧

The Mythic Evolution of the Beatles

By the end of the 1960s, the Beatles' savior mythos had firmly rooted. Their temporal mythology had been soundly established by their historical import, their archetypal mythology (reflected in their story as well as their art) had been largely created and experienced across the world, and their communal mythology, which had been growing with each passing year (or album, or song), had solidified to the point where their status as generational, even spiritual, leaders was widely acknowledged. Though the Beatles' end as a working partnership was drawing close, their ubiquitous fame, innovative artistry, and cultural significance was showing no signs of slowing, they were in fact as influential and salient as ever before.

The redeemer drama of the Beatles is clearly illustrated in the animated film *Yellow Submarine*—released into theatres in the fall of 1968—which presents them as mythic heroes in a story equally evocative of their iconic music, historical narrative, and centuries of monomythic literary invention. The film was created with nearly no involvement from the Beatles themselves aside from a few new songs and a short, taped segment that provides the film's coda, and yet it is a timeless mythic saga, ironically birthed from the dream-state wherein archetypal symbols originally manifest and resonate.

The *Yellow Submarine* film was inspired by the "Yellow Submarine" song, which came to Paul McCartney while he was falling into slumber. As he explains, "I was laying in bed in the Asher's garret, and there's a nice twilight zone just as you're drifting into sleep and as you wake from it; I always find it quite a comfortable zone, you're almost asleep, you've laid your burdens down for the day and there's this little limbo-land just before you slip into sleep. I remember thinking that a children's song would be quite a good idea and I thought of images, and the color yellow came to me, and a submarine came to me, and I thought, 'Well, that's kind of nice, like a toy, a very childish yellow submarine.'"[1]

Songs emerging from the land of dreams is not uncommon, and for Paul, "Yellow Submarine" wasn't even the first time this had occurred. Famously, his classic standard "Yesterday" came to him in a dream with the structure and melody fully formed.[2] Two other notable Beatles songs, "Nowhere Man" and "Across the Universe," came to John Lennon in just such a hypnagogic state,[3] and Rolling Stone Keith Richards's proto-rock riff for "(I Can't Get No) Satisfaction" manifested in similar fashion.[4] What sets "Yellow Submarine" apart is the archetypal nature of the song itself, and the film based on the dream world it suggests.

King Features, the animation company that had earlier produced the Beatle cartoons, also made *Yellow Submarine.* Their creative team of writers and animators distilled the Beatles' archetypal mythology down to its most fundamental allegorical elements: the Beatles sail across dangerous seas, transform into Sgt. Pepper's Lonely Hearts Club Band, and rescue the good people of Pepperland from the Blue Meanies—the savior restoring the community to its pristine state and bringing redemption and peace to the innocent community victimized by dark forces. The story climaxes with the elemental statement, "All You Need is Love," and ends with an invitation for the people of the world to join in a song of camaraderie, "All Together Now." This straightforward morality tale—Joseph Campbell's monomyth in glorious psychedelic Technicolor—reveals the essential construct of the Beatles' overarching mythos: a hero's journey through the deep sea of our collective unconscious, seen through the looking glass of music and art, and experienced by way of sights, sounds, and symbols.

The enormously popular Beatle cartoons debuted in September 1965 and ran through September 1969, with the last two seasons consisting of repeats. By 1967, when the final episodes were produced, the team at King Features was racing to keep pace with the Beatles' sprawling story and increasingly sophisticated music and lyrical content. As the Beatles were the first living persons to be animated into a cartoon series, their temporal history couldn't be ignored. After two seasons of predictable storylines wherein the boys were typically seen running from screaming fans to the frenetic pitch of their early, Beatlemania-era songs, by the fall of '67, children watching the show were following the bouncing ball to lyrics such as: "She said ... I know what it's like to be dead."

The second-to-last episode produced, which initially aired October 14, 1967, has the Beatles fall into a well and land in the "inner world," portrayed as a primeval, mystical locale. There, they perform the song "Tomorrow Never Knows" in an ancient temple, essentially transforming into high priests in a religious ceremony. Mystery school symbolism notwithstanding, contending with the Beatles' evolving image and music primed King Features for a timely feature of the group, and the first full-length animated film to be produced in Britain in fourteen years.[5]

Using the simple imagery from the song depicting a sea voyage by submarine, King Features created the story of a mythic journey reminiscent of literary works of fantasy by such authors as Homer, Jonathan Swift, H.G. Wells, and Jules Verne. The narrative arc of *Yellow Submarine* indeed bears strong resemblance to that of the Old English epic poem *Beowulf* (composed circa 700 CE), a fact made explicit in the liner notes of the *Yellow Submarine* soundtrack album. In that story, the hero Beowulf travels by sea, vanquishing monsters along the way, to save a feasting, drinking, and music hall called Heorot from the evil spirit Grendel. Similarities to classical literature aside, the screenwriters of *Yellow Submarine*, which included Lee Minoff (who wrote the original story based on the song), Erich Segal (author of *Love Story*), and (un-credited) Liverpudlian poet Roger McGough (who provided puns and double-entendres), were, as with the animators and production team, under considerable pressure to create the film in less than ten months, and also forced to craft a story hewing to a soundtrack of Beatle songs, and even references to Beatle songs not in the film itself ("Help! Help! Won't you please, please help me!" and "You're not half the lad you used to be!" etc.).

Dr. Robert R. Hieronimus, author of *Inside the Yellow Submarine: The Making of the Beatles' Animated Classic,* shares (in an unpublished chapter from the book) his view that these elements were created unconsciously, an organic development inspired by scope of the Beatles' music and historical narrative, and the love and respect afforded them by the King Features creative team: "Most of the co-creators of this film insist they were too busy with their deadlines and the frenzied, script-less beginnings of their production to create the multi-layered allegories many of us fans read into it."[6] After extensive interviews with everyone involved, he stressed that "there was no deliberate or conscious effort to make a film with classical, mythological or symbolic meanings of any kind.... It appears that the co-creators of *Yellow Submarine* were driven by the level of excellence they admired in the Beatles, and the admiration they felt for the group was expressed through their film. The result neatly fits the pattern established by others inspired to create a classic; a pattern of a mythology repeated through the ages in innumerable forms."[7]

Art Director Heinz Edelmann concurred: "It was a communal effort, done under pressure, so nobody had the time to really control one's input.... I knew that part of my subconscious would go into these things, but I chose to disregard that. I simply did not want to know what's happening. I mean, otherwise, I couldn't have done the work.... It became a sort of reservoir of the collective unconscious at the point of the flower revolution."[6]

Yellow Submarine is of the rarest class of artworks that both vividly reflect their time-period and yet remain timeless, and even more so because it moves hearts of all ages. Its function is now like that of the illustrated children's books read in Sunday school, imprinting the minds of the young with vibrant color, simple presentation, and, as with all monomyths, the "greatest story ever told." *Rolling Stone* noted that "Yellow Submarine" is the "gateway drug that turns little children into Beatle fans, with that cheery sing-along chorus,"[8] while the British magazine *Punch* observed, "The Lennon-McCartney songs used in the film seem to have been conceived and brought forth in the pure simple spirit of mystical innocence, like the paintings of Chagall.... The animation style ranges from storybook simplicity to pop art and psychedelic shimmer."[9] A contemporary review in the *New York Times* stated: "*Yellow Submarine* is a family movie in the truest sense—something for the little kids who watch the same sort of punning stories, infinitely less nonviolent and refined, on television; something for the older kids, whose musical contribution to the arts and longings for love and gentleness and color could hardly present a better case; something for parents, who can see the best of what being newly young is all about."[10]

That such a lasting work of archetypal mythology could arise from simply the symbolic *inspiration* of the Beatles (and not from their direct artistic involvement) is telling; their story was so already so pervasive and thrilling that *Yellow Submarine*, in a sense, wrote itself. If the tacit understanding of the Beatles' savior mythos was expressed artistically through the creators of the film, a phenomenon that followed soon after suggests that the public at large had also intuited the deeper symbolism at play, leading them to the likelihood that the Beatles' narrative was reaching its conclusion.

In September 1969, a wide-spread and persistent notion took hold within the ranks of the Beatles' faithful that Paul McCartney had died. Curiously, the conception captured the public imagination at precisely the same time as the actual break-up of the Beatles, though there would not be an announcement of such for over six months. Within a matter of weeks following the final recording sessions for the *Abbey Road* album—the last time the four Beatles would create music together—the "Paul is Dead" fable emerged, a seeming mass-premonition of the "death" of the Beatles, and in turn the 1960s.

The seeds of the story had actually been circulating for several years. In February 1967, a short paragraph appeared in the *Beatles Book Monthly* fanzine under the heading "False Rumour" that quickly summarized and denied the essentials: "Stories about the Beatles are always flying around Fleet Street. The 7th January was very icy, with dangerous conditions on the M1 motorway, linking London with the Midlands, and towards the end of the day, a rumour swept London that Paul McCartney had been killed in a car crash on the M1. But, of course, there was absolutely no truth in it at all, as the Beatles' Press Officer found out when he telephoned Paul's St. John's Wood home and was answered by Paul himself who had been at home all day with his black Mini Cooper safely locked up in the garage."[11]

The threadbare rumor laid dormant for nearly three years, until, on September 17, 1969, a college student at Iowa's Drake University published an article in the *Drake-Times-Delphic* titled "Is Beatle Paul McCartney Dead?" that added a crucial element to the story by implying that the Beatles themselves had been giving the public clues to Paul's death through hidden messages within songs and album covers.[12] A few weeks later, the story was embellished by an anonymous caller to Detroit's radio station WKNR-FM, and disc jockey Russ Gibb, intrigued by the conspiracy theory, spent the next hour debating it with callers on-air. The station then added fuel to the fire a few days later with a special two-hour broadcast titled "The Beatle Plot." The tale then spread rapidly, culminating in coverage from major news outlets, including *LIFE* magazine, who interviewed a very-much-alive Paul for a cover story titled "The Case of the 'Missing' Beatle: Paul is still with us."[13]

The rumor itself was essentially as follows: In November 1966, Paul McCartney had been decapitated in an automobile accident in England. The remaining Beatles, attempting to maintain their commercial dominance and continue growing their financial fortunes, concealed this fact by replacing Paul with a double, who they found in the winner of a Paul McCartney look-alike contest named William Shears Campbell (the infamous "Billy Shears" from the

"With a Little Help from My Friends" song). As time progressed, the Beatles became guilt-ridden with the deception and decided to communicate the truth to their fans by inserting clues into their songs, album covers, gatefold sleeves, and various LP accoutrements (the *Magical Mystery Tour* booklet, the White Album poster, etc.).[14]

The list of "clues" found by sleuthing fans is exhaustive and has grown exponentially in the years since the initial suspicion took hold (a Google search in 2018 on the topic "Paul is Dead" offered approximately 473,000 results). Without going down that rabbit-hole here, it can be said that they range from the slightly curious to the coincidentally eerie to the abjectly insane, and they continue to be proffered by countless believers in the "hoax" supposedly perpetrated by the surviving Beatles, though John, George, and Ringo all denied the story numerous times. The details of the speculation are not germane to this study; what is interesting here is the similarity to revelatory responses and practices of past religious cults, and the acute timing of the phenomenon suggesting a cultural intuition of the break-up of the Beatles that was indeed occurring in tandem, and in secret.

Faced with the potentially alarming prospect of losing the Beatles, fans and followers resorted to a deep study of their "religious scriptures," in this case Beatle songs and album cover imagery, in search of hidden messages and revelations that could help them make sense of the loss and light the way forward. This response to crisis mirrors the practices of the Rastafarians in Jamaica in the 1930s, as noted earlier, and the Judaic people of Palestine in the period directly preceding Christianity. This community, reeling from their subordination by Rome and the increasing corruption within their sacred second temple, pored through their holy books seeking clues concerning a coming Jewish messiah. The practice continued to be employed by the Apostles;[15] St. Paul particularly stresses that his understanding of the gospel is reliant on revelation and scriptural study.[16] The point is that, when faced with a physical or existential disturbance, religious cults turn to their history in the attempt to augment and thereby advance their belief system.

This is precisely how mythology evolves, and the response of the '60s generation to the impending demise of the Beatles follows this pattern closely.

Barbara Suczek, in a 1972 article for the sociological journal *Urban Life and Culture*, pointed to the religious implications of the Paul is Dead phenomenon. She contended that "many aspects of the McCartney death story suggest an abortive attempt to apotheosize Paul McCartney," noting the curious inconsequence of whether the rumor was actually true or not: "The fact, or lack of it, of the death of Paul McCartney seemed similarly irrelevant to its public. The inference, then, is that the Paul McCartney of this story was a symbol, a social construct that no longer required the facts of a personal existence to sustain it." Citing the examples of Osiris, Adonis, Dionysus and Jesus, Suczek suggested, "The untimely death of a beautiful youth who is subsequently transformed into or revealed to be a god is a recurrent mythical theme and is presumed to reflect the cyclical process in nature. ... It may be that the McCartney rumor represents an aborted attempt to re-create such a myth ... [This] may be a process whereby socially valued qualities of an exemplary youth can be abstracted into an idealized model and thus preserved from the eroding onslaught of ongoing reality."[17]

The social psychology of rumor is also illuminating. Studies of urban legend show that when something of serious significance occurs and facts are not readily available, often this type of "myth" is quickly generated collectively by word of mouth to fulfill the narrative. A "collective explanation process" is, according to social psychologists Prashant Bordia and Nicholas DiFonzo, a primary feature in the transmission of rumor: "Rumor discourse has been conceptualized as an attempt to reduce anxiety and uncertainty via a process of social sense-making."[18]

Urban legends typically contain information that is frightening (or at the least negative) with the potential to affect a great number of people. The young are especially vulnerable and tend to spread these rumors quickly. A 2001 study found that "the younger the mean age of 'infection,' the more contagious the rumor in question," and further that "reluctance to change one's mind about a rumor can occur when there is no dispositive evidence that the rumor is false, so rumors of distant events may be more persistent than local rumors."[19] Of course, it is nearly impossible to logically disprove a negative, so even when Paul was proven to be alive the "replaced by a double" trope enabled the fantasy to persist. Essentially, it was not possible to prove the Beatles *weren't* complicit in the hoax, even if "Paul" was still with us.

The latent fear of the end of the Beatles implicit in the "Paul is Dead" rumor may be best explained by the hypothesis that their community was experiencing the group's mythic narrative in real time, as participants and catalysts as much as fans and followers. The Beatles' massive following knew instinctively that the story was coming to its conclusion because it was happening to *them* as well. In truth, from the time the Beatles ceased live performance (their metaphoric "death" foreshadowing the inevitable demise of the group) their future had been in question, and increasingly, on record and in public, they seemed less a unit and more a vehicle for the individual expressions of the four members. It is noteworthy that the initial spark of the rumor occurred shortly after the Beatles stopped touring, and yet before the single "Strawberry Fields Forever/Penny Lane" announced their return to "form"— the six month wait since *Revolver* was the longest of their career, and in contrast to the early to mid-1960s, when Capitol released new Beatle product every two months on average, this absence was even more pronounced.

It's not surprising that Paul would be the one singled out for symbolic deification as the Beatles fractured; by late 1969 he was essentially the only "Beatle" left in the group, or at least the only one still solely and strongly identified *as* a Beatle. John and Yoko were consumed with their peace effort and releasing solo albums and singles; George was writing with Eric Clapton ("Badge"), jamming with the Band in Woodstock, and even performing with Delaney and Bonnie; and Ringo was making films. We now know each of these three temporarily quit the group at various times, and though this was unknown to the public it could be felt in the Beatles' music, where Paul had clearly assumed the role of leader (this is often explained by the others as Paul forcing himself into the position, though it is safe to say that necessity was a prime motivator, even given his natural ambition). For the final three years of the Beatles' recording career, he accounted for six of their single A-sides ("Hello Goodbye," "Lady Madonna," "Hey Jude," "Get Back," "Let it Be," and "The Long and Winding Road"), while John composed two ("The Ballad of John and Yoko" and "Come Together"), and George, one ("Something"). Also, as the only unmarried Beatle (until his nuptials with Linda Eastman in March '69) and acknowledged "cute" one, Paul had maintained his status as a sex symbol, which uniquely positioned him for the "untimely death of a beautiful youth" theme the rumor expounded. Symbolically, Paul's "death" would naturally signify the "death" of the Beatles as well.

Then, as we well know, came the literal end to the Beatles' working partnership, a heartbreaking development for millions of fans and the generation at large. Somehow (because it certainly wasn't planned), the Beatles managed to once again infer a balance of opposites even as they fragmented, this time through the dual nature of their final albums, *Let it Be* and *Abbey Road*, which respectively provide both a tragically human and gloriously godlike end to their shared career.

The disintegration of the band is documented in the both the album and the film, *Let it Be*. Recorded in early 1969, the album was delayed so it could accompany the release of the film in May 1970, and because the ragged nature of the recordings required an arduous editing and post-production process. This makes *Let it Be* the final album the Beatles would release, but *Abbey Road* was indeed the last album the Beatles recorded. After the semi-debacle of *Let it Be*, where the group's increasing deterioration as a creative unit finally began to weaken the power of their music, remarkably the band decided to record one last album of the high-quality worthy of their status. It is their mythic swansong, and as strongly as *Let it Be* chronicled the end of the Beatles as a functioning group, *Abbey Road* cemented the enduring power and grace of the mythic Beatles.

The two albums appear at first glance to be studies in contrast, their basic conceptions, production values, and even titles and working titles opposing, and yet in a larger sense they are conjoined twins. *Let it Be* had begun as a project entitled "Get Back" and was an explicit attempt by the group to revisit their roots, even featuring a song, "One After 909," that was among the first John and Paul composed together as teens. It was planned to be a window into the Beatles' creative process and evolution of the form and content of the songs themselves. The construction of the album would be filmed, showing the Beatles in the studio as they developed the music, and, in addition to this somewhat novel (at the time) "fly on the wall" approach to documentary, the album would then be recorded live, without the artifice of studio tricks and embellishments. The endeavor was an attempt by the Beatles to humanize (really, demythologize) themselves in the eyes of the public, while recapturing the spark and magic of their partnership.

The basic concept of the project, summarized by the chorus of the title song, "Get back to where you once belonged," is evocative of an ancient mythic symbol, the *ouroboros*, which is represented by the circular image of a serpent (or dragon) consuming its own tail. Originating in Egyptian iconography circa 1400 BCE (the first known use being in a funerary text carved inside the tomb of King Tutankhamen),[20] the symbol can be found in Hindu, Gnostic, and Hermetic traditions, among others. Jung clarifies, "In the age-old image of the ouroboros lies the thought of devouring oneself and turning oneself into a circulatory process, for it was clear to the more astute alchemists that the *prima materia* of the art was man himself. The ouroboros is a dramatic symbol for the integration and assimilation of the opposite, i.e. of the shadow. This 'feed-back' process is at the same time a symbol of immortality, since it is said of the ouroboros that he slays himself and brings himself to life, fertilizes himself and gives birth to himself."[21]

The concept of "return to source" is also reflected by the *Abbey Road* album. As noted earlier, the word "Abbey" derives from the Aramaic *abba*, which means "father." EMI's Abbey Road studio in London was the Beatles' creative home, where they recorded nearly every song and album, all produced by George Martin, their musical and symbolic father. All except the final sessions for the Get Back project, where Martin had left the group to their own devices out of disappointment and frustration with the bickering, lack of focus, and deterioration of both the music and his collaborative role. He was genuinely surprised when Paul asked him to produce one more album for the Beatles, assuring that even John would work "the way we used to do it."[22] In this sense, *Abbey Road* is also an album where the Beatles would "get back to where they once belonged," a fact punctuated by both the title and the album cover implying a "Road to the Father" motif, and the music therein representing a true return to form, which for the Beatles meant yet another compositional and sonic innovation. *Abbey Road* is widely regarded as their best "sounding" album; the production value enhanced by recent advances in recording technology and the employ of a brilliant young engineer, Alan Parsons (who would go on to engineer Pink Floyd's seminal *Dark Side of the Moon* three years hence). The album is also the first where George Harrison's songwriting quality truly matched that of the Lennon-McCartney team, his "Something" and "Here Comes the Sun" at last equaling the best work of his esteemed colleagues. George's full maturation on *Abbey Road* broadened the album's creative palette considerably, and in the process expanded the Beatles' artistic purview once more.

Abbey Road was conceived as a crowning achievement that would both equal their best studio work and provide a fitting finale to their illustrious recording history. A working title, "Everest," (though originating from an in-joke relating to engineer Geoff Emerick's cigarette brand) more than hinted at the immortality they felt they had earned and wished to preserve—for a time it was even planned that the album cover would be a photograph of the four at the summit of Mount Everest.[23] Paul was particularly determined to create a masterwork; his medley of songs (with some from John) end both the album and the Beatles' recording career in exhilarating fashion and brings the group's raw musicianship and collaborative power front and center. Ringo's first and only drum solo on a Beatles record, leading into a string of searing, alternating guitar solos by John, Paul, and George, crescendos into a final statement equally befitting both the archetypal savior and the cyclical nature of the ouroboros: "And in the end, the love you take is equal to the love you make." The *"Abbey Road* suite" is, in these climactic passages, everything the Beatles had hoped to achieve with the Get Back project—their creativity as a group expressed through the essential power of direct and ultimately transcendent rock & roll.

In the end, both *Let it Be* and *Abbey Road* can lay claim as the Beatles' final album, one recorded last but released first, one recorded first but released last. Both albums provide fitting denouements; even their final single, "The Long and Winding Road," is an eloquent testament to the shared journey of the '60s generation and the eventual return to source that awaits all living things.

Then, the Beatles were together no more. Still, their mythic resonance continued to progress and inform the culture even as the four went in separate directions. For their adoring public, it couldn't *really* be the end; the savior, they were convinced, would soon return. After the break-up and throughout the '70s the world still questioned, in essence, "When will the Beatles get back together?" It is telling that there were hardly any books written about the Beatles in the '70s given the immensity of their story and the breadth of their ongoing influence. Like the early Christians, who seemingly waited decades before they thought to write down the stories of their savior, the writers, historians, and musicologists during the "solo years" seemed likewise convinced that the Beatles' story wasn't over, that a second coming was imminent. Of course, that all changed on December 8, 1980.

John Lennon's death was an event of truly mythic import, a "where were you when" moment as indelible as the Beatles' *Ed Sullivan* appearance had been nearly two decades prior. Tragic though it was, it further aligned John (and, in turn, the Beatles) with the mythic savior archetype in a manner more visceral than even his potent personal story and revolutionary art could inspire. With this single shocking incident, the temporal, archetypal, and communal mythology of the Beatles became one and the same; the historical reality, existential implication, and mass shared experience forever united through the loss of a global spiritual martyr. John, in death, instantly became an even greater symbol of love, peace, and transcendence than during his extraordinary and inspirational life.

Commenting on the impact, *Time* magazine summarized, "The outpouring of grief, wonder and shared devastation that followed Lennon's death had the same breadth and intensity as the reaction to the killing of a world figure: some bold and popular politician, like John or Robert Kennedy, or a spiritual leader, like Martin Luther King Jr. But Lennon was a creature of poetic political metaphor, and his spiritual consciousness was directed inward, as a way of nurturing and widening his creative force. That was what made the impact, and the difference—the shock of his imagination, the penetrating and pervasive traces of his genius—and it was the loss of all that, in so abrupt and awful a way, that was mourned last week, all over the world."[24]

The death of the savior in mythology is an allegorical construct, a way in which the resurrection drama both reflects the human experience and offers inspiration and insight by example. Though scores may believe otherwise (or, to be more specific, believe that a person can be divine in a literal sense and thus able to achieve the impossible), human resurrection does not occur in our temporal world. The sadness felt by countless millions was a response to the finality of his death; John would not be back in a physical sense, and the Beatles would never "reform." And yet, like the mythic gods, John Lennon and the Beatles live on. The undiminished power of their voices, the transcendent beauty of their music, and the timeless truth of their message lives on in the realm of pure vibration—recorded sound—reminding us who we were, inspiring us in the now, and offering hope for a positive future. It is the sound of love, and it belongs to everyone.

A symbol always transcends the one who makes use of it and makes
him say in reality more than he is aware of expressing.
–Albert Camus

THE FAB FOUR ELEMENTS

❖ ❖ ❖

The Mythic Symbolism of the Beatles

In his 1964 book *The Act of Creation*—an elaborate and compre-hensive general theory of human creativity—novelist and cultural theoretician Arthur Koestler observes, "For man is a symbol-mak-ing animal. He constructs a symbolic model of outer reality in his brain and expresses it by a second set of symbols in terms of words, equations, pigment, or stone. All he knows directly are bodily sen-sations…the rest of his knowledge and means of expression is symbolical. To use a phrase by J. Cohen, man has a metaphorical consciousness."[1]

Semiotics is the study of precisely this feature of human per-ception—the ability/potential to create, employ and receive signs (such as words) and symbols (such as numbers) for thinking, communicating, and preserving knowledge. Often, these signs are both expressed and received unconsciously, communicated through a basic image or figurative impression, and many of our iconic figures in modern media unwittingly transmit symbols that reflect and activate the archetypal realm. In his book *The Quest for Meaning: A Guide to Semiotic Theory and Practice*, Marcel Danesi writes, "Pop culture (hero) representations are, more often than not, based on recycled codes dressed up in contemporary garb to appeal to contemporary audiences. In contemporary mass culture, many representations have a mythic origin…and are thus guided by unconscious or latent code features (setting, character, etc.) that define their style and form."[2]

To be sure, semiotics is a vast and burgeoning area of academic science. It is also intrinsically subjective, or at the least open to many interpretations, many of which may be in some sense equally "true." After all, if the signs under scrutiny are (often) being implied and understood unconsciously, there is no accurate "map" to consult and thereby determine the desired effect or the overt perception of a symbol transmitted through, what appears on the surface, a simple image or representation. Thus, interpreting the Beatles through this lens requires a somewhat intuitive analysis, as they communicated to the culture at large through a wide variety of artistic mediums, and it is likely that neither they nor their audience were overtly conscious of the archetypal signage implied. Michael R. Frontani, in his book *The Beatles: Image and the Media*, summarizes, "To consider the Beatles' image is to contemplate an evolving and complex array of signs that carry with them cultural meanings."[3]

If it is true the Beatles convey profound meaning to millions of people, what exactly are the "signs" the collective perceives and resonates with—specifically, the archetypal suggestions imbedded in the Beatles' essential image? We've discussed several aspects of the Beatles' savior symbolism that can be described as signs implying resolution of duality or spiritual transformation, for instance: the title of the *Revolver* album, the color of *The Beatles* (White Album) album cover, and the name of the Beatles' record label, "Apple." Here, we focus on several essential signs hidden in plain sight within the fabric of the Beatles' image that may have helped to provide the unconscious foundation of their archetypal mythology.

Because the group cycled through so many musical styles and figurative incarnations, it may appear at first glance that their image shifted and evolved along with their art, in effect, morphing into a different representation with each single and album. Though it is tempting to refer to the Beatles' image as one that changed many times over the years, it may be more accurate to say that it deepened and widened, while remaining remarkably true to the essential elements that defined the core of that image from the beginning.

From the outset of their fame, the most striking and noteworthy aspect of the Beatles' image is also their most broadly encompassing and mythically suggestive sign: their *hair*. During the Beatlemania period, the Beatles' hairstyle was a principal focus of the press and a notorious point of contention in the escalating generational tensions. Seemingly overnight, hair length became the source of a seminal cultural dispute, suddenly denoting everything the two age groups considered socially acceptable, or not. For baby boomers, long hair may have represented and expressed freedom, individuality, change, and evolution; for their parents, it was a disrespectful act of defiance and a clear indication that the social order, which had recently been defended with the blood of family and friends, was in danger of collapse.

Given various societal and anthropological theories on hair symbolism, this is not surprising. Hairstyles have long been signifiers of social standing and are also strongly associated with religious traditions and belief systems. For example, practical cuts for the working class, extravagant styles for the ruling class, unkempt and unruly hair for the financially challenged, and regularly groomed and styled cuts for the merely prosperous are immediate visual clues suggesting economic status. Hair length has often designated group membership, such as conservative or liberal, military or civilian, man or woman. The baldness of Buddhist monks, the tonsure of Western monks, the dreadlocks of Rastafarians, and the headscarves, yarmulkes, or turbans of followers of many orthodox faiths are examples of hairstyles indicating religious affiliation.

Perhaps because a full head of hair is naturally associated with youth, it has long been a symbol of physical health and sexual power. In his 1958 essay "Magical Hair," anthropologist Edmund Leach (building on the "hair as phallic symbol" theories advanced by psychoanalyst Charles Berg)[4] posited that "long hair = unrestrained sexuality; short hair/partially shaved head/tightly bound hair = restricted sexuality; and closely shaved head = celibacy."[5]

Classical mythology offers many narratives centering on a "cut hair = castration" allegory, the Old Testament story of Samson being one of the most famous examples.[6] In that tale, Samson, leader and judge of the Israelites, is betrayed by his lover Delilah, who robs him of his strength when she shears his head of the long hair that is the source of his physical power. And what virility it was—wrestling and slaying a lion, killing one thousand men with the jawbone of an ass, and binding three hundred live foxes together by their tails. The sexual symbolism within the Samson story makes explicit the unconscious conflation of hair with sexual potency and activity; the metaphor can also be found in the Greek myth of Medusa, the Norse legend of (Thor's wife) Sif, and the Brothers Grimm fairy tale Rapunzel, among other variations.

The Beatles' employ of hair as an attractor of youth, and their generation's adoption of the style as a means of establishing group unity and independence posed an existential threat to the establishment, who appeared to react with anger and derision as a means of defense. Perhaps the most alluring element for the young, and most perplexing for the old, was that the long hair of the Beatles and their contemporaries announced a larger cultural shift away from traditional gender roles and towards a new, or at least modern, expression of sexual androgyny. Given the feminized image of the Beatles and the sexually pursuant behavior displayed by their female fans, it is clear conventional values were rapidly realigning. As the youth embraced this more relaxed approach to gender and sexual behavior, their social mores and politics followed suit, which increasingly fueled the divide with their elders as the decade unfolded.

It is noteworthy that Jung believed that the "Self" archetype of his analytical psychology (which he identified with the mythic savior archetype) is "androgynous and consists of a masculine and feminine principle."[7] This reflects his theory of two primary conceptual archetypes of the unconscious mind: the "anima" and the "animus." Respectively, this is the inner feminine personality within the male unconscious, and, equivalently, the inner masculine personality within the female unconscious. Though these archetypes are described through the language of gender, for Jung they are not demarcations in a sexual sense, but energies that require incorporation into a balanced whole for an individual to increase self-awareness. It follows that the integration of these energies would be a prevalent aspect of mythic gods.

Consequently, from ancient times we have worshipped androgynous deities. To list but a few, the Egyptian Atum, Roman Minerva, and Greek Artemis are gods displaying both male and female aspects, or simply not defined by gender at all. Though the Hindu god Vishnu is primarily understood as male, he takes on many forms and is often portrayed as a figure split down the middle, equally male and female. Ganesha is another Hindu deity who, though usually referred to as male, contains feminine elements. As a half-human, half-elephant creature, the notion of dual nature is explicit; the juxtaposition of a distinctly feminine face with a protruding phallic trunk is further suggestive of an inherent androgyny. Even the "Son of Man" is described, in the book of Revelation, as appearing with female aspects—sporting breasts and wearing a dress and a brassiere of gold.[8]

In 1968, concerning the suggested androgyny of the Beatles and its effect on their fans, Evan Davies, in the *Journal of the History of Ideas*, proposed, "The cult is one in which masculinity is minimized and femininity idealized.... The intensity of Beatlemania is indicative of strong and complex motivational factors, some appearing to have [a] religious and love basis. It is possible that the modern era in Western society is passing through a transition from expressive paternalism to an era of semi-maternalism, in which love will acquire an idealistic orientation. The transition represents a revulsion against many emotional concomitants of the previous period, and Beatlemania is but one of the behavioral symptoms."[9]

In her book *Where the Girls Are: Growing up Female with the Mass Media*, Susan J. Douglas draws attention to the Beatles' gender-blurring image and its effect on their female followers: "When we watched these joyful, androgynous young men, we saw not just a newly feminized, distinctly friendlier form of manhood. We also saw our *own* reflection.... Without ever saying so explicitly, the

Beatles acknowledged that there is masculinity and femininity in all of us."[10] She suggests that as the Beatles evolved so did the inspiration they provided to feminine concerns: "By 1968, we weren't chasing the Beatles in the streets, regarding them as love objects; we were taking their politics to heart, regarding them as political role models and cultural gurus. Inside our heads now, embedded in lyrics envisioning the overthrow of existing society and the birth of a new one, was a new persona, a politically defiant girl."[11]

Douglas also notes the effect of the early Beatle songs—often seen as innocuous love ditties despite their compositional originality—and speculates that "because they sang so directly to and about young women, and did so without pandering to them, this reaffirmation was especially compelling to girls."[10] In fact, the Beatles sang not only directly *to* young women, they also embraced songs *by* female vocalists and songwriters, five of which appeared on their first two albums. Meredith Willson's "Till There Was You," made famous by Shirley Jones in the film version of the Broadway musical *The Music Man*, was a staple of their Hamburg years and performed by the group during their first appearance on *Ed Sullivan*. In addition to this standard, seen at the time as a crucial (if obvious) olive branch to the older generation, the Beatles performed and/or recorded various "call and response" numbers from then current girl-groups, including the Marvelettes, the Shangri-Las, the Ronnettes, the Donays, and the Cookies. The Shirelles' song "Boys," often Ringo's spotlight tune in concert, even retained its feminine gender perspective in the Beatles' version.

The Beatles' hairstyle had its genesis with several fans they befriended during their extended residencies in Hamburg. One of their German chums, Jürgen Vollmer, had been wearing the style since the mid-1950s, and the Beatles became enamored with it, eventually adopting the fashion themselves. The first to sport the look was Stuart Sutcliffe, the ill-fated early Beatle who, shortly after he left the group to remain in Germany, passed away unexpectedly from a brain hemorrhage. George was the next Beatle to comb his hair forward, followed soon after by John and Paul. Drummer

Pete Best refused to join the others and insisted on keeping his pompadour and duck-tail, one of several reasons he was eventually dismissed from the group.

It is important to note, in the context of the Beatles' hair as semiotic sign, that the German name for the style is *pilzen kopf,* which translates as "mushroom head." If the distinct cut was a noticeable signifier of androgyny, it was also an implicit visual cue foreshadowing the foray into various psychedelic drugs explored by the Beatles and their generation as the '60s progressed.

In contemporary terminology, an *entheogen* is a psychoactive substance used in a religious context. There are many examples in the modern era of entheogens playing a central role in religious ritual, including the use of peyote by indigenous Americans; ayahuasca by the tribes of the Amazon basin; ibogain by the African Pygmies; and psilocybin by the Mazatecs in contemporary Mexico. It is also speculated that the entheogenic experience may be a key facet (if deeply veiled in symbolism) of many ancient mythologies and a possible mystical influence on still widely followed religions, including Hinduism, Judaism, and even Christianity.[12, 13]

To be concise, the entheogen theory of religion suggests that various myths are oblique descriptions of psychotropic plants and compounds and the numinous states they induce. Due to the threatening implications of this hypothesis in terms of conventional religious and cultural beliefs, scholars considering this view have by and large struggled for peer review and often seen their university careers jeopardized. Research is further complicated by the secretive nature of the ancient rituals themselves, the opaque methods used by those who wrote about them, and the many academic fields required to address the essential issues (mycology, ethno-botany, philology, etymology, archeology, etc.). For these reasons, studies of the topic have existed mostly on the scholastic fringe, but increasingly several core tenets of entheogenic religious theory are reluctantly being accepted as likely, or at least possibly, true.

The query begins at the dawn of recorded history, with clues communicated through suggestive symbols and narratives found in the world's oldest religious texts. While many may surmise that the Old Testament, and the Pentateuch in particular (Genesis, Exodus, Leviticus, Numbers, Deuteronomy), comprises the planet's earliest surviving works of spiritual literature, the Avesta (the "bible" of Zoroastrianism) was composed during the same time period (approximately 1,000-500 BCE) and the works attributed to Homer (the earliest examples of classical Greek mythology) also likely date to this era. Holy writings of the ancient Indians and Egyptians (the Vedas and Pyramid Texts respectively) are much older, dating well into the second and even third millennium BCE. What theorists find intriguing are certain analogous elements in these works and others, particularly references to plants and potions that confer divinity and immortality with striking similitude.

A major character in the Rigveda is *Soma*, the Hindu moon god who is a sacred symbol for both a plant and the godlike state the plant produces. Soma is associated with the deities Vishnu and Shiva[14] and is the root of the word *Somavara*, i.e. Monday in the Indian calendar. In its full aspect, Soma is what the gods drink, what makes them deities, and what brings them immortality: "We have drunk Soma and become immortal; we have attained the light, the Gods discovered."[15] Researchers have proffered many potential psychotropic plants as the basis of the sacred Soma, the most prevalent (and thus debated) being the Amanita muscaria mushroom, as first proposed by R. Gordon Wasson in his 1968 book *Soma: Divine Mushroom of Immortality.*

The Zoroastrians in ancient Persia held religious rituals known as Yasna celebrations wherein a plant called *Haoma* was consumed to similar effect. According to Encyclopedia Britannica, "Haoma was regarded by Zoroaster as the son of the Wise Lord and Creator (Ahura Mazda) and the chief priest of the Yasna cult. He was believed to be incarnate in the sacred plant that was pounded to death in order to extract its life-giving juice so that those who consumed it might be given immortality." The article also suggests these rites were a "remarkable anticipation of the mass in Christianity."[16] Russian archeologists may have discovered the secret ingredient in

Haoma when, in 2009, they discovered embroidered woolen textiles in Mongolia dating to the first millennium BCE which depict an ancient Zoroastrian ceremony featuring a king or priest holding a mushroom.[17]

Greek mythology is replete with references to *ambrosia* and *nectar* as the food and drink, respectively, of the gods. The two terms may have been originally interchangeable, and it is notable that the Greek roots of the word "nektar," denote immortality (*nek* means "death" and *tar* or *tere*, originally from Sanskrit, means "cross over, pass through, overcome."). Also significant were annual Greek festivals known as the *Eleusinian Mysteries* (dated by some as early as 1500 BCE),[18] which centered on the resurrection myth of Demeter and Persephone and offered a sacred rite of passage to chosen initiates, which included the drinking of a potion called *kykeon* that delivered a revelatory state. In a stone sculpture excavated from the wall surrounding the temple at Eleusis, Persephone and Demeter are seen holding mushrooms.[19] Some scholars[20, 21] have proposed that kykeon likely contained the hallucinogen ergot, a fungus that grows on barley accessible in Greek agriculture of the period. Ergot was synthesized by chemist Albert Hoffman in 1938, producing the drug we know today as LSD.

Egyptian mythology contains a symbol known as the *Eye of Horus* that is closely identified with the Egyptian deities Horus and his father Osiris. The Eye of Horus (represented by a glyph of a single eye) signifies numerous concepts, including health, protection, and restoration; in one of the myths, Horus gives his eye to Osiris to assist in his resurrection.[22] There is evidence to suggest that the Eye of Horus also symbolized a sustenance that conferred divinity and immortality.[23] British Museum Egyptologist and philologist Sir E. A. Wallis Budge writes, "The gods nourished themselves with celestial food which was supplied to them by the Eye of Horus, that is to say, they supported their existence on the rays of light which fell from the sun which lit up heaven, and they became beings whose bodies were wholly of light. In other places we read of 'bread of eternity' and 'beer of eternity.'"[24]

The Abrahamic traditions also contain references to a divine plant or bread—*manna*—that brings nourishment, light, and immortality. The Islamic *Hadith* quotes Mohammed as saying: "Truffles are a kind of 'manna' and their juice is a medicine for the eyes."[25] Of course, manna plays a crucial role in the Moses story, where it appears "when the dew settles"[26] and provides sustenance to the Israelites for forty years in the desert.[27] In the Gospel of John, Jesus explicitly declares himself to be the manna of the new covenant: "I am the living bread which came down from heaven. If any man eat of this bread, he will live forever."[28] In the Sermon on the Mount (in the King James Bible), he tells his followers: "The light of the body is the eye: if therefore your eye be single, your whole body shall be full of light" (changed, for some reason, in most modern Bibles, to "if your eye is healthy.")[29, 30] These echoes of earlier Indian, Persian, and Egyptian myths, which can be understood as anything from literal divine fiat to deeply-veiled allegorical symbolism, speak to the syncretistic nature of ancient mythologies, at least at their most enigmatic interiors.

Fast forward two millennia: the Beatles release the number one single "Lady Madonna" in March 1968, at the very moment they are camped on the banks of the Ganges River in Rishikesh, India, furthering their study of Transcendental Meditation with Maharishi Mahesh Yogi. On the B-side of this new single is a George Harrison-penned song, inspired by a poem from Lao-Tzu's *Tao Te Ching*[31] and containing the lyrics: "Without looking out of your window, you could know the ways of heaven.... Arrive without traveling, see all without looking." The song, recorded in Bombay with local Indian musicians playing traditional instruments, is titled "The Inner Light."

The influence of psychotropics in the roots of religion may still be an area of active (if not raging) debate, but there is no question they played a huge role in the evolving mythos of the classic rock era. The advent of psychedelic music was likely the most important line of demarcation between early rock & roll and the late '60s designation of "rock" music, and the Beatles, while not the only artists to explore the terrain, are certainly the genre's most famous and influential musical and cultural ambassadors. MacDonald contends: "The Beatles' psychedelic music represents a state of mind different from ordinary reality: a magical, all-beautiful, all-loving vision in which opposites are peacefully reconciled."[32] He surmises that their song "Tomorrow Never Knows" from *Revolver* "introduced LSD and Leary's psychedelic revolution to the young of the Western world, becoming one of the most socially influential records the Beatles ever made."[33]

"Tomorrow Never Knows" may have contained the first overt references to entheogenic principles in Beatles' oeuvre, however by the time of *Revolver*, psychedelics were influencing both their compositional and production process and could be deeply felt in their music. The song "She Said, She Said" was inspired by an acid trip the Beatles took with Byrds Roger McGuinn and David Crosby in Beverly Hills in August 1965. At the party, actor Peter Fonda (who had supplied the drug) was explaining that he knew "what it was like to be dead," after he had suffered a nearly fatal self-inflicted gunshot wound as a child.[34] The Beatles became uncomfortable with his tale, and, according to Fonda, John at one point exclaimed, "You're making me feel like I've never been born."[35] Both phrases were incorporated into the song, which also features complex meter changes, manipulated tape speeds, and eclectic drum patterns that underscore the psychedelic suggestion of the lyric.

The Beatles continued to compose and record music inspired by entheogens through late '67, with the *Revolver, Sgt. Pepper,* and *Magical Mystery Tour* albums (and singles from the time) offering implicit lyrical and aural allusions, mostly written by John ("Day Tripper," "Rain," "I'm Only Sleeping," "Strawberry Fields Forever," "Lucy in the Sky With Diamonds"); though Paul's "Penny Lane" also inferred the surreal aspect of the psychotropic journey through the sly inference that winter and summer are occurring simultaneously, the "pouring rain" versus "blue suburban skies," settings of the verse and chorus, and the jarring dissonance of the final bars suggesting that the clear vision of the song has now returned to the dull perspective of ordinary reality. Perhaps the most overt reference is found in the joint Lennon-McCartney composition "A Day in the Life" and its memorable line: "I'd love to turn you on." Though considered by many the Beatles' supreme opus on record, the song was banned by the BBC due to this unambiguous phrase.

In June 1967, fresh on the release of *Sgt. Pepper*, Paul became the first rock star to publicly admit to having taken LSD. In an interview with the British magazine *Queen* and reprinted in *Life* magazine as part of a feature titled "The New Far-Out Beatles," he described the experience: "After I took it, it opened my eyes. We only use one-tenth of our brain. Just think what we could accomplish if we could only tap that hidden part. It would mean a whole new world."[36] George's recollections of his initial forays also spoke to the drug's revelatory power: "It was something like a very concentrated version of the best feeling I'd ever had in my whole life. It was fantastic. I felt in love, not with anything or anybody in particular, but with everything. Everything was perfect; in a perfect light."[37]

The Beatles officially renounced the use of drugs (though never voiced regret) in favor of meditation in August 1967. Paul explained, "You cannot keep on taking drugs forever....Now it's over and we don't need it any more. We think we're finding other ways of getting there."[38] Of course, history shows the Beatles did not stop taking drugs, including psychedelics, and that the members struggled, to various degrees, with harder substances later in the decade, including cocaine and opiates. John and George were both arrested for marijuana possession in the late '60s, and Paul's 1981 pot bust in Japan, an international news story, kept the Beatles/drugs conflation at the forefront of their mythos well into their third decade. The more reclusive John and George continued to explore entheogens periodically, such as when, in 1978, George composed the song "Here Comes the Moon" (which could be described as a modern hymn to Soma) while tripping in Hawaii.[39] John, in his and Yoko's interview with *Playboy*, was forthcoming regarding his ongoing use: "A little mushroom or peyote is not beyond my scope, you know, maybe twice a year or something....People are taking it [acid], though, even though you don't hear about it anymore. People are still visiting the cosmos."[40]

The psychotropic suggestion of the German name for the Beatles hair style (*pilzen kopf*/mushroom head) provides one key to understanding semiotic meaning that may be inferred or understood unconsciously; we often name or describe things based on physical resemblance. We also bestow titles, monikers, and nicknames to people due to their past actions or future expectations. Consider the "last" names of both Jesus Christ and Gautama Buddha. In each case they refer to titles given by their followers; the name "Christ" meaning "anointed" in Hebrew ("messiah" in English), while the designation of "Buddha" denotes "awakened" or "enlightened one" in the East. In the case of Jesus (*Yeshua*, which translates as "Savior" in Hebrew), even his given name is said to be predestined in the Gospels.[41, 42] The point is that, even if one knew absolutely nothing of these two characters other than the implications of their names, one would have a remarkably accurate impression of their cultural meanings and archetypal functions.

In terms of the names "The Beatles" (which they gave themselves) and "The Fab Four" (the nickname given them by their followers), we find a depth of semiotic inference aligning once again with the mythic savior archetype. In English, *be* means "to exist." In Hebrew, *bea* means "to ask, to seek." The Latin word *beatificus*, the origin of the English "beatific," means "making happy," while the Greek *beatitude* connotes supreme happiness.

The word "Beatles," in addition to its etymology (and twentieth century cultural associations with the "Beat Movement" and "Beat Music"), also suggests a powerful ancient symbol, the scarab beetle. The scarab represents the Egyptian solar deity Khepra, who in his myth pushes the sun across the sky, mimicking the beetle's practice of rolling the dung of ruminants (elephants, sheep, cattle) in a ball across the ground. The scarab beetle's eggs hatch from within these balls of dung, which the Egyptians saw as a potent metaphor for rebirth and resurrection. Khepra was therefore represented as a god or Pharaoh with the head of a beetle.

John Lennon wanted the insect itself to be the image conveyed in the name, openly admitting the direct inspiration of Buddy Holly's

Crickets. When asked about the origin of the name "Beatles," he often replied with the apocryphal story that it came to him in a dream, where he was visited by a man on a flaming pie, who said, "From this day forward you are Beatles with an 'A.'" In more serious mode, he said, "I wanted it to be Beat music when you read it and little crawly things when you said it."[43]

The scarab is often represented as a central feature of the Ankh, the Egyptian precursor of the Christian cross and likewise a symbol for eternal life. The *cross* in its primal form is a universal, ancient symbol that communicates myriad concepts simultaneously. Beyond cultural/religious denotations (Egyptian, Christian, etc.) which place—overlay, really—their chosen deity onto the primitive geometrical figure, the cross is a multi-layered metaphor for the integration of opposites in both the material and spiritual realms.

With its vertical line suggesting divine ascension/descension and its horizontal line representing the physical plane, their union can be understood as the point at which all is resolved in heaven and earth. The cross infers the division of the world by the four elements and pinpoints the intersection of the four cardinal directions. It marks the axis of the yearly cycle—its spokes representing the equinoxes and solstices—and thus communicates the nexus at which all time converges, the eternal now. As it is not bound by a surrounding box or circle, the image also implies infinity. These concepts—demonstrating balance, harmony and the resolution of duality—make the cross an extremely effective symbol to represent the possibility of divinization and communicate the integrative essence and timeless nature of the savior archetype.

The Beatles are a remarkable semiotic conduit for the mythic themes inherent in the cross. First, they communicate the actual geometric figure in a wide variety of promotional imagery. Consider the front and back covers of the album *Let it Be* and the front cover of the United Artists soundtrack album *A Hard Day's Night*, where the four Beatles are shown in equally-sized individual square portraits—the negative space between the four images is the cross symbol in relief. This method of presenting the group through the balanced symbiosis of their four faces has been used by photographers and artists countless times to produce literally billions of impressions of them over the last half-century.

Other paths to understanding the Beatles' resonance with themes associated with the cross can be found through special attention to their number (four), their distinct individual personalities, and the equilibrium inherent in their meta-personality or group identity.

Numbers have been understood for millennia to represent metaphysical concepts, and for this reason many belief systems have incorporated astrological and numerological elements into their mythologies. The idea that numbers have a divine nature is most commonly associated with the Greek philosopher Pythagoras, however it is likely his "school of thought" was a synthesis of ancient traditions that long predate his teachings.[44] The Pythagoreans evolved the practice, however, through their study of and emphasis on musical ratios. Plato describes the Pythagorean philosophy of the "Music of the Spheres" in his *Republic*, which posits the divine nature of numbers because they express perfect harmonic ratios in both heaven (celestial bodies) and earth (sound vibration and frequency): "As the eyes, said I, seem formed for studying astronomy, so do the ears seem formed for harmonious motions, and these seem to be twin sciences to one another, as also the Pythagoreans say."[45]

The Egyptian Book of the Dead teems with complex numeric rituals and incantations required to achieve successful passage into the spirit world. For millennia, the Hebrew Bible has been studied through a system known as *gematria*, which seeks to identify hidden divine meaning in the numeric values of the letters and words in the scripture. This is the basis of the Kabbalist religion and practice and owes to the fact that the Hebrew alphabet was constructed so that its letters corresponded to numeric counterparts; the potential for hidden messages was seemingly built into the very fabric of the language. Christian Mysticism delves deeply into similar study, as reflected in a quote attributed to early Christian mystic St. Augustine of Hippo: "Numbers are the Universal language offered by the deity to humans as confirmation of the truth."[46] The apocalyptic books Daniel and Revelation are but two examples of biblical scripture containing numeric descriptions long believed to hold hidden symbolic meaning.

Likely due to the universal nature and understanding of mathematics, these traditions and more ascribe remarkably similar mythic meaning to the primary numbers, with the first four describing the act of creation itself in symbolic form. The *Tao Te Ching* teaches, "Tao begets One, One begets Two, Two begets Three, and Three begets all things."[47] The Beatles—The Fab Four—reflect the mythic characteristics of the numbers one through four in the order they joined the band, their usual listing (John, Paul, George, and Ringo), and their individual narratives both within and without the group.

The number one is identified with the Creator and pure potentiality. It is the number through which all others emerge and is contained in all primary numbers; as such it is the most essential number, without which nothing else may manifest. The number one represents the Sun, the godhead, the original, the creative spark, the first cause. It is considered the masculine principle—the *yang* in eastern symbology, and God the Father in Western traditions.

John Lennon was the creator of the Beatles. He was often referred to as the leader, or "first Beatle," and was the oldest of the original group. It was his final choice to include each of the other Beatles in the band, and he was first to functionally exit the group and become a "solo" artist. He claimed, accurately, "I started the band. I disbanded it. It's as simple as that."[48] John was the *yang*; his introduction of sexuality into the Beatles' mythos through his relationship and collaboration with Yoko Ono literally exposed his penis through album covers and experimental films. He was an artistic and cultural pioneer, and, of all the Beatles, the most personally singular—he alone stands as a global cultural icon nearly equal to that of the Beatles as a group.

The number two represents duality, harmony, and the splitting of the number one into separate but equal parts (without that split, there is no physicality). Two implies the dualism of the natural world and suggests the potential balance between the spiritual and physical realms. It represents the Moon, the part, the compliment, the mirror. In the East, the number two is the *yin*, the receptive feminine energy balancing the creative masculine energy of the *yang*, the number one.

Paul McCartney was the ideal partner for John Lennon, complimenting him in countless ways as an artist, composer, and band member. Paul's diplomatic and cooperative personality balanced John's aggressive tendencies and softened his rougher edges—on stage, in the studio, and with the media and fans—harmonizing the creative team at the core of the Beatles. As songwriter, singer, performer, and musical force, Paul was co-leader of the Beatles. In brief, Paul was John's equal.

John has been oft-quoted on his choice to become musical partners with Paul, who he saw "had talent" but who he also clearly felt was a potential threat to his dominance of the group: "I was the singer and the leader, and I made the decision to have him in the group or not. Was it better to have a guy who was better than the people I had in, obviously, or not? And the decision was to let Paul in, and make the group stronger."[49] As the younger of the two, and the second to join the band, Paul would always be listed after John, though in order only.

The number three is the synthesis of one and two, and thus initiates action and motion. Three represents the idea, the concept, the expression, the creative alchemy between one and two. It completes the triad of Father, Mother, and Child, expressed in Egyptian mythology as Osiris, Isis, and Horace, and in the Hindu pantheon as Shiva, Parvati, and Ganesha. It implies relationship, family, and mediation.

As the third to join the Beatles, George Harrison's inclusion suggested the idea of a band. With George, they were no longer a duo, they were a group; in fact, they didn't even become the Beatles in name until after George joined. As the youngest member, George's attachment signaled the concept of band as family.

Blossoming later than John and Paul as a songwriter and singer, he was initially their junior in terms of ability and importance to the Beatles' musical canon, but as the child eventually grows beyond the confines of the family home, George's maturation necessarily altered the dynamic of the band. As the third composer, George hastened the inevitability of future solo careers, as a single album didn't offer space for each artist to express themselves fully. The number three is inherently dynamic, and therefore unstable.

The number four classically represents material manifestation, making concrete the dream created through the alchemy of one, two, and three. It marks the resolution of the active principle into a stable framework, and thus signifies symbolic completion. Like the square, which denotes stability, the number four implies balance and foundation, and, as with the cross, integration, wholeness, and perfection.

When Ringo Starr replaced Pete Best as the drummer of the Beatles, that undeniable alchemical reaction took place, certainly in terms of the Beatles' image, and quite obviously in the creative growth of the group as well. In hindsight, we can see the addition as the final piece of the puzzle. Indeed, their decision to include Ringo seems to have been based on the intuition that he would provide just that—a missing element. The Beatles had already secured a recording contract with Pete Best—there was no external pressure to make the change. In fact, given Pete's popularity with the fans (and girls, in particular) and the longtime support of his mother Mona to the group's efforts, the move was a risky one. Manager Brian Epstein was against it, and producer George Martin made it clear that he would be using a session drummer (initially, anyway) in the studio regardless of who was the Beatles' drummer on stage.

And yet it was a decision that brought completeness to the Beatles. It is well known that Pete was never really one of them; he seemed to lack the power of personality the others so naturally emanated, and he never bonded with them the way they did with each other. His drumming, while solid enough to propel them through their club years, never felt to them like the foundation they sought for their music. George remembers that when Ringo would sit in for Pete during the dog days of Hamburg, "it seemed like 'this is it.' "[50] Tony Barrow, Beatles press agent during their touring years, recalls asking Lennon the difference between Pete Best and Ringo Starr. "Pete was a good drummer; Ringo is good Beatle," was John's dry but quite telling explanation.[51] It shouldn't surprise that a number of the Beatles' most famous and beloved songs were either sung by Ringo ("Yellow Submarine," "With a Little Help from My Friends") or had their titles inspired by him ("A Hard Day's Night," "Tomorrow Never Knows"). He was an essential, creative member. He was a Beatle.

The name "Ringo Starr" is itself a powerful semiotic sign communicating several mythic themes simultaneously. The first connotation would naturally be the *ring*, which, like the ouroboros, is a symbol for the cyclical nature of life, the integration and assimilation of opposites, and eternity (the reason it accompanies a wedding vow). The name Ringo Starr also calls to mind the *halo* (a *ring* around a *star*), completing the Christian inference begun with the saintly names John, Paul, and George. The halo is inspired by the light (aura, corona) surrounding celestial bodies, and is a visual metaphor for spiritual enlightenment. Given our primitive focus on the cosmos as inspiration for attributes of gods, it naturally became a defining characteristic in art depicting deities and saints in many religious traditions. Ringo was experienced, by the audience, as the halo above the other three Beatles; he was physically behind and above them in concert, one of their most indelible visual images (for the first *Ed Sullivan* performance, Ringo was placed on an elevated, ring-shaped platform). Of course, a star floats above, shines light, and draws wise men to knowledge. Plus, his name is Ring-O! The name itself contains a ring—which accents and deepens the visual and auditory power of the symbol.

Groupings and divisions of things, concepts, and systems into four parts are ever-present in our material world. In addition to the four elements (earth, air, fire, and water) and the four cardinal points (north, east, south, and west), we have four seasons (winter, spring, summer, and autumn), four moon phases (full, waning, crescent, and waxing), and four spatial dimensions (length, breadth, width, and depth). Card decks are separated into four suits (clubs, spades, hearts, and diamonds in playing cards and swords, wands, discs, and cups in the Tarot). In Western classical music, common time is based on four beats per measure, and is the most frequent rock/pop time signature. Four beats—four Beatles.

The totality suggested by the number four can be seen in creation narratives and the assembly of spiritual literature. In the Abrahamic traditions, there are four rivers flowing from a single source in their stories of paradise. There are four letters in the Hebrew name for God, "YHWH," known as the Tetragrammaton. We see groupings of four in the organization of sacred scripture: The four Vedas in Hinduism (the Rigveda, Yajurveda, Samaveda, and Atharvaveda); four Gospels in the New Testament (Matthew, Mark, Luke, and John); and four Sacred Books of Islam (the Taurat, Zabur, Injil, and Quran).

Jung writes about the inherent symbolism of the number four, explaining that it is "an age-old, presumably pre-historic, symbol, always associated with a world-creating deity,"[52] and further that "symbolic structures [which] refer to the process of individuation tend to be based on the motif of the number four... the natural unhampered manifestations of the center are characterized by four-fold-ness.[53] ... Psychologically, it denotes concentration on and preoccupation with a center."[54] His concept of the four functions of the psyche—thinking, feeling, sensing, and intuiting—adhere to this pattern, and provide the basis of the *Myers-Briggs Type Indicator* used in modern personality profiling and psychometric testing.

The Beatles themselves highlight the numbers one through four in their recordings. Two of their albums, *Please, Please, Me* and *Revolver*, begin with the exclamation, "One, Two, Three, Four," and it is reasonable to say these are two of the most famous "count-ins" in the history of popular music. In fact, the second of the two (leading into the song "Taxman" on *Revolver*) can be heard as a comment on the first, wherein the excited "live" sound of Paul's count-in to

"I Saw Her Standing There" on their first album is replaced with stuttering tape effects, suggesting that the recording process has supplanted live performance as the modus operandi of the Beatles.

The songs of the Beatles contain their most famous mythic signs, in that they contain predominantly explicit messages that are communicated and understood at the conscious level. It is hard to miss the integrative valuation of mutual support in "We Can Work it Out," "With a Little Help from My Friends," and "All Together, Now;" the sense of joy and fulfillment emanating from "I Feel Fine," "Here, There and Everywhere," and "Across the Universe;" the utopian ideals of "Give Peace a Chance" "Imagine," and "Happy Christmas (War is Over);" the solar genuflection in odes "Good Day Sunshine," "Sun King," and "Here Comes the Sun;" nor the philosophy of love and acceptance in "The Word," "All You Need is Love," and "Let it Be."

A similar semiotic rubric can likewise be applied to many other artists, as the Beatles were not the only icons of the classic rock era to communicate distinct archetypal mythologies through their music, art, and narrative. If the Beatles represented the transformative and transcendent ideals of their generation and thus embodied a savior archetype for their time, Bob Dylan brought mystical poetic prophecy into the '60s zeitgeist and became its greatest sage. Also the Rolling Stones, who illuminated our darkest depths through their earthy hedonism and infernal blues; the Beach Boys, whose hymns of eternal youth celebrated the innocence of a generation on the verge of adulthood; Joni Mitchell, whose layered expression of the divine feminine called for gender equality and environmental responsibility; and the Who, whose fierce negation of the material world cleared the way for spirit to soar. These artists and more also became gods and goddesses to legions of followers in the 1960s and are still worshipped by millions to this day. It is to them we now turn.

It is perfectly possible, psychologically, for the unconscious
or an archetype to take complete possession of a man and
to determine his fate down to the smallest detail.

–Carl Jung

THE INNER GROOVES

❖ ❖ ❖

The Pre-Fab Mythic Archetypes of Rock & Roll

As with the creation of the world, it is impossible to pinpoint exactly when rock & roll began. The term itself, with its implication of both unbridled sexuality and charismatic religious fever, had been a part of the musical (and, to some degree, Baptist Christian) lexicon since the 1930s, appearing with increasing frequency as the 1940s drew to a close. While there has never been a consensus from historians on either the musical or cultural beginning of the genre, there is a near universal recognition, certainly in hindsight, that the explosion of rock & roll, with all its connotations, became uniquely visible in the unrestrained, ecstatic gyrations of a single person: Elvis Presley. In other words, though the "world" of rock & roll may have been created in fits and starts, it wasn't communally "experienced" until the arrival of Elvis, who anthropomorphized the music into an indelible human image, one that was instantly mythic in stature and impact. Recall John Lennon's oft-quoted statement: "Before Elvis there was nothing."[1]

Psychologist Marie-Louise von Franz, who wrote numerous books on the archetypal foundations of fairy tales, contends that creation myths describe "not the origin of our cosmos, but the origin of man's conscious awareness of the world."[2] The character of Adam in the Judaic mythos can thus be understood as a symbol for the evolution of human consciousness; his initial androgyny splitting into two equal parts an allegory for the resulting dualities of the natural world, the motif deepened by the story of the forbidden fruit of the Tree of Knowledge, i.e. "of good and evil," and that of man and woman's banishment from the Garden of Eden. Joseph Campbell asserts that the Garden is a metaphor for the human psyche;[3] as such the fall from grace in creation myths is an allegory of our struggle to resolve the multiplicity of the conscious world with the pristine wholeness of our deep unconscious.

In the rock mythology, Elvis recalls in numerous ways the original human archetype of Adam, representing duality in many forms and the anticipation of resolution as symbolized by the mythic savior, in Elvis's case the Beatles. The description of Jesus Christ in the epistles of St. Paul (and writings of other Christian mystics) as the "last" Adam is indicative of the psychic path of transformation and transcendence that began with the Fall: "The first man, Adam, became a living being; the last Adam became a life-giving spirit."[4] Likewise, Elvis was a harbinger of this development in the rock mythology; his character incorporating myriad musical, cultural, and figurative dualities. In addition to his merging of country and blues styles into a novel musical alloy, Elvis's persona harmonized societal divisions of rural and urban culture; religious demarcations of good and evil; racial perceptions of Caucasian and African American; and physical expressions of male and female, all aspects of the prototypical "rock star" we would see emerge again and again. Elvis was a "white" who sang "black," a poor country boy who became a rich Hollywood star, a sexually charged performer who sang reverent gospel hymns, a man who moved like a woman, and, by nearly unanimous accounts from both genders, possessing a striking, unmistakable androgynous beauty.[5] He was also (significantly in terms of his personal psychology) a surviving twin who felt throughout his life that he carried the spirit of his lost brother, Jesse Garon, in his own soul.[6]

The dualities balanced by Elvis permeate the rock mythology, often expressed in the stories that define many of our biggest stars and most successful groups. Consider the images and personal narratives of the Mamas and the Papas, Fleetwood Mac, and ABBA; in each case we see two married (or essentially bonded) couples whose private dramas and sexual tensions must be resolved for great art to emerge. The mirrors within these groups are even more exaggerated in famous "family" acts such as the Everly Brothers, the Bee Gees, the Jackson 5, the Carpenters, and Heart, where the clear physical and vocal resemblance of the members is essential to their image and sound. The hard rock and heavy metal bands take this duality motif to an almost comical level with their "good versus evil" operatics, underscored by their duality-laden names: Iron/Butterfly, Blue/Cheer, Vanilla/Fudge, Black/Sabbath, Judas/Priest, AC/DC, Quiet/Riot, and Guns/Roses, etc.

Often in mythic narratives, the ensuing story is initiated by a character described as the *herald*, and Elvis fulfills this role in the rock pantheon. Frequently functioning as a "divine messenger," the herald is familiar in both classic literature and poetry and modern works of film and television drama. A salient contemporary example would be the character of M in the James Bond mythos, who, early in nearly every story, gives Bond his orders and sends him on his quest. In some cases, the herald is not even a human character but a found or won physical object, such as the Golden Ticket in *Willy Wonka and the Chocolate Factory* or R2D2's projection of Princess Leia that launches *Star Wars*.

The herald is ubiquitous in classical mythology, to the degree that Joseph Campbell lists its function as one of the primary stages of the Hero's Journey: "The Call to Adventure." The Greek god Hermes, for instance, is the emissary of Zeus in Homer's *The Odyssey*, acting as a divine agent assisting the Greeks in their war with the Trojans. As with his Roman equivalent Mercury, he is characterized with winged feet and cap and carrying a *caduceus*, a winged staff wrapped with two snakes (also called a "herald's staff"). In *The Iliad*, the herald role is filled by Iris, a goddess messenger with wings on her feet and shoulders who also represents the rainbow, itself a symbol for divine messages in many traditions (such as the myth of Noah and the flood). In Norse mythology, Loki often plays the part, issuing threats or challenges that initiate the consequent drama. The *trickster* aspect of Loki is shared by Hermes and other heralds; the proclamations by these deities may bring good and/or bad trials and outcomes to the hero protagonist.

The Gospel stories are replete with heralds, who announce both Jesus's birth and the beginning of his ministry; indeed, the Gospels themselves and various Old Testament prophets can also be understood as heralding his arrival and divinity. Mark, the first Gospel to be composed, opens with the verses: "The beginning of the good news of Jesus Christ, the Son of God. As is written in the prophet Isaiah, 'See, I am sending my messenger ahead of you, who will prepare your way.' "[7] Matthew and Luke both describe angels announcing Mary's immaculate conception and Jesus's impending birth. In Matthew, an angel appears to Joseph in a dream to explain how and why his virgin fiancée has become pregnant and implore him to carry on with the wedding and name the child Jesus.[8] In Luke, where the birth narrative is elaborated in a story known as "The Annunciation," the angel Gabriel appears to Mary to inform that "the Holy Spirit will overcome you," that she will conceive a child, and he will fulfill a divine purpose.[9] Then, once Jesus is born, an angel appears to shepherds to bring them the good news, followed by a "multitude of heavenly host" (angels) praising God and promising peace.[10]

Luke also features a story, known as "The Visitation," wherein the conception of John the Baptist (here described as Jesus's cousin) is foretold by an angel to John's elderly father Zechariah. Then, when Zechariah's wife Elizabeth is six months pregnant, her sister Mary (who had just conceived the Christ-child) comes to visit, and Luke reports that the infant John in Elizabeth's womb "leaped for joy!"[11] This narrative, suggesting John and Jesus are related, that John was born first, and that he recognized Jesus's divinity even from within the womb, explicitly ascertains John the Baptist as a herald of Jesus. This is, of course, deepened by the story, related in all four Gospels, that three decades hence John baptizes Jesus in the river Jordon, further establishing his divinity and the beginning of his ministry. John even makes his own role explicit: "I baptize you with water; but one who is more powerful than I is coming."[12]

The influence of Elvis on the Beatles and their contemporaries is incalculable. Though they were also inspired to action by the artistry of Chuck Berry, Bill Haley, Little Richard, and Jerry Lee Lewis, et al. (and a multitude of blues musicians, folk balladeers, and standards singers), it was Elvis who was the most influential, lighting the path for all future popular musicians and establishing the rock genre as the most commercially successful of the twentieth century. Paul McCartney recalls seeing for the first time a picture of Elvis in a local British paper: "He just looked perfect. That's it. That is the Guru we have been waiting for."[13] John Lennon draws an unmistakable line between Elvis and his own career: "Nothing really affected me until I heard Elvis. If there hadn't been an Elvis, there wouldn't have been the Beatles."[14]

The relationship between Elvis and the Beatles is therefore an allegorical equivalent to John the Baptist and Jesus; like John, Elvis paved the way for a more potent and fully realized savior, and both were eclipsed in the middle of their "ministry" by archetypes with deeper cultural and symbolic significance. When the Beatles first appeared on *Ed Sullivan*, Elvis sent a telegram wishing them luck that Ed referenced to viewers—a passing of the torch or "touch of grace" that associated Elvis with the new music revolution, but now more as a standard-bearer receding as a vital force. The King was, in a sense, abdicating his throne to his four princely sons, who would hence reign as a collective, honoring their aging father's legacy by expanding and deepening his mythic promise.

After Elvis issued the "call to adventure" to the coming generation of rock gods, and yet before the arrival of the savior in the form of the Beatles, there were two artists that further chiseled the bedrock of the music and the mythology. Representing archetypes that often prefigure the savior in classical mythologies, they provided crucial, direct influence on the Beatles artistically and symbolically.

At the dawn of the 1960s, after Elvis's enrolment in the United States Army and the deaths of Buddy Holly, Richie Valens, and the

Big Bopper, entered an implausibly young singer with the voice
of a grizzled sage. Singing penetrating and pertinent poetry to
the timeless musical forms that had evolved out of centuries of
American folk music and crystallized in the folk milieu of the late
'50s and early '60s, he was the definition of an enigma, untrace-
able and untrained. Singing of change and justice, salvation and
annihilation in a common voice to the elemental chords G, C, and
D, his words inspired millions, bringing with them passion, a call
for action, and hope for a better tomorrow. Fans and media soon
began referring to him as a prophet.

Robert Zimmerman emerged in the New York City folk scene
with a self-concocted identity. He changed his name to Bob Dylan
and told audiences, artists, and record producers fantastic tales of
iconic Americana in place of his life story, while in actuality he grew
up middle class in a small Minnesota town, dropped out of college,
and moved to New York to be a singer. The reality was common to
the point of being trite, but Dylan seemed to intuitively understand
a performer's power to create an identity in the eyes of the audience
that may have little to do with what is temporally "true." He acknowl-
edges, "I felt right at home in this mythical realm made up not
with individuals so much as archetypes."[15] It didn't matter what the
technical facts of his past or his present were, the character of Bob
Dylan was mercurial, cagey, and above all, mysterious. In fact, it was
directly after Dylan was "outed" as a middle-class Midwesterner in
the media that he forsook all coherence and respect for reporters
and interviewers, answering nearly every question with bald-faced
fabrications, doublespeak, and insouciant jabs.

People were eager to accept the notion of a teenage Dylan on
a Steinbeckian dustbowl pilgrimage, learning guitar techniques
from Leadbelly's grandson, or bargaining for his mystical talent
at a rural crossroads. His early songs captured the zeitgeist of a
novel time period, and utilized tones, themes, and forms heretofore unemployed in contemporary folk trends. His anthems were
not tales or threats of death, downbeat and full of despair like so
many traditional and contemporary American folk songs; they were

hopeful and inciting, calling believers to arms and promising that a better world was forthcoming if those who could see clearly would only take up their swords, shields, and pens to fight for truth and justice. The times, Dylan insisted, would change.

A *prophet* is fully flesh and blood, as opposed to a god or demi-god (who is half human and half divine). They may be uniquely gifted with wisdom, temperance, perspective, poetic language, or clairvoyance; often the words they say or write are even considered to be the god speaking through the human being, as if the prophet were a celestial stenographer. Western religious prophets, such as Moses and others in the Old Testament, tend to show up in highly contentious and seemingly hopeless situations; they may possess warlike qualities, inspiring their followers to overturn an oppressive or unrighteous ruler, often by violence. In Eastern traditions, such as Daoism and Buddhism, the prophet archetype (personified in quasi-historical characters like Huineng, Zhuangzi, Lao-Tzu, and Bodhidharma) takes the form of the hermetic sage, achieving enlightened perspective through isolation and meditation rather than divine ventriloquism. This Eastern adept also inspires change in his followers, however abstract—an adjustment in morals, or in governing, or in the way the individual views the world and his or her place in it.

Three common themes appear frequently in the prophet archetype: inspiration, words, and mystery. The prophet rouses people to change the world they live in, whether in terms of a power structure, their personal actions, or simply their own points of view. He wields an uncanny propensity for language and foresight which reaches beyond his given limitations. The prophet also hides most of his carnal and psychic life behind the veil of enigma, and usually wanders—he comes from somewhere else, brings people along for part of his journey, and, once their positions have shifted, keeps moving, like a leaf blowing in the wind or (forgive me) like a rolling stone.

Dylan's early songs certainly lent themselves to prophetically over-toned extrapolation. The sad, wizened hopefulness of "Blowin' in the Wind" and the farseeing call to arms of "The Times, They Are A-Changin'" affected listeners like urgent, divinely inspired sermons. While written in the nomenclature of the rural American common man, lyrics to "A Hard Rain's A-Gonna Fall" read like something directly out of the Bible: unflinching Old Testament authority mixed with Revelations-style eschatological clairvoyance, allusions to prophetic wandering, meditation on a mountaintop, and even walking on water.

His version of wandering, confusing to fans and music journalists as it may have been, is in fact the central theme in many of his most iconic and enduring songs, such as "Like a Rolling Stone" and "Tangled Up in Blue," both of which are about mobility and the dissolution of identity. These enigmatic aspects are arguably Dylan's most interesting traits to filmmakers, who over five decades have continued to explore him as a wandering poet in movies with titles such as *Don't Look Back*, *No Direction Home*, and *I'm Not There*.

Highly proficient at self-mythologizing, Dylan was equally adept at dodging media-imposed labels, though the press and public persisted in painting him as a prophet long after he had publicly shunned the role. It is relevant to note that even his denials of this definition are often of an elliptical and undeniably prophetic nature: "I really was never any more than what I was; a folk musician who gazed into the gray mist with tear-blinded eyes and made up songs that floated in a luminous haze.[16] ... To do it, you've got to have power and dominion over the spirits. ... see into things, the truth of things—and not metaphorically, either—but really see, like seeing into metal and making it melt, see it for what it was and reveal it for what it was with hard words and vicious insight."[17]

Dylan's most significant cultural contribution was to make it acceptable—and eventually standard—to combine serious poetry with popular music, which provided a medium for passionate lyrical ideas that were farther-reaching and more accessible and immediate than words on a page. Indeed, since Dylan, the role of the poet in Western society has been all but supplanted by the singer-songwriter, and many of the most culturally relevant post-Dylan poets (Leonard Cohen, Lou Reed, Patti Smith) eventually made their deepest (or at least widest) impact through songwriting.

As Homer melded poetry with storytelling, illustrating the human being in relationship to mythology and the world, and Shakespeare elevated the poetry of playwriting, emphasizing the human being in relationship to society, so Dylan brought visceral poetry to the musical song, stressing the individual and their relationship to themselves. Dylan's lyrical and melodic voice was a culmination of centuries of musical and literary evolution, encompassing and crystallizing songwriting into a singular form that seemed to have been waiting out in the aural ether for the right moment to unveil itself. No one redefined poetry in the twentieth century more than Bob Dylan, and in that sense, he certainly stands with Homer and Shakespeare as a prophet in terms of his literary influence, a view sympathetic with the Nobel Committee, who awarded him the literature prize in 2017—the first ever for a writer from a primarily musical tradition.

When Dylan "went electric," the masses did not take the abandonment of their prophet gracefully. The hostile reaction following Dylan's foray away from folk music and into rock & roll in 1964-5 (following his exposure to the Beatles) may well be the ultimate fan backlash of the media age. Former fans catcalled (*Judas!*), threw things at the stage as he performed, and even called in death threats, while the media hounded him with endless prods about his artistic integrity and responsibility to the people. When he retreated quietly to upstate New York in the attempt to live an ordinary life with his family, his followers found him, camped on his lawn, stole his garbage, and broke into his home. Dylan describes the difficulties he endured: "Demonstrators found our house and paraded up and down in front of it chanting and shouting, demanding for me to come out and lead them somewhere—stop shirking my duties as the conscience of a generation."[18]

Writers and fans expressed the same dismay and sense of betrayal over his hermetic, countrified, late '60s *New Morning* period as they did over his initial foray into rock & roll. Then, in the late '70s and into the '80s, when Dylan followed the acclaimed *Blood on the Tracks* and *Desire* with a trilogy of Christian albums and followed that somewhat baffling phase with a near decade of artistic apathy, the reaction was repeated. He was still Bob Dylan; he still owed the world the truth, which he was unfairly hiding behind these constant character slips.

Perhaps the most remarkable thing about Dylan as a cultural entity is his almost complete lack of any definable linear identity. Whereas the mythos of, for instance, the Beatles, the Rolling Stones, and the Beach Boys contain distinct and well-known personal stories that informed their art and help identify their archetypal essences, for Dylan it is the non-existence of dramatic narrative that allows him to remain obscure and mysterious. Moreover, he seems to be as opaque to himself as he is to his following. In an interview with *Newsweek,* he offered, "I don't think I'm tangible to myself. I mean, I think one thing today and I think another thing tomorrow. I change during the course of a day. I wake and I'm one person, and when I go to sleep I know for certain I'm somebody else. I don't know who I am most of the time. It doesn't even matter to me."[19]

Author Jonathan Lethem, who interviewed Dylan for *Rolling Stone,* described the difficulty in piercing the prophet's veil: "As ever, Dylan is circling, defining what he is first by what he isn't, by what he doesn't want, doesn't like, doesn't need, locating meaning by a process of elimination. This rhetorical strategy goes back at least as far as 'It Ain't Me, Babe' and 'All I Really Want to Do' ('I ain't looking to compete with you,' etc.)."[20] To the media, the audience, and even, perhaps, himself, Bob Dylan is ineffable, unknowable, and can only be seen in relief against a background he creates for himself.

It is this elusive and puzzling nature of Dylan that allowed his myth to root and persist for well-over a half century, even as the physical flesh-and-blood *man* still roams the roads. While many other rock gods who did not die during their tragically beautiful youth seem to carry their aging flesh awkwardly as disjointed living relics somehow connected to the glory of a mythic past, Dylan, with his inscrutable identity and bizarrely epic "Never Ending Tour" (which, like his "Rolling Thunder" tour of the '70s, could not scream "wandering prophet" more loudly), remains the reluctant, confounding, sometimes unintelligible and yet continually inspiring prophet.

In a religious context, prophets express the fundamental ethics of the belief system and the hope of fruition through a coming savior or great spiritual awakening. However, they represent far more than a conceptual place-holder; their facility with words and inspired thought are not only aspects shared by the savior deities themselves, the pronouncements of prophets often inspire the saviors directly, becoming integral aspects of their novel spiritual philosophy. The *Rishis* (seers) in India are believed to have composed the sacred Vedas, bringing the pantheon of Hindu deities to life through the printed word, while the Judaic prophets, whose words comprise the bulk of Old Testament teachings, are continually cited by Jesus, St. Paul, and other Christian writers as the basis for moral laws supporting the holy precepts of the new covenant. As such, the prophet provides the spiritual foundation and societal context that guides the savior as he enacts the edifying and exemplary passion play.

The essential link between prophet and savior is pronounced once more in the rock mythology, where the reciprocal relationship of Dylan and the Beatles is symbolized by game-changing pivots in the history of each artist: Dylan's turn to electric music as a way of amplifying the power of his voice in the new music landscape defined by the Beatles; and his introduction of cannabis to the group, which, along with his example of social consciousness and lyrical depth, inspired the progressive quality of their songwriting and awakening cultural stance in 1965-66.

Also predating the arrival of the Beatles and proving to be among their most vital influences was an artist who, like the prophet

Dylan, represents an elemental aspect of the savior. As this young man distilled the hopeful enthusiasm of teenage America into symphonic rock & roll anthems exalting a never-ending summer, his dramatic personal saga symbolized our individual and collective search for transcendence, in this case through innocence.

In the summer of 1961, as President Kennedy's "New Camelot" was defining a sunny American spirit of forward-thinking vim and vigor, Brian Wilson entered a recording studio for the first time. Along with his two brothers, a cousin, and a high-school chum, he recorded his own composition, "Surfin'," which quickly became a strong local hit in Los Angeles and (surprisingly, given the dominance of the folk boom in full swing) reached number seventy-five on the national charts. Within a few months, Brian (and his group, the Beach Boys) would be signed to Capitol records, and he would soon thereafter be given total creative control in the studio. Over the course of the next five years, he would compose, arrange, produce, sing, and perform on twelve gold albums and over thirty Top-40 singles that capture the optimism, promise, and sheer joy of youth while painting an aural picture of a heaven-on-earth called California.[21]

Clearly, the experience of childhood is expressed directly in a great number of '60s-era Beach Boys songs: "When I Grow Up (To Be a Man)," "All Summer Long," "I'm So Young," "Fun, Fun, Fun," "Be True to Your School," and "Wouldn't It Be Nice," to name but a few. And of course, the overt topics explored in their early recordings were essentially toys, locales, and concerns for kids: surfing, hot rods, motorbikes, skateboards, hamburger stands, drive-ins, the beach, first love. In addition to the obvious references in the songs, Brian personally exhibited many characteristics that suggested a child at play. He likely has the most famous falsetto singing voice (also called the "head" or "childhood" voice) in the history of popular music; his high tenor often carrying the main melody and his sweeping top harmony one of the Beach Boys' sonic hallmarks. As well, countless anecdotes from his (well-known to fans) personal narrative—playing grand piano in a sandbox, installing a tent and tumbling mats in place of furniture in his living room, holding business meetings in a swimming pool, employing the sound of chewing vegetables as percussion—bolster his "man-child" image in the popular imagination.

The *child* is a universal archetype that represents the essence of purity, imagination, creativity, and unlimited potential. According to Jung, this character is symbolic of the developing personality in the individual, the primordial memory of our origin in the collective unconscious, and "potential future." He writes, "The child symbolizes the pre-conscious and the post-conscious essence of man. His pre-conscious essence is the unconscious state of earliest childhood; his post-conscious essence is anticipation by analogy of life after death."[22] In other words, the child, while being a metaphor for the individuation process in every human being, is a symbol for the pristine state from which we collectively emerged (Eden), and our hope for spiritual wholeness after death (heaven). It is the anthropomorphic character representing our archetypal concept of *paradise.*

By the time the Beach Boys surfed onto the airwaves in the early '60s, California had long been a destination both dreamed of and sought after, the natural conclusion of a manifest destiny ideal that began the instant Europeans sailed to the shores of the Americas and continued charging west. From the outset, the "New World" was imagined as an earthly paradise and approached with the passion of a religious quest. In a journal entry dated October 1500, Christopher Columbus suggested that his recent "discovery" was divinely inspired and the culmination of biblical prophecy.[23]

In Eastern traditions, paradise is associated with an enlightened state of mind to be actively sought in this world (nirvana), the final release from perpetual reincarnation and endless suffering (Samsāra), and the eternal condition of peace and spiritual understanding that is the final destiny of all souls. In Tibet, these concepts coalesced into the legend of an earthly heaven located in the highest reaches of the Himalayas. First described in ancient Sanskrit texts[24] and elaborated upon in the Kalachakra Tantra,[25]

Shambhala was a Buddhist "pure land" that existed as much in the spiritual realm as it did the material. Though never discovered, it was imagined as a place of enlightenment, peace, and tranquility, and believed to be where the teachings of Gautama Buddha were preserved.[26] The Eastern emphasis on paradise as a conceptual rather than physical destination is paralleled in the "dreamtime" of the Australian Aborigines, which is believed by its practitioners to be a psychic immersion into time before memory, also encompassing their notion of the land of the dead, i.e. heaven.

In the Abrahamic religions, paradise is conceived as a fertile primordial garden, a gift from God lost forever to terrestrial Man in a tragic fall from grace. It is also imagined as the final resting place of the soul, a heavenly afterlife rewarded to the righteous. Western response to paradise has tended to focus on the accumulation of power and wealth, often with an emphasis on the ultimate dominance of Christianity over "pagan" belief systems. In the West, paradise is seen as something to be *acquired*; in the East, it is understood as something to be *realized*.

In many paradise myths, the concept of perfect harmony is implied, and often specified. The depiction of heaven in the book of Revelation offers numeric measurements describing the exact ratios and dimensions of the physical city.[27] Given that the word for "heaven" is indistinguishable in many languages (including Old English) from the word for "sky" (or "firmament"), it follows that notions of paradise would contain astronomical and arithmetical emphasis; the inclusion of "sacred geometry" underscores the primacy of mathematical theory and harmonic relationships in the physical construct of our temporal reality, and thus is fundamental to our concepts of perfection.

The harmonies composed and arranged by Brian Wilson for the Beach Boys are generally acknowledged as the gold standard of the rock era. Allmusic.com calls them "the most intricate, gorgeous harmonies ever heard from a pop band,"[28] while Dylan simply opines, "Jesus, that ear. He should donate it to the Smithsonian."[29] Multiple Grammy-winning songwriter Jimmy Webb explains, "One of the secrets of how their voices blend is that they use very little vibrato, which is really old-style church singing from five or six hundred years ago.... They sang very straight tones. The voices all lie down beside each other very easily; there's no bumping between them because the pitch is very precise."[30] Oscar- and Emmy-winning sound engineer Eugene Gearty clarifies: "[Brian] was far more complex than the Beatles (and mostly like Stravinsky) in orchestral music, where the key changes and key centers change four or five times within a pop tune...which is unheard of."[31]

Water, in many religious traditions, is believed to be the bringer and restorer of life. In the Quran, Muhammad tells of the four waters which flow "beneath" the garden of life,[32] suggesting at once the four elements in balance and the primordial waters from which humanity emerged: "Here is a Parable of the Garden which the righteous are promised: in it are rivers of water incorruptible; rivers of milk of which the taste never changes; rivers of wine, a joy to those who drink; and rivers of honey pure and clear."[33] In Christianity, water's redemptive and purifying power is folded into the ritual of baptism and exemplified in Jesus's miracle healing of the paralytic at Bethesda.[34] In a verse known as the "Water of Life Discourse," Jesus says: "Whosoever drinketh of the water that I shall give him shall never thirst; but the water that I shall give him shall become in him a well of water springing up unto eternal life."[35]

In paradise mythologies, magical water is often the elixir that bestows eternal life. "Fountain of Youth" legends reach from the Americas to the Far East. Tales of the fountain on a mythical island in the Bimini area of the Bahamas were said to have inspired Spanish explorer Juan Ponce de León's expedition to what is now Florida, and though that story is apocryphal (he was likely searching for gold), it fascinated the Western imagination for centuries. A similar fantasy persisted throughout Europe during the Middle Ages and Renaissance, attesting to a magical kingdom of "Prester John" that was said to border biblical Eden and contain a fountain of youth. A fraudulent but widely circulated and believed "letter" from the kingdom attested to a grove "at the foot of Mount

Olympus, from where a clear spring issues, containing all kinds of pleasant tastes. ... If someone who has fasted for three days tastes of this spring, he will suffer no infirmity from that day on, and will always be as if he were thirty-two years old."[36]

As the premier surf group of the rock era, nearly every Beach Boys song is immersed in a water setting or motif. While the music itself—cascading vocal harmonies, slick guitar licks, rushing rhythms, and melodious percussion—often implies the sounds of water, the subject matter explores multiple concepts associated with the element. It could be joyful ("Catch a Wave"), romantic ("Surfer Girl"), melancholic ("The Lonely Sea"), adventurous ("Sloop John B."), metaphoric ("Sail on, Sailor"), foreboding ("Till I Die"), contemplative ("Surf's Up"), or rejuvenating ("Cool, Cool Water"). For Brian Wilson, the ocean reflects human experience, expressed as allegory for the struggles and triumphs of individuation. In his oeuvre, water represents life itself.

Gold and precious jewels are plentiful in paradise myths, from the depiction of heaven in Revelation ("The wall is built of jasper, while the city is pure gold, clear as glass")[37] to the legend of Prester John ("The sand and gravel are nothing but precious stones and gems").[36] Indeed, the title *El Dorado* in Spanish means "The Golden One," which refers to the gold dust covered king who was believed to rule over an enchanted city (or lake) overflowing in gold coins and emeralds. Over the centuries, many fruitless expeditions were undertaken across several continents to find El Dorado (in the Andes), Shambhala (in the Himalayas), and Prester John's kingdom (in India, China, and Africa), but these supernatural oases always remained just beyond reach in the temporal realm.

The gold in Beach Boys' music is the "Golden State" itself, California. Venerated in such standards as "Surfin' USA" and "California Girls," Brian Wilson's songs of a mythic California, with its golden sun, beaches, bodies, and blondes. inspired dreams of paradise across the globe. Longtime *Rolling Stone* editor Anthony DeCurtis summarizes: "There was a distinct cultural identity to California music, once the Beach Boys defined it. They created this idea of California as a 'state of mind.' The Beach Boys came along as representatives of this kind-of California end-point of the American Dream, the heaven, the Eden, the final delivery. And there it was, a perfect bundling of those ideas. 'Surfin' USA'—that just said it all."[38] Elijah Wald contends, "The most enduring legacy of the surf craze may have been the creation of a rock & roll utopia, removed from R&B, schoolyards, or gritty city streets. A mythic California...would remain one of rock's most popular escapist fantasies."[39]

For the Beach Boys, the state that inspired a gold rush and built a Golden Gate Bridge is nearly a member of the band, so vital is its contribution to their music and mythos. Further, the paradise motif is so crucial to their appeal that their only later-day commercial successes are highly dependent on it. In 1974, after the Beach Boys had suffered several years of critical and commercial decline, Capitol Records, in attempt to squeeze the last penny out of their catalog, released a double album compilation of their early '60s hits: *Endless Summer*. The title itself suggested immortality and paradise, while the cover featured a painting of the group in a paradisiacal setting, peering through island flora with the ocean waving in the background. To general shock and surprise, *Endless Summer* went number one, became the best-selling album of the year, spent 155 weeks on the Billboard chart, and landed the now-bearded, thirty-something group on the cover of *Rolling Stone*. Then, in 1988, after a decade of poor sales and critical rebuke, the band released the single "Kokomo," an explicit ode to an imaginary island paradise—it became a global chart-topper and one of the biggest hits of the decade. As for the mythic Kokomo in the song, the location is somewhere "off the Florida Keys," in the very waters once believed to source the Fountain of Youth.

The symbols the Beach Boys share with classic paradise mythologies—perfect harmony, healing water, eternal youth, gold—are all metaphors for purity and incorruptibility, which are in turn qualities associated with infancy and childhood. The grief of innocence lost fuels the archetype of the child, which—while *we* age (and eventually die)—retains its exemplary pureness and remains focused on the future, in a sense allowing and encouraging us to believe in our own regenerative process. Be it the garden of our deepest collective memory, the yearning for physical and psychological wholeness in our present, or visions of our final release from suffering, paradise is the resultant allegory of lost youth, glorified in the archetypal mind yet irretrievable in the material world.

The child is such a potent archetype that, in addition to its relationship to paradise, it also contains many distinct "faces," or sub-personalities, within its essence. The *magic child* archetype (for example, Alice in Wonderland, the Little Prince, and Pippi Longstocking) represents the essence of creativity and the spirit of pure potentiality. This defines the modus operandi of Brian's instinctive compositional and production process; his innovations in the recording studio, experimental vocal approaches, and novel multi-tracked instrumental combinations affected a sea change in music production and established a future industry standard. Derek Taylor, in a 1967 press release that began with the infamous laud "Brian Wilson is a genius," marveled, "He alone in the industry is at the pinnacle of the pop pyramid—full creator of a record from the first tentative constructions of a theme to the final master disc. Brian is writer—words and music—performer and singer, arranger, engineer, and producer with complete control even over packaging and design."[40]

The *abandoned child* (like Snow White, Cinderella, and Dorothy in *The Wizard of Oz*) is the archetype that embodies childhood traumas of abuse and neglect. The psychological and physical harm Brian endured from his cruel father Murray is well documented and widely believed to have contributed to his mental illness. The emotional strain was repeated in Brian's collaborative relationship with combative band member and frequent lyricist Mike Love (who resisted Brian's move away from surf-and-car-centric pop music), and the increasing lack of support for his creative process by the other Beach Boys and their record label. Though the commercial success of the global number one single "Good Vibrations," released in October 1966, provided Brian a temporary respite from the pressure, as sessions for his ambitious *Smile* project wound well past several anticipated release dates, the group's impatience and Capitol's demand for fresh commercial product eventually proved too much for his fragile psychology. Brian's ensuing nervous breakdown marked the end of his creative stewardship of the Beach Boys and with it his function as a leading artistic innovator for his generation.

Brian's retreat in 1967 triggered his embodiment of the *eternal child*. This archetype (think Peter Pan, Forrest Gump, and Pee Wee Herman) is the part of human nature that chooses to exist in a state of perpetual innocence and refuses to mature. Essentially, Brian's family, band, record company, and fans demanded he remain in stasis; his urge to develop as a composer and producer in effect squelched by the monetary desires of his support system. To say he complied with their wishes is an understatement—hiding in his bedroom for a period of years, gorging himself on sweets, declining to contribute to the creative process of the Beach Boys unless he was given "treats" (cheeseburgers, ice cream, cocaine), and, when he could be coerced to work, reverting to the childish subject matter of his early efforts indicates that Brian had deserted his personal evolution, whether out of hopelessness, petulance, misguided jokery, or mere psychological incapacity. His one widely acknowledged musical innovation following his breakdown, the elegiac "Till I Die" from 1972's *Surf's Up*, witnesses a man resigned to a tragic fate and unable to imagine the healing of his deep wound.

In religious traditions, the child is frequently expressed through the miraculous birth stories and infancy/childhood narratives of the savior gods, creating the archetype of the *divine child*. Myths surrounding the births and childhoods of Krishna (in the *Bhagavata Purana*), Buddha (in the *Buddhacarita*), and Jesus (in the Gospels and Gnostic texts) share key features, such as the instant recognition of divinity or kingship, visitation of Magi, i.e. wise men, and gifts of precious jewels and substances. We also see fantastic birth/childhood legends attested to Confucius, Pythagoras,

Alexander the Great, Joan of Arc, various Caesars, and biblical heroes such as Moses, Samuel, Solomon, and Daniel. Jung suggests that these "intimations and pre-figurations of the Incarnation" are essentially "stages in the process of becoming conscious."[41] The holy purpose that is incarnate in the divine child (the younger version of the fully-evolved savior) begins humanity's process of evolving consciousness.

In the rock pantheon, only Brian Wilson's narrative contains testimonies of a musical infancy and prodigious talent while still in his formative years. According to biographer Peter Ames Carlin, when his father sang the melody to "When the Caissons Go Rolling Along," a one-year-old Brian flawlessly hummed the melody back in unison; by the age of two, he was obsessed with George Gershwin's "Rhapsody in Blue."[42] In his early teens, mostly self-taught on piano, Brian deconstructed the complicated harmonies of pop-jazz vocal groups the Four Freshman and Hi-Los and began arranging vocal parts for his family to sing at gatherings. All this, while being deaf in one ear.

One of the most familiar myths of the divine child is a story in Luke, known as the Disputation, where members of Jesus's family and community are journeying home to Nazareth after having participated in the feast of the Passover in Jerusalem. When they notice that Jesus is not among them, they return to find the twelve-year-old boy in the temple, "sitting in the midst of the teachers, both listening to them and asking them questions. And all who heard Him were astonished at His understanding and answers."[43] A similar story in the apocryphal *Infancy Gospel of Thomas* describes the wise child Jesus confounding his teacher, Zaccheus, who exclaims, "I cannot understand his speech at all. This child is not earthborn. ... I worked anxiously to have a disciple, and I found myself with a teacher."[44] Jung comments, "The motif of the growing up of the hero is discernable in the wisdom of the twelve-year-old child in the temple, and there are several examples in the gospels of the breaking away from the mother."[45]

In 1964, Brian began working with a group of top LA session musicians known as "The Wrecking Crew" to produce Beach Boys music, effectively replacing his family with experienced professionals able to decipher his increasingly sophisticated compositions. Drummer Hal Blaine remembers: "[He] was just a child, really, and we were seasoned studio musicians.[46] ... There were times when Brian would say something that didn't make sense to us as trained musicians. He was some kid ... there would be a glance around the room, like 'What? Are they kidding?' And then they took the world by storm; every time you turned on the radio, there they were. Then there was tremendous respect ... you realized what Brian was saying, even if it wasn't the way we were used to it being said."[47] Bassist Carol Kaye adds, "He heard sounds—combinations of sounds—that were not written before."[48]

The motifs of the child and paradise are explicit in the subject matter and legacy of Brian's most personal works: *Pet Sounds* and *Smile*. Widely considered a masterpiece and definitive recording in the history of popular music, *Pet Sounds* marks Brian's transition from child to adult, its postmodern production values, emotional cohesiveness, and musical invention mirroring the evolution of a generation maturing beyond the concerns and language of youth. The album begins with an echo of infancy—a music-box—leading into "Wouldn't It Be Nice," a song of yearning for the sexual freedom of adulthood. It ends with a heartsick ballad, "Caroline, No," mourning the lost idealism of young love. *Pet Sounds* can be heard as loosely depicting the arc of a love affair, but at a deeper level it is about the maturation of the child—it is at once excited, longing, and positive, but also tentative, as if sensing the impending loss of something sadly irretrievable. The "pet" sounds in the album's final moments—dogs barking while chasing after a train receding into the distance—deftly summarize the archetypal essence of the *Pet Sounds* song cycle.

Famously and accurately, the album is considered a primary influence on the Beatles' *Sgt. Pepper*, which has been described by George Martin as the Beatles' attempt to "equal" *Pet Sounds*.[29] While this is usually understood solely in terms of similar musical and production philosophies, in fact, *Pet Sounds* sparked the initial context of the Beatles' magnum opus. The first songs recorded for *Sgt. Pepper*—"Strawberry Fields Forever," "Penny Lane," and "When I'm Sixty-Four"—began the project at large by exploring childhood memories,[49] these early sessions following soon after John Lennon and Paul McCartney were first awed by the qualities of *Pet Sounds*. Though "Strawberry Fields Forever" and "Penny Lane" were released as a double A-side single and ultimately not included on the album, and the childhood motif mostly discarded in favor of the "mythic band" concept, *Sgt. Pepper* retained the sense of childlike playfulness, creative invention, and innocent daring that typified Brian's working methods generally and *Pet Sounds* specifically.

Encouraged by the critical acclaim of *Pet Sounds* and the commercial success of "Good Vibrations" (which began production during the *Pet Sounds* sessions), Brian endeavored to take his creative vision even further with *Smile*, an album he described as a "teenage symphony to God."[50] Conceived as a double LP imbued with spirituality and humor, the concepts surveyed on *Smile* are evocative of Brian's own archetypal import: the mythos of Manifest Destiny, the spiritual maturation of the individual, and the exploration of sound as essential communication. Several abstract thematic movements reveal themselves within the content of *Smile*, including an "Americana" section that takes the listener on a bicycle ride from Plymouth Rock to Hawaii; a "Life Cycle" section beginning with a young woman finding God through her sexual awakening ("Wonderful") and ending with an old man finding God through his inner child ("Surf's Up"); and a section, "The Elements," that evokes earth, air, fire, and water through musical and vocal onomatopoeia.

Though most of the original sessions recorded over a ten-month period in 1966-67 have been made public over recent years, *Smile* remains the most legendary unreleased album of the recording era. For many mavens, the lack of *Smile* irrevocably altered the course of popular music history—leading to cries of "what could have been" had the work been absorbed into public consciousness during the heady days of *Sgt. Pepper* and the Summer of Love. Still, it is hard to imagine the album being more indicative of the archetypal child than it has in absentia, where it became a modern recast of the grail legend in the rock mythos. Like the fabled cup of the Arthurian tales, *Smile* is permeated with mythic significance, but ultimately represents a conceptual paradise that is forever sought but can never be found.

The folklore contained within *Smile* itself, and that which has grown around its enigmatic creation and eventual demise, has been widely chronicled; suffice to say its failure to see timely release in 1967 marked both the retreat of Brian Wilson and the energy of the child in the classic rock era. DeCurtis laments: "By the end of the '60s everybody understood that [Brian] was one of the great geniuses, even if initially it didn't seem as if he was on a level with the Beatles or Bob Dylan, by the end of the '60s it was very apparent, and it was also very apparent that he was a damaged figure."[38] With respect to rock & roll's mythic pantheon, it might be said that Brian ceased to be crucial to the evolving mythology. When the generation lost its innocence, the child disappeared.

The story of Brian Wilson is a disturbing cautionary tale, a reminder of the emotional devastation of child abuse, the dangers of excess (be it drugs, food, money, fame, or art), and the fine line between exhilarating creativity and debilitating madness. Ironically, what is often unnoticed in Brian's mythos is his near supernatural resilience, which has borne out with a highly unexpected string of personal, commercial, and critical successes in the twenty-first century. The sad image of a broken, bed-ridden man long overshadowed the very fact of his strength and fortitude in the face of seemingly insurmountable pressures. Jung explains, "It is a striking paradox in all child myths that the child is on the one hand delivered helpless into the power of terrible enemies and in continual danger of extinction, while on the other he possesses powers far exceeding those of ordinary humanity. Myth emphasizes that the child is endowed with superior powers and, despite all dangers, will unexpectedly pull through."[51]

During the pivotal period of the years 1965-67, the creative evolutions of the Beatles, the Beach Boys, and Bob Dylan were so closely aligned as to essentially produce one over-arching musical narrative, both signaling the future of recorded sound and marking what many consider the creative apex of popular music in the twentieth century. John Lennon, the instinctual artist and poet, had clearly been most affected and influenced by Dylan, while Paul McCartney, the natural musician and melodist, had his ear honed on the Beach Boys, likely understanding that the classical forms he was then learning under George Martin's tutelage were already being expanded to new heights in the rock soundscape by Brian Wilson. After *Pet Sounds*, however, even the characteristically reticent Lennon (in terms of complimenting other musicians and writers) was effusive with praise for Brian's talents and stature.[52] McCartney was simply floored by *Pet Sounds*.[53] Recognizing that the gauntlet had been thrown, and with the exercise of several familiar Wilson approaches and techniques—piano-centric compositions, striking contra-punctual bass lines, soloing orchestral instruments, and sectional approaches to structure—he responded with the most expressive and conceptually eloquent music of his career ("Eleanor Rigby," "For No One," "Penny Lane," "She's Leaving Home," "Hey Jude," and the *Abbey Road* suite).

Unlike the Beach Boys, Dylan was never a serious competitor to the Beatles on the charts or in the studio, however culturally and philosophically he maintained the standard to which they would aspire in terms of socio-political relevance. That the early '60s zeitgeist deemed folk music a vital social tonic with gravitas while pop music was considered fallow and ultimately disposable lessened the relative importance of the Beatles, and certainly the Beach Boys, initially in the minds of serious critics and intelligentsia. For the Beatles themselves, Bob Dylan's influence on their writing (most noticeable during Lennon's self-confessed "Dylan period" but also a creative template for his wildly surreal "I Am the Walrus") is only matched by Brian Wilson's effect on their music, a view shared by George Martin.[54]

However widely acknowledged in retrospect, the understanding of this dynamic was still very much under the radar in the 1960s. For the mainstream press and typical youth of the period, there was another entity that clearly represented the Beatles' most visceral and formidable opponent. Because, mythology.

Without Satan, with God only, how poor a universe, how trite a music!
—Olaf Stapledon

STANDING IN THE SHADOW

❧ ❧ ❧

The Shamanic Verses of Rock & Roll

The Rolling Stones emerged in 1962 out of a shifting assortment of blues aficionados playing in various configurations in London clubs, when guitarist Brian Jones formed the nucleus, named the band, and became its nominal leader. Seven years later, mired in drug, alcohol, and sex addiction, a series of arrests, and a trail of violent, psychotic episodes, Jones was dead, while his handpicked group—Mick Jagger, Keith Richards, Bill Wyman, Charlie Watts, and (Jones's replacement) Mick Taylor—were being billed as the "The World's Greatest Rock & Roll Band" and encouraging fans and listeners to "just call me Lucifer."

The *devil*, which means "slanderer" and "accuser," is a most curious archetype in that, despite its weighty significance and primeval origin stories, it is a relatively recent addition to mythic and religious conception. While the "problem of evil" has long confounded human understanding in general and religious theologies particularly, the personification of absolute evil is essentially absent in classical Egyptian, Judaic, Greco-Roman, Northern, and Eastern mythologies. Though characters such as the Egyptian Set, Greek Hades, Roman Pluto, and Norse Loki often exhibit evil aspects—trickery, lies, vanity, and a compulsion to thwart the noble efforts of the other deities (and sometimes murder them)—they don't operate as lone actors; they occupy a seat in the celestial boardrooms of their respective pantheons, and are often siblings of the munificent gods (Osiris, Zeus, Jupiter, Thor, etc.).

The designation *Satan* translates as "adversary." In the Old Testament, Satan plays the role of heavenly prosecutor, serving at the behest of Yahweh, as in the book of Job where he suggests testing the title character's faith at a meeting between the two deities.[1] The first Book of Samuel describes a character named Saul who is tormented by "an evil spirit from the Lord," implying that good and evil are aspects contained within the purview of Yahweh and not separate, dueling entities.[2] In the Jewish *Book of Jubilees*, Satan (under the name "Mastema," i.e. "hostility" in Hebrew), here described as a "prince" presiding over fallen angels that had been "given him" by Yahweh, implores the testing of Abraham's faith and stands next to Yahweh while Abraham prepares to sacrifice his son Isaac.[3]

The character of the devil as we have come to understand him in the West—overseeing the damnation of souls, ruling over an eternal prison, both source and consequence of *all* evil—first became noticeable in the Zoroastrian religion of Persia circa 500 BCE (an account in the Avesta of Zoroaster's temptation by Ahriman in the desert predating that of Jesus' by five centuries),[4] wherein the notion of salvation became increasingly valued, assuming critical importance with the advent of Christianity. Gerald Messadié, in his book *A History of the Devil*, maintains, "The Devil found as fertile ground in this theme as bacteria might in a Petri dish—because if you say 'salvation' you also say 'damnation,' and once you say 'damnation' you've already said, 'the Devil.'"[5] The same principle informs the rock mythos; once you say, "the Beatles," with their positive, light, spiritual implications, there instantly comes to mind an equal, opposing force, "the Stones," with their negative, dark, carnal connotations.

From their earliest days as a group, the evolution of the Rolling Stones was dependent on the influence of the Beatles. The Stones were signed by Decca Records' A&R executive Dick Rowe (who had personally rejected the Beatles after their audition a year prior) at the encouragement of George Harrison. Once recording, the group struggled to break through on the charts with their blues and Chuck Berry covers until their first real hit, "I Wanna Be Your Man," was personally gifted to them by John Lennon and Paul McCartney. Progressing through the '60s, everything the Beatles did provided the Stones opportunity to react alternatively, while remaining (publicly at least) generally subservient and grateful to bask in the glory of the group so instrumental in their own earliest commercial recognition.

Once they had a toehold in the industry, the Stones were marketed and sold as the shadow opposite of the Beatles. In 1963, aspiring pop impresario Andrew Loog Oldham became the Stones' manager and quickly set about molding their dangerous image, inspiring articles with such titles as "Would You Let Your Daughter Go Out with a Rolling Stone?"[6] The ruse caught on quickly; within a year, serious journalists were extolling the moral chasm between the groups, as evidenced in Tom Wolfe's infamous quip, "The Beatles want to hold your hand; the Stones want to burn your town."[7] Regarding Oldham's operating philosophy, Richards states, "Nobody took the music seriously. It was the image that counted— how to manipulate the press and dream up a few headlines."[8] Jagger explains, "Andrew wanted to make the Rolling Stones into the 'anti-Beatles'…like in a movie where you've got good guys and bad guys…it wasn't just an accident; he thought the Rolling Stones would suit that image."[9]

It is ironic that the Beatles were themselves "cleaned up" by manager Brian Epstein, who perceived that a socially acceptable image would benefit their career, just as Oldham intuited a contrary approach for the Rolling Stones. Still, it is telling that the moral demarcation between the two groups was so swiftly accepted by the press and public at large. Though other British groups initially provided a greater commercial challenge to the Beatles—The Dave Clark Five, the Animals, and the Kinks, among others—the Stones quickly took advantage of their contrived adversarial status with a string of hit singles espousing content the likes of which had never been heard, or even allowed, on Top 40 radio. These songs all leveled accusations against mainstream society.

"(I Can't Get No) Satisfaction," the song that turned the Rolling Stones into international stars (and remains their signature tune more than a half-century later), rails against commercialization while implying sexual frustration, positioning the band in dramatic relief to the Beatles, with their early odes to romantic love and who represented the height of commercial success. Here, in stark contrast to the Beatles' oft-repeated refrains of "Yeah, Yeah, Yeah!" the Stones exclaimed "No, No, No!" The very title of the song recalls Satan's dissatisfaction with his standing in the celestial hierarchy; in most tales of his separation from God, it is Satan's hubris and desire to be worshipped as equal to God that leads to his fall from heaven.

The Stones' existential complaints continued with "Get off My Cloud," championing alienation and antisocial behavior; "Nineteenth Nervous Breakdown," mocking suburban depression and their "dismal dull affairs;" "Mother's Little Helper," attacking the hypocrisy of concealed drug use by the older generation; "Paint it, Black," surrendering to nihilism and declaring "I wanna see the sun blotted out from the sky;" "Let's Spend the Night Together," challenging prevailing sexual mores; and "Have You Seen Your Mother, Baby (Standing in the Shadow)," exposing a dearth of dark psychoses lurking within the human unconscious.

Emboldened by their increasing notoriety, the Stones turned up the heat and began using the devil metaphor as an overt reference to their role in the rock mythos and their function as an entity pushing moral and ethical boundaries. Album titles became explicit, beginning with the ominous *Aftermath* and continuing with, among others, *Their Satanic Majesties Request, Let It Bleed, Exile on Main St.,* and *Goat's Head Soup.* The songs became unambiguous as well, most notably "Sympathy for the Devil," a paean to the psychologically deep-seated animalism within human nature. Inspired by Jagger's reading of the Mikhail Bulgakov novel *The Master and the Margarita* (a Faustian satire on atheistic Soviet Russia), the song drew attention to the trial and death of Jesus Christ, religious wars, the Bolshevik revolution, Nazi atrocities, and the assassinations of

John and Robert Kennedy, ultimately decrying the folly of deny-
ing our innate shadow aspects and impugning our fundamental
complicacy in the manifestations of evil, "when after all, it was you
and me."

Sympathy for the Devil (originally titled *One Plus One*) is also the
title of the first theatrically-released film to feature the Rolling
Stones. Directed in 1968 by French auteur Jean Luc Goddard, the
experimental documentary focuses on the construction and recording of the song itself by the Stones at Olympic studio in London,
interspersed with various footage (including Black Panthers
brandishing weaponry, literary selections in an occult bookstore,
bloodied female bodies, Nazi salutes, and Marxist propaganda)
mirroring the social upheaval of the period. Beyond the revealing
coincidence that their most controversial and archetypal song happened to be what the Stones were composing when Goddard joined
them in the studio, the film also captures the noticeable dissolution of Jones, the band's chemically debilitated founder who would
drown in his swimming pool less than a year later.

The demonic allusions suggested by the Stones' music and
image had, by the end of the '60s, also manifested in their personal lives and unfolding band narrative. During the period of
"flower power" optimism, the Stones seemed somewhat wilted; the
album *Their Satanic Majesties Request* (though the title would elicit
the expected conventional backlash) was met with critical distain
and derided as a blatant attempt to ride the Beatles' psychedelic
baroque-pop coattails. They barreled back to infernal form, however, in 1968 with the single "Jumping Jack Flash" and accompanying video in which the group dropped the trappings of psychedelia
in favor of nightmarish make-up (on the single's sleeve they are
seen flaunting knives, masks, and blood-red tridents). The ensuing
album *Beggars Banquet* was hailed a rock masterpiece; the revolutionary left considered it a lucid response to the incendiary political divide, while the Beatles' "Revolution" (the B-side of the "Hey
Jude" single) was criticized as a non-committal hedge by many in
the same community. The line of demarcation between the ethos

of the two groups had been sharply reestablished; while the Beatles were flashing peace signs and meditating with the Maharishi, the Stones were wearing war paint and declaring "the time is right for fighting in the streets."

In October 1969, *Life* magazine, in an article discussing the revolutionary atmosphere in the US and around the world, coined what has become a ubiquitous expression: "Sex, Drugs, and Rock."[10] Though a modern spin on the old adage, "Wine, Women and Song" (which dates back several hundred years to a couplet composed by, ironically, Martin Luther),[11] the phrase has come to describe the self-indulgent philosophy and debauched rock & roll lifestyle typified by the Rolling Stones in the popular imagination. If "The World's Greatest Rock & Roll Band" supplied the rock, its two most infamous members, Mick Jagger and Keith Richards, provided the sex and drugs, respectively.

The Stones' conflation with illicit drug use first became international news when Jagger, Richards, and singer Marianne Faithfull were arrested during an LSD party at Keith's country estate in February 1967. Famously, Richards answered the judge at his trial: "We're not worried about petty morals."[12] Soon-after, Jones was arrested for possession of marijuana, cocaine, and methamphetamine, and by the time of his drug-related death in July 1969, Richards was addicted to heroin. The narcotic would become central to Keith's personal mythos for the next decade, culminating in a Toronto arrest in 1977 for heroin trafficking (the fifth time he would be arraigned on drug charges), an incident that nearly ended the band as he faced a multi-year prison sentence. During these years, drugs (particularly heroin) became a common trope in the Stones' lyrics; what began with the detached subject matter of "Mother's Little Helper" quickly moved into more explicit autobiographical territory with allusions to addiction in songs such as "Monkey Man," "You Can't Always Get What You Want," "Sway," "Can't You Hear Me Knocking," "Sister Morphine" and "Dead Flowers."

While Richards became his generation's exemplar of the supreme rock wastrel, Jagger became its most flamboyant sex symbol, taking

Elvis's and the Beatles' latent androgyny to extremes while reducing sexuality to unapologetic carnality demanding satiation. Press accounts from the Stones' heyday seemed incapable of avoiding Mick's sexually provocative connotations, much as they were helpless to steer descriptively clear of the religious fervor manifesting during Beatlemania: "Jagger, with eyes surrounded with sparkles, slithered and strutted ... [and] sang like a demon;"[13] "Unisexual liberation dandyism to a degree so pronounced that prancing Mick Jagger now performs wearing Cleopatra-style eye make-up in green glitter;"[14] "He has become a veritable spastic Nureyev, a demonic eye-riveting force;"[15] "He is bathed in crimson light, half man, half woman, a slithering, swirling figure of raw sexual power and attraction;"[16] "Some say his satanic quality, his sexual ambivalence, his sensual vitality have a way of whipping people into extraordinary emotional states."[17]

For Oldham, the path to creating the Stones' image had from the beginning centered on drawing attention to the sexual expression in their music and the outrage he bargained (correctly) it would elicit from parents of their fans. He explains that when he first saw the band perform, their appeal was clear in his mind: "There was no production ... it was just a Blues roots thing. ... Even so, I knew what I was looking at. It was sex."[18] In stark contrast to the largely asexual music of the Beatles, who focused first on romantic and then universal love, Rolling Stones music is obsessed with sex while love is verboten; their earliest compositions warn the female listener not to "Play with Fire" or expect anything more than a "Heart of Stone." The sexual context naturally expanded to include control and domination ("Under My Thumb"), blatant condescension ("Stupid Girl"), illicit under-age conduct ("Stray Cat Blues"), and even rape and murder ("Midnight Rambler," "Gimme Shelter").

A variety of Rolling Stones imagery also emphasizes aggressive, male-dominant sexuality. The Stones' sexually evocative "Tongue and Lips" logo, likely the most famous band emblem in popular music history, was inspired by Jagger's own lascivious facial features and the Tantric sex deity Kali.[19] Their suggestively-titled 1971 album *Sticky Fingers* sports the notorious "zipper cover" (conceived by Andy Warhol) showing a well-endowed penis outlined beneath a jean-clad crotch. Promotion for their 1976 album *Black and Blue* included a billboard on Sunset Boulevard in Los Angeles featuring a bound and bruised woman and the phrase "I'm Black and Blue from the Rolling Stones—and I love it!" that was taken down after protests from the organization *Women Against Violence Against Women.*

As with the Beatles, the Stones' archetypal influence grew to the degree events occurred, as to seem almost mystically inspired. Akin to John Lennon being pursued to play the role of Jesus in Weber and Rice's *Jesus Christ Superstar,* Jagger and Richards were approached in 1968 by avant-garde filmmaker Kenneth Anger and offered the roles of Lucifer and his henchman Beelzebub respectively in the occult-inspired, homoerotic *Lucifer Rising.* Though they ultimately rejected appearing in the film, Mick composed and recorded a soundtrack, which was eventually used in Anger's cinematic short *Invocation of My Demon Brother.* Jagger's girlfriend Faithfull, though, accepted the part of Lilith—a character from Jewish folklore believed to be the demonic first wife of Adam (and who copulated with Samael, an archangel possessing many of the traits of Satan)—while the role of Lucifer ultimately went to Bobby Beausoleil, who would shortly thereafter join the Manson family and personally commit first-degree murder.

Though the Stones' flirtation (or collision) with the occult may have been suspected by the public, their association with archetypal evil became unequivocal on December 6, 1969 at Altamont Speedway in Northern California. Headlining a free concert of their own design, the attempt to upstage the recent Woodstock festival manifested violence, injury, theft, and murder; amidst the unruly throng of 300,000 occurred four deaths, including the infamous stabbing of a young man by members of the Hells Angels motorcycle gang acting as "security" for the event. The mythic significance of Altamont as germane to the Stones' legacy is fundamentally akin to the death of John Lennon in context of the Beatles' savior mythology; both events synergized the temporal, archetypal, and communal mythologies of their subjects, permanently cementing their respective core ethos.

One of the key tropes in angelology (or demonology, to be more specific) is the casting out of Satan (and angles loyal to him) by God following a primordial "war in heaven." This drama, alluded to in Luke[20] and expanded upon in Revelation[21] (and several pseudepigraphical works including the books of *Enoch* and *Jubilees*), seems to have its genesis in a passage from the Old Testament book of Isaiah that includes the verse, "How art thou fallen from heaven, O Lucifer, son of the morning! How art thou cut down to the ground."[22] Predating Isaiah's reference, however, is likely an ancient astrological concept. In the Hebrew (and Latin) language, the planet Venus is called "Lucifer." Venus (the Morning Star) was seen as a challenger to the light of the Sun (the Day Star), thus the word Lucifer also provides the Hebraic adjective, "luciferian," meaning "light-bringing," and in English we have the derivatives "lucid," "lucent," and "translucent." Still, regardless of its etymology and/or original context, the name became interchangeable with that of Satan, and conceptions of his fall from heaven were further incorporated into Christian theology through the works of, among others, Origen (*Principles*), St. Thomas Aquinas (*Summa Theologiae*), and Jonathan Edwards (*Wisdom Displayed in Salvation*); and explored in the arts through the epic poetry of Dante Alighieri (*The Divine Comedy)* and John Milton (*Paradise Lost*).

The motif is underscored in the mythos of the Stones; they were the "challengers" to the Beatles, and their "fall" can be seen allegorically in their leaving native England to become tax "exiles" in 1972. Decamping to the south of France, the band set about recording *Exile on Main St.* in the basement of Richards's newly-leased mansion, Villa Nellcote, which had once been a Gestapo headquarters during the Nazi occupation (doorknobs and floor-vents in the villa were said to have been decorated with swastikas). In many ways, this period of Stones history has become its most mythically charged; it is described as extremely decadent with rampant drug use and frequent clashes with law enforcement, and the music that emerged from the bowels of Nellcote has ultimately been praised by many as the Stones' best (or at least most idiosyncratic) work.

The idea of an ongoing war between light and dark forces is perhaps best understood through Jung's psychological concept of the *shadow* archetype, which describes the hidden, dissociated aspects of the human unconscious. When not integrated into the conscious personality, the shadow is often projected outward and can become the basis for what is now understood as multiple personality disorder—religious scholar Elaine Pagels delineates Satan as a "reflection of ourselves and how we perceive 'others.'"[23] In many religious worldviews, this fractured state is understood as demonic possession, and exorcism believed to offer the spiritual remedy. The frightening potential of the unassimilated shadow has been explored in a vast array of literary works, such as Robert Louis Stevenson's *The Curious Case of Dr. Jekyll and Mr. Hyde,* Oscar Wilde's *The Picture of Dorian Gray,* and Edgar Allen Poe's *The Tell-Tale Heart* and *William Wilson.* Most obviously in modern cinema, the shadow motif is central to the *Star Wars* mythos, with its "moral imperative to resist the dark side of the force" grand narrative.

While Hollywood will likely continue to rely on dramatic battles to illuminate our struggle to triumph over the power of shadow energy, Jung believed that evil wasn't something to *defeat,* but rather to understand and *incorporate*: "The more negative the conscious attitude is, and the more it resists, devalues, and is afraid, the more repulsive, aggressive, and frightening is the face which the dissociated content assumes.[24] ... Recognition of the reality of evil necessarily relativizes the good and the evil likewise, converting both into halves of a paradoxical whole."[25] Apocryphally, Jesus also infers this, warning in the *Gospel of Thomas*: "If you do not bring forth what is within you, what you do not bring forth will destroy you."[26] Given that it seems healthy, vital even, to illuminate our demons so that they may be understood, and their power deflated, modern culture may owe the Stones far more than mere sympathy. Like Lucifer, the Morning Star, they shone a spotlight on our darkest passions.

The Rolling Stones' identification with the physical and not spiritual world is metaphorical of the devil's arch relationship to the savior; numerous biblical passages describe Satan's lordship over the earth in distinction to Jesus's reign in heaven.[27] The "battle" between the Beatles and the Stones can thus be understood as a modern allegory of the spirit/body dichotomy at the heart of the human experience. Similarly exemplified in the generally divergent concerns of classical and jazz music—the former emphasizing structure and order, the latter stressing emotion and intuition—the clash was magnified once more in the rock mythos as the Stones' impulsive blues tested the Beatles' mannered pop. The process continues still as the Stones' physical longevity scales the Beatles' brief but impeccably chiseled celestial summit for the title of world's greatest rock & roll band.

In the '60s, as the Beatles exemplified a communal transcendence, the Rolling Stones instigated chaos and instability, and the age-old existential conflicts materialized. The ballast provided by mediator gods was then required to restore equilibrium. Resolving existential dualities in the temporal world is the purview of the *shaman* (or *medium*), an archetype which, like the prophet, concerns a human being inspired by divine forces and tasked with negotiating a merger of the physical and spiritual realms.

From the model Siberian Shaman to the *vegestalista* of the Amazon basin, a multitude of distinct shamanic types have existed throughout history and are still in practice across the globe (such as the Latin American *curandero*, the South African *sangoma*, the Melanesian *dukun*, the Japanese *itako*, and the Aboriginal *kadji*). The traits variously ascribed—balancer of energy, intuitive physician, connector to sky gods, soul traveler, link to animal spirits, fertilizer of land and women, exorcist of evil spirits, perilous hallucinogenic explorer—make the designation somewhat of a catch-all term, however several encapsulating themes bind the many traditions: exercise of ceremonial magic, ritual healing of individuals and communities, and the guiding of souls through the experience of both metaphoric and literal death. To these ends, the shaman/

medium (sometimes with the aid of entheogens) issues invocations, commands, prayers, curses and/or spells, and often employs chanting, drumming, music, and song to create a psychic space for the molding of reality through concentrated will.

The conflation of rock & roll with shamanism has been and continues to be used with such frequency that it would be hopelessly cliché if not so clearly apt. The rock icons usually mentioned in this discussion—Jimi Hendrix, Jim Morrison, and Janis Joplin in particular—seem to be of otherworldly nature, guided by forces unavailable to the community at large, and possessing the ability to affect change through the application of focused psychic energy. Beneath the superficial (though quite evocative) costuming they sported—feathers, hats, capes, furs, beads, bells, and shells—were artists who mirrored the archetypal shaman in terms of symbolic ritual, community role, and personal narrative.

With his preternatural mastery of the guitar, Jimi Hendrix, the *magician* of the rock pantheon, established the instrument as a shamanic device in both symbol and practice. Though the electric guitar was first distinguished as the central instrument of rock & roll by Chuck Berry, Hendrix transformed it into ritual tool and magical wand; in his virtuosic hands, the guitar could figuratively morph into a plethora of archetypal symbols: woman, phallus, serpent, vehicle, weapon, etc. Pete Townshend of the Who describes the totemic import of the instrument, and specifies its significance for Hendrix: "The guitar gave me something that was *more* than something on which you played a tune.... [This] was definitely true for Jimi Hendrix. As a Shaman, which he was, he was able to channel light or something."[28]

For his audience, Hendrix employed the guitar as a means to translate a unique sonic language, transporting listeners into a realm of new experience. Reflected in both the name of his band—The Jimi Hendrix Experience—and the title of his startling debut album—*Are You Experienced*—the notion is bolstered by the LP's cover image, a low-angle, infrared-tinted, fish-eye lens photograph distorting the vividly-adorned Hendrix—wearing a psychedelic coat with large painted eyes—and his similarly coiffed band. The altered image expands the size of Hendrix's hands considerably, and it is notable that in some Northern traditions the shaman wears enormous gloves and mask while conducting healing rituals.[29]

Released in May 1967 in the UK and three months later in the US, *Are You Experienced* enthroned Hendrix in the upper reaches of rock royalty—he would soon thereafter assume the mantle of world's highest-paid performer. A dazzling showman (playing the guitar left-handed and upside down, to boot), his use of controlled feedback, distortion, flanging, chorusing, and the recently-invented wah-wah pedal quilted a sonic tapestry unlike anything heard previously. His music—liquid lightning guitar runs, slippery chord progressions, entrancing stereo phasing, and cosmic dream-drenched lyrics—suggested a medium operating outside the bounds of ordinary reality.

The function of the magician archetype can perhaps best be understood through the symbolic imagery of The Magician card in the Major Arcana of the Tarot, a system which is—beyond its supposed purpose of providing clues that may predict potential future—at its core a depiction of archetypal narrative illustrating the process of initiation. On a table in front of the magician are a sword, wand, disc and cup (the four suits of the Tarot), representing his mastery over the four elements. In his right hand, the magician raises a wand toward the sky, and with his left points to the earth. This gesture, evocative of the ancient Hermetic creed "As above, so below" (which in modern parlance would describe the symbiotic and causal relationship between the macrocosm and microcosm), establishes the Magician as the point of connection between the uncreated and created, the metaphysical and the physical, and intention and action.

Hendrix's most iconic song, "Purple Haze," announces *Are You Experienced* with a dissonant intro—a jarring and somewhat sinister sounding triad of notes rarely employed in prior twentieth century popular music. Known as the "Devil's Interval," the tri-tone produces a restless sound that elicits a feeling of unresolved tension (it has since been employed in many now-omnipresent hard rock riffs such as Deep Purple's "Smoke on the Water" and Black Sabbath's "Iron Man").[30] The song then marches to a strident, anxious beat until catharsis comes in the form of Hendrix's unforgettable turn of phrase: "'Scuse me, while I kiss the sky." With this evocative line, Hendrix infers the shaman's inter-dimensional ability and intimate relationship with the sky gods.

Sky imagery abounds in Hendrix's personal narrative and musical canon. In 1961, he enlisted in the United States Air Force and became a paratrooper with the 101st Airborne Division, achieving twenty-five successful jumps and achieving the rank of private first class before a broken ankle precipitated an honorary discharge.[31] In 1969, he appeared at the historic Woodstock Festival (delivering his renowned rendition of the "Star Spangled Banner" to effectively close the event) with an ensemble he dubbed the "Electric Sky Church." Though it never became formalized, Hendrix often used the Sky Church moniker to describe his core group of musicians, the modus operandi of his live concerts, and even his specific style of music.[32] In the years since his death, numerous posthumous releases have adopted the cosmos/sky motif as album titles, including: *Rainbow Bridge, First Rays of the New Rising Sun, Midnight Lightning, Valleys of Neptune*, and *Both Sides of the Sky*.

The shaman's perceived ability to ascend into the heavens (and descend into the underworld) is made possible, mythically, by way of the *axis mundi*, a concept representing the center (or navel) of the world, the point of connection between earth and heaven, and hub of the four cardinal points on the physical plane. Also known in various traditions as the *World Tree, Yggdrasil Tree, Cosmic Pillar,* or *Sacred Ladder*, we see the notion expressed in symbolic structures such as the maypole, the totem pole, the church steeple, and—in rites ranging from Burning Man to selecting a pope—a column of smoke. Dante's journey in his epic poem *The Divine Comedy*, from the depths of the underworld to the heights of heaven by way of a chain of spiral formations, can be understood as a voyage along the axis mundi.

Mircea Eliade contends the axis mundi is "only rarely accessible to privileged individuals, the heroes and demigods" and that "the shamans climb it on their celestial journeys."[33] An aural simulation of this voyage can be heard on Hendrix's second album, *Axis: Bold as Love*, in the spiraling, stereo-phased, over-driven feedback of the opening track, "EXP." Following his voice-manipulated exclamation, "Now, if you'll excuse me, I must be on my way," the swirling sonic flight leads, appropriately, into the song "Up From the Skies." Then, to close the album, on the title track "Bold as Love," Hendrix instructs the listener to "just ask the Axis."

If Hendrix was able to "channel light," as Townshend suggested, and (metaphorically) ascend into the heavens, the descent into the underworld was similarly expressed by Jim Morrison and the Doors. Not to be confused with the concept of hell, the underworld in this context represents the land of the dead, the eventual destination of all living things in the temporal realm.

Lord Byron famously wrote, "Whom the gods love, die young,"[34] an edict that seems particularly accurate with regards to scores of rock stars who burned incandescent during their brief careers, only to pass away as their fame was reaching its zenith. Byron's decree seems even more prescient with regards to the shamanic rock gods, and most of all Jim Morrison, who ostensibly raced towards his own early demise as a form of both artistic expression and self-fulfilling prophecy, creating a modern "doomed-hero" archetype in the process.

Frank Lisciandro, Morrison's close friend and personal photographer, clarifies: "Jim was interested in the subject of death, he was not afraid of the subject of death. He wrote about death, sang about death, and he spoke freely about it. He wasn't interested in suicide; he was interested in pushing the boundary of life to point where it came very close to death, so that he could experience, taste, feel, sense what it must be like ... he put himself in jeopardy many times to experience that."[35]

Morrison's fascination with death permeates the music and lyrics of the Doors. Foreboding, funereal, and often frightening, the band sonically expressed their singer's perilous personal narrative and death-obsessed poetry, while Morrison himself became increasingly unpredictable and hazardous, to himself, his band, and (given his predilection for inciting audiences to riot) his generation at large. The death imagery in many iconic songs of the Doors—"Break on Through (To the Other Side)," "Soul Kitchen," "Light My Fire," "When the Music's Over," "Riders on the Storm," and "The End"—belies Morrison's personal obsession and in turn establish him as a figurative *psychopomp* for the '60s generation, a distinct type of shaman who guides the soul through the experience of death.

Classical mythology sports such psychopomps as the Egyptian gods Thoth (judge of the dead), Anubis (god of mummification and protector of graves), and Nehebkau (guard of the underworld); while Hermes (cosmic messenger and spirit guide), Charon (ferryman to the underworld), and Hecate (goddess of crossroads, entranceways, and necromancy) perform similar functions in the Greek pantheon. Eastern traditions contain characters that have psychopompic traits, such as Izanami, the Shinto goddess of creation and death, and the Buddhist Mrtyu-Mara, the death aspect of the demon Mara. The Judaic and Islamic religions give us Azrael, the "Angel of Death" who extracts souls from bodies and maintains records of the living and the dead (a likely predecessor of our more recent conception, the Grim Reaper).

A psychopomp need not be a human figure; they can take the form of birds, animals, and reptiles (consider the ancient Egyptian depictions of the ibis-headed Thoth, the canine-headed Anubis, and the double-serpent-headed Nehebkau). In Christianity, there is the fourth "Horseman of the Apocalypse" in the book of Revelation, the rider of the pale horse named "Death."[36] In literature, Edgar Allen Poe's mesmeric poem "The Raven" insinuates the titular bird as a psychopomp; when asked its name by the narrator, the raven's only reply is also the work's interminable refrain: "Nevermore."

The shape-shifting ability of the psychopomp (exemplary of the shaman's primal connection to animal spirits) is pronounced in the mythos of the Doors, where Morrison's zoomorphic designation as the "Lizard King" and his Mr. Hyde-like alter ego "Mr. Mojo Risin'" (an anagram of his given name) imply this mercurial facility. Certainly, the name "The Doors" is suggestive of passing from one realm into another. Morrison admitted that, in his mind, the name "correlates with death,"[37] and his thoughts on the subject imply a relationship far more intimate than that of the average person: "People fear death even more than pain. It's strange that they fear death. Life hurts a lot more than death. At the point of death, the pain is over. Yeah—I guess it is a friend."[38] Even his perception of temporal reality suggests a shamanic point of view: "I used to see the universe as a mammoth, peristaltic snake....I think [this] motion is the basic life movement—swallowing, digestion, the rhythms of sexual intercourse."[39]

In the song "Peace Frog" from the Doors' album *Morrison Hotel*, Morrison directly communicates an experience he had as a child that he felt bestowed his mystical essence: "Indians scattered on dawn's highway bleeding; ghosts crowd the young child's fragile eggshell mind." He includes a longer description of the event in his posthumous spoken-word album *An American Prayer*: "Me and my mother and father, and a grandmother and a grandfather, were driving through the desert, at dawn, and a truck load of Indian workers had either hit another car, or just—I don't know what happened—but there were Indians scattered all over the highway, bleeding to death."

It is common for a shaman to be recognized as such by their community, and/or personally accept the role at a young age. Morrison's tale of witnessing the dead Native Americans, though it may be somewhat exaggerated (his family expressed doubts about its accuracy), is precisely the type of formative experience—be it real or a dream—that signals a shaman's unique disposition. It is said that for months as a child, Jimi Hendrix clung to a broom day and night pretending it was a guitar, a dependence that raised concerns from the social worker at his elementary school (and a fruitless attempt to persuade the school or his father to buy him a real one).[40] Modern culture makes little priority of finding and nurturing the psychically-gifted child, and Morrison struggled throughout his life with family estrangement; once famous, he frequently and falsely claimed to interviewers that his parents were dead.

Jim Morrison's death itself remains one of the most enigmatic episodes of the rock era, forever accentuated by the equally mysterious music of the Doors, which continues to reverberate through popular culture as a reliable aural symbol of dissolution and fatality (such as in the film *Apocalypse, Now!*, where their song "The End" is used to convey the insanity associated with war and the dreadful mantra of personal obsession). At once an entirely predictable event and yet shrouded in mystery to this day, the questions surrounding Morrison's demise—the lack of autopsy, the cause of death determined vaguely as "heart failure" (or even the laughable "natural causes"), the persistent urban legends that he faked his own death—have the effect of deepening its significance. His iconic status continues to grow with time, and his death remains the essential episode in his story, such as when he adorned the cover of *Rolling Stone* a decade after his passing under the banner: "He's hot, he's sexy, and he's dead."[41] Though mystery also surrounds the death of Hendrix, it is the sonic frontier he explored, magical abilities as an instrumentalist, and enduring musical influence that define his legacy; while for Morrison it is his death that ultimately makes his music transcend and his mythic role resonate.

Like Elvis, the Beatles, and Mick Jagger before them, the rock shamans also symbolized androgyny, with Morrison's "Dionysian" beauty and sensitive poetry and Hendrix's feminine attire and feline personality softening the more dangerous aspects of their archetypes. It was also a key distinction of the female rock shamans, Grace Slick and Janis Joplin, both of whom exhibited androgynous elements at a time when fluid gender identification was commercial anathema for female singers and performers.

Slick, lead singer (along with Marty Balin) of the psychedelic San Francisco sextet the Jefferson Airplane, was a striking beauty and former model who chose to downplay her natural allure in favor of cultural, not sexual, provocation. The first of the female rock icons, Slick presented a shocking persona relative to other popular female vocalists of her time, side-stepping the demure femininity typified by the "canaries" of the standards era, the reverence of the gospel-infused soul singers, the stylized choreography of the Motown chanteuses, and the boy-obsessed posturing of the girl-groups. Creating an insubordinate role for women in popular music, Slick was a counter-culture rebel who mocked convention and challenged society to follow her example. Most palpable in the daring content of her self-penned anthem "White Rabbit," with its clear endorsement of hallucinogens as perception gateways ("Feed your head"), Slick exhibited many characteristics of the *witch* archetype, and (undoubtedly to the older generation in the '60s) an apparently wicked one at that.

In a spellbinding voice set over a haunting rock bolero, Slick sang "White Rabbit" not as popular entertainment, but as incantation; her 1966 performance of the song on the television program *American Bandstand* while wearing a nun's habit and go-go boots punctuating the inciting nature of both the song and her archetypal character. Slick would continue to provoke with unruly antics, such as appearing (in 1968 with the Airplane) on the *Smothers Brothers Comedy Hour* in blackface and ending the song "Crown of Creation" with the Black Power fist-salute, a guise and gesture she repeated on the January 1969 cover of *Teenset* magazine. Posing in her (actual) Girl Scout uniform was less shocking but still subversive, while performing in concert dressed as Adolph Hitler[42] and becoming the first person to say the word "fuck" on American television (singing the word "motherfucker" on *The Dick Cavett Show* in 1970) proved the lengths she would go to rouse complacent mainstream viewers.

The Oxford-English dictionary defines the word "Maleficium" as (1) "An act of witchcraft performed with the intention of causing damage or injury; the resultant harm;" and (2) "A potion or poison, used especially in witchcraft." There are of course many examples in fairy tales and classic literature conflating witches with toxic concoctions, such as the Evil Queen with her poisonous apple in *Snow White and the Seven Dwarves*; the Wicked Witch of the West utilizing poppies to thwart Dorothy in *The Wizard of Oz*; and the Three Witches in William Shakespeare's *Macbeth*, with their chilling spell: "Round about the cauldron go; in the poison'd entrails throw... Double, double toil and trouble; fire burn, and cauldron bubble."

In a well-known anecdote, Slick once set out to dose President Richard Nixon's drink with LSD. An alumnus of Finch College, she was invited (under her maiden name, Grace Wing) to a tea party at the White House by Trisha Nixon, the president's daughter who had also attended the New York finishing school. Bringing along as her guest the notorious Yippie leader Abbie Hoffman, the two were turned away as security determined their true identities (both were listed on a then current FBI list of subversives). Slick recounts their foiled plot in her autobiography: "The plan was for me to reach my overly-long pinky fingernail, grown especially for easy cocaine snorting, into my pocket, fill it with six hundred mics of pure powdered LSD, and with a large entertainer's gesture, drop the acid into Tricky Dick's teacup."[43] When asked why she would attempt such a brazen trick by Marie Osmond during an interview on *The Donny and Marie Show* in 1998, Slick replied "To get him *really different*."[44]

Eliade aligns witchcraft with shamanism,[45] however the practice has long been shunned and feared by mainstream society (unlike that of the shaman whose healing purpose is welcomed), resulting in centuries of atrocity against those accused. The Bible contains a great many laws forbidding sorcery and equating it with heresy, and the 1487 German text *Malleus Maleficarum* (usually translated as *Hammer of Witches*), which called for the total extermination of witches and offered explicit prescriptions to carry out that task, was second only to the Bible in book sales for nearly two hundred years.[46]

In the 1960s, Grace Slick brought the witch archetype to the fore once again in popular culture, and though it was no longer an offense carrying a vigilante-induced death sentence, it is doubtful she would have persisted into her mature years during the millennium 800-1800 CE. Her late-1960s San Francisco contemporary Janis Joplin, however, would not live beyond her mid-twenties, and though her death was nominally a product of drug addiction, the archetype she embodied suggests that an early demise was a distinct possibility. Joplin represented a type of female medium/shaman best described as an *oracle*, and while the archetypal witch typically lives far into old age, the oracle offers the community at large her psychic energy until her physical body is depleted completely; when she perishes another oracle is chosen, and the process repeats.

Oracles were prevalent throughout classical antiquity, and the practice of giving voice to the deity while in trance state remains in spiritual traditions throughout the world. History's most famous example is undoubtedly the Pythia, more commonly known as the Oracle of Delphi (technically, the oracle was the location of the rite—usually a chthonic cave or underground structure—or the forecast the god delivered through the priestess, however the designation was to become synonymous with the ritual practitioners themselves). Believed to be the mouthpiece of the Greek god Apollo, the Delphic Oracle was a religious institution that reigned in Hellenic culture for over one thousand years (from approximately 800 BCE to 400 CE), until the oracles were demonized by the early Christian church fathers and abolished by Roman authorities.[47] During this time, the Oracle of Delphi was likely the most powerful and influential woman in the world, her purview attested by dozens of philosophers and writers in ancient Greece, including Plato, Sophocles, Euripides, Herodotus, Aristotle, and authors unknown in the *Homeric Hymn to Delphic Apollo*, composed circa 700 BCE.

Of course, there wasn't just *one* oracle at Delphi (or the many other sacred sites). Given the perilous ritual performed, the Pythia are believed to have had a very short life expectancy, one reason young priestesses chosen for the role were expected (or ordered) to relinquish ties to family, spouse, and even personal identity. Plutarch describes the ceremony conducted at Delphi in his *Moralia* (a collection of first century essays), alluding to "prophetic vapours" to which the Pythia were subjected, and recounting the death of one: "She went down into the oracle unwillingly...and at her first responses it was at once plain from the harshness of her voice that she was not responding properly; she was like a labouring ship and was filled with a mighty and baleful spirit. Finally, she became hysterical and with a frightful shriek rushed towards the exit and threw herself down, with the result that not only the members of the deputation fled, but also the oracle-interpreter Nicander and those holy men that were present. However, after a little, they went in and took her up, still conscious; and she lived on for a few days."[48]

Many theories have been proffered and excavations undertaken to determine the physical cause of the Pythia's trance. As the site at Delphi sat above a subterranean spring (that has since been redirected as a water source for the modern city), some have contended that methane, ethane, or ethylene gas would escape from the fissure and fill the room,[49] which seems somewhat corroborated by Plutarch. Others have speculated that the Pythia would eat or smoke the poisonous Oleander plant,[50] or even be subjected to near-fatal doses of venom, possibly from a cobra or krait snake.[51]

Anyone with cursory knowledge of Janis Joplin's life and career will see many parallels with the vocation and plight of the ancient oracles—the estrangement from community, the years of exposure to toxic substances, the hyperactive state she assumed during live performance. Shortly before her death, Janis expressed that all she had was her muse: "Women [in] the music business give up more than you'd ever know...you give up a home and friends, you give up children and friends, you give up an old man and friends, you give up any constant in the world except music. That's the only thing you've got, man, after you boil it down, the only thing you got left in the world is that music, man."[52]

Janis was a societal outsider from a young age. She was reportedly bullied throughout her childhood and teen years, taunted for her weight, acne, and care-free "beatnik" personality, and suffered the insult of being voted "Ugliest Man on Campus" by a fraternity at the University of Texas, where she attended college her freshman year.[53] Also struggling throughout her life with (mostly) closeted bisexuality, dysmorphia, and various addictions (drugs, alcohol, sex), the loneliness continued even after she became a major star and beloved to millions of fans. She lamented, "On stage I make love to 25,000 people; and then I go home alone."[52]

Unlike the other '60s rock gods, Janis's most famous and enduring songs were written by other people, establishing her as a channel; receiving musical energy and directing it through her primal voice. Her distinct choice of material—tunes such as "Piece of My Heart," "Ball and Chain," "Cry Baby," "Down on Me" and "Work Me, Lord" (the title of which could suffice as an oracular credo)— speaks to both her unique gift and the curse she labored under. The description she often gave regarding her unique style of music, Kozmic Blues (which informed the title of her first solo album, *I Got Dem Ol' Kozmic Blues Again Mama!*), was, like Hendrix's "Electric Sky Church" explanation, a glimpse inside her personal psychology and perhaps an attempt to put into words the supernatural source she suspected was using her as a vessel.

Even more than her music, it was Janis's seemingly possessed delivery that captivated and entranced her audience. It is noteworthy her frantic stage presence was not a style she developed consciously, but something she claimed overtook her: "I don't know what happened. I just exploded. I'd never sung like that before ... I stood still, and I sang simple.... But you can't sing like that in front of a rock band. You have to sing loud and move wild with all that in back of you.... I just want to feel as much as I can, it's what 'soul' is all about."[54]

Janis's intensely emotional performance style recalls the *sibyls*, enchanted prophetesses known for their wild, hysterical forecasts who may have been the first of the Delphic Oracles in early Greek antiquity. The philosopher Heraclitus's description of their manner and method, circa 500 BCE, reads like a review of a Janis Joplin concert: "The Sibyl, with frenzied mouth uttering things not to be laughed at, unadorned and un-perfumed, yet reaches to a thousand years with her voice by aid of the god."[55]

While the isolation, neglect, and abuse Janis experienced as a child may have fueled her signature wailing vocal style, it also likely contributed to the severe addiction to alcohol, methamphetamine, and narcotics she battled throughout her adult years. In October 1970, soon after finishing her second and ultimately most successful solo album *Pearl*, she died from a heroin overdose, only sixteen days after Jimi Hendrix had also suffered a drug-related death. Though she would often boast to friends that her addictions would not prevail, Janis seems to have intuited the risk inherent in her mythic role: "People, whether they know it or not, like their blues singers miserable. They like their blues singers to die afterwards. ... Maybe my audiences can enjoy my music more if they think I'm destroying myself."[56] Kozmic Blues, indeed.

Prototypal queens of rock & roll, Grace Slick and Janis Joplin forged new pathways for women in popular music, Slick offering example for future image-morphing female media stars who challenge society, and Joplin erasing conventional stylistic lines; she is possibly, along with Aretha Franklin, the most emulated female vocalist of the past half-century. But though they may represent the role alongside Jimi Hendrix and Jim Morrison, the shaman archetype, with its primary concern of resolving duality and emphasis on catharsis and transformation through physical ritual, is essentially androgynous. Therefore, while Grace and Janis achieved enduring fame and influence, they also forfeited some aspects of their perceived femininity, resonating more masculine or even asexual characteristics.

It says much about our modern understanding and value of the *divine feminine* that very few women from the classic rock era enter the mythic category. As it was born in a time and place previously dominated by a particularly male-centric brand of Christianity, it perhaps follows that the classic rock pantheon is comprised primarily of male deities, in contrast to the mythologies of antiquity, which were populated with both male and female gods in mostly equal measure and status, and often presented as dual aspects of the same concept. Further, the deeper feminine qualities of inner wisdom and intuitive process, concerns of ecology and equality, possession of hidden knowledge, emphasis on truth and integrity, and role as creator, nurturer, and protector of Earth and humanity were the attributes of countless mythic goddesses of the ancient world.

In the late '60s, as they witnessed the inevitable entropy of their cultural idealism, the baby boomers began their retreat from the harsh socio-political realities of that time: failure of the flower children, the injustice of the draft and the Vietnam War, race riots and the unrest of the Civil Rights movement, and murders of Robert Kennedy and Martin Luther King, Jr. Evident in the growing singer-songwriter community coalescing in Southern California's Laurel Canyon, the new zeitgeist emphasized a move back to nature and a look inward for a sense of meaning and purpose. When the counterculture began to lose hope in its ability to change society through the masculine qualities of force, argument, and will, it was the perfect moment for the traditionally feminine traits of patience, wisdom, and empathy to take their places. The time of the goddess had come.

The Tao that can be told is not the eternal Tao.
The name that can be named is not the eternal name.
–Lao Tzu

PURE AND EASY

⚜ ⚜ ⚜

The Divine Feminine and Spirit of Rock & Roll

During the twentieth century, feminist and post-feminist seekers of Western spirituality became increasingly dissatisfied with their patriarchal options. Christianity, as it was largely practiced, tended to limit women to the mutually exclusive roles of virgin, mother, and whore, none of which offered much in the way of power, respect, or intellectual stimulation to a growing demographic that was beginning to demand all the above. Along with these nascent cultural attitudes, "goddess" religions became the feminist antidote to Christianity, whose celestial, omnipotent male deity came to symbolize masculine oppression and patriarchy to many spiritual progressives.

Second-wave feminism began in the early '60s and spanned the entire rock epoch, coinciding with the burgeoning sociological sea change deemed the "sexual revolution." Men and women who fought for "women's liberation" during this period focused on equal rights between the sexes, reproductive choice for women, and more amorphous inequities, such as cultural attitudes, biases, expectations, and double standards that left little room for individuality in women who wanted to stay on society's approving side. Slowly, these once-radical movements gained traction and incorporated themselves into the counterculture, and eventually the mainstream ethos.

The "goddess movement" grew out of later second-wave feminism, surfacing in the 1970s. Perhaps because the rock gods were able to channel mythic concepts directly without the self-consciousness that accompanied more nominally religious movements (art as usual moving a bit faster than larger societal institutions), Joni Mitchell emerged as the *goddess* of the rock pantheon a few heartbeats before the movement brought discussions of the divine feminine into spiritual pop culture.

Joni has said in interviews that it was not until 1965 that women in North America had the chance to be considered creative artists, and she cited that year as the true beginning of her career.[1] She has also spoken about the many female musicians in her family who were forced to give up their artistic passions to perform the tasks of housewifery. Their creative sacrifices filled her with a feeling of responsibility to see her own talents and ambitions through as far as they would go: "I thought, 'Maybe I'm the one who has the gene that has to make it happen for these women.'"[2]

Her life story was laced with a mythic tincture from the start. At the age of nine, Joni was hospitalized for polio and told by her doctors that she likely would never walk again. After receiving the devastating news that she may not be well enough to return home for Christmas, the sad, crippled girl sat gazing at an old tree and in desperation, began to pray to it. She promised the tree that if she were able to walk again, and go home for the holiday, she would "pay [it] back." Soon after, she regained her strength, and returned to her family that December.[2]

Like Bob Dylan and Robert Johnson before him, Mitchell invokes the "supernatural bargain" myth to partially explain the scope of her extraordinary life. However, while Dylan alluded to the myth literally and overtly to the point of facetiousness, Joni made her plea not to the devil, but to nature, aligning her narrative with the "Earth Mother" early on. A tree is a widely recognized symbol of the earth and life itself, and in the Mitchell myth, this tree is characterized as a supernatural healing entity. There is no oath drawn in blood, no preternatural talent obtained in exchange for her soul, just a sick child asking for the strength to walk. In return, she offers a vague promise of repayment, the implication being that this tender would unfold in the form of her life's work. It is noteworthy that, unlike the traditional crossroads legend, Joni's version does not credit her talent to the deity; the tree, or what it may represent, gives only health, only life. It is her responsibility to repay this divine gift with her own talents, to cultivate and create until her life meets the weight and magnitude of its own miracle.

Her resonance with goddess mythology compounded when she became a mother during her first year at art school. She married folksinger Chuck Mitchell (not her daughter's father), hoping to provide for her newborn and somewhat conceal the illegitimacy of her pregnancy; after the birth (and her husband's sudden loss of interest in parenthood) she put the child up for adoption. The choice to give up her daughter would haunt Joni throughout her twenties—she would often spot young girls in the audience at concerts or on the street and wonder if the child could be hers.[3]

Mitchell's story of motherhood recalls the Greek myth of Demeter and Persephone, the earth mother goddess who loses her daughter to the unknown and is wrought with sorrow until she returns. Persephone becomes the goddess of the springtime when she resurfaces from the underworld, since when her daughter is gone, Demeter becomes so depressed she neglects her duties and the earth suffers its winter. Notably, Joni's nickname and eponymous love song to her absent daughter was "Little Green." "Just a little green, like the color when the spring is born," are lyrics in the song, which was so emotionally weighted for the grieving mother that she didn't release it until 1971's *Blue,* four years after it was written.

The concept of the goddess in contemporary goddess worship, first popularized in 1948 by Robert Graves' book *The White Goddess,* is three-parted, expressed by the cyclically aging Maiden, Mother, and Crone. The Maiden is the beautiful, innocent young woman, past childhood, but not yet hardened by the evils of the world. The Mother is the mature nurturer, teacher, and strong protector. The Crone is the wise-woman, no longer a sexual being able to procreate, but privy to secrets, sagacity, and magic. Because she is so

closely associated with nature, the goddess does not age in a linear fashion; her relationship to time is cyclical as the seasons. The
aging Crone again becomes the Maiden as surely as winter turns to
spring.

The drama of "Little Green" aligned Joni with the mother
archetype, however, since she gave up her daughter and eventually
divorced, she was also able to inhabit the role of maiden, the pretty,
young, single woman of the liberating '60s. And the profundity of
her lyrics, along with her effortless-seeming proficiency with melody, musical instruments, and alternate guitar tunings summoned
the energy of the wise woman, or crone. Joni managed to embody
all three goddess personae simultaneously.

The strength of her songwriting also allowed her to circum-
vent the dreaded "muse" classification. Mitchell was not the inspiration for creators—she was a creator herself. While many women,
even performing women, were relegated to the muse role in the
'60s, Mitchell was no such thing. Recalling her initial effect on
the male-dominated Laurel Canyon coterie, Leah Cohen Kunkel
(Cass Elliot's sister) says, "When Joni would sing over that guitar,
men were riveted—they stopped what they were doing, they were
absolutely enamored. Before that it was always women [in the
Canyon] riveted by the male guitarist—this was the first time it
changed. Joni got introduced to the cream of the pop rock world,
and she was accepted right away."[4] The men of Laurel Canyon
describe her as "this ethereal blonde" who would occasionally
descend an odd staircase and bless them with her other-worldly
songs. She was perceived as mystical, almost untouchable (even
by men who touched her repeatedly); Graham Nash, in recalling
their intensely romantic cohabitation, states, "I looked at Joni as a
goddess, and she was."[5]

The media, for its part, handled Mitchell clumsily, often
attempting to paint her as a consort, the type of goddess least
threatening to patriarchy, even after she had risen to a considerable level of fame and established herself as one of the most important songwriters of the twentieth century. While her male musical

comrades thought of her as a peer, in the early '70s *Rolling Stone* dubbed her "Old Lady of the Year,"[6] and published a chart linking her romantically with slews of famous male musicians.[7] Years later, Joni commented, "There was no free love. It came with great strings attached. It was free for men, but not for women, same as it ever was."[2] On the heels of the sexual revolution, but before Gloria Steinem and Germaine Greer became household names, the women of the '60s walked a tightrope between geisha and immaculate mother. Reprise, Joni's record label, advertised her first album with the tagline: "Joni Mitchell is 90% virgin." As with the Christian Mary, whenever virginity is proffered as a defining characteristic, the unspoken correlate is sex; with this line they alluded to that link overtly.

The media's preoccupation with her attractiveness aside, what really distinguished Joni from the other (mostly male) musicians of the late '60s was her lyrical depth and acumen. Though a gifted composer of melody and structure, it was the content and direction of her works that caught the public, and other songwriters, by surprise. Her brooding lyrics, set to unconventional tunings, revealed a multi-dimensional, searching voice. Regardless of whether the "I" in a given song was Mitchell herself, a friend, or a fictional character, each was an incisive, self-contained sketch of the human psyche, the inner voice longing to be heard.

In addition to the goddess's role as the divine body (nature, sex, birth, regeneration) she is also associated with our emotional and interior lives. The Greek Sophia of early Gnostic Christianity is wisdom personified. In the Daoist concept of yin/yang, the feminine aspect, yin, is ruled by emotion, passivity, and the element of water. In classical Greek mythology, Athena represents wisdom and the strategic aspects of war. The Tarot's High Priestess card symbolizes the inner guiding voice and the emotional world, both of which are elusive and veiled in mystery.

Joni's most iconic songs are those that place inner wisdom in relation to nature, the lines often blurring until the listener starts to question where the human psyche ends, and the earth begins.

"Both Sides, Now" illustrates the fallacy of human perception using the metaphor of clouds, while "Big Yellow Taxi," one of the first popular songs to address environmental concerns, criticizes sprawl, deforestation, wanton commercial development, and consumerism. "The Circle Game" is a simple yet poignant commentary on the human lifecycle and time, and "Woodstock" combines scientific and religious imagery into a beautiful declaration of the physical body, and a lament for its disconnection from the earth as the source of life.

An intuitive approach to her music was discernable, exemplified in her use of a wide array of alternate guitar tunings, many which she invented herself. Composing in these subtle yet complicated keys came natural to Joni and lent much to the ethereal quality underlying much of her work. She explains the process as one of literally aligning a particular sonic set and setting to specific queries posed by her own psyche: "Chords are depictions of emotions. These chords that I was getting by twisting the knobs on the guitar until I could get these chords that I heard inside...feel like my feelings. I called them, not knowing, 'Chords of Inquiry.' They have a question mark in them."[2]

Mitchell was and remains a mystery. Her musical catalogue is arguably one of the recording era's most challenging, ultimately resistant to any formal definition, often quite trying for inflexible fans of any specific genre and demanding of a genuine contemplation and self-reflection from the listener. And, ironically, for an artist so identified with transparency and intimacy, she long held the audience at arm's length, taking extended sabbaticals from the stage and public appearance, guarded against the potential of idolatry to encroach upon the purity of her creative expression, and always resistant to the ego-boosting gratifications of celebrity. She recalls how the success of the critically acclaimed *Blue* and her ever-quickening deification were early red flags that her creative process could be usurped by the demands of industry and expectations of fans. She reasoned that to remain true to both herself and her followers she would have to speak with an increasing authenticity: "I took it upon myself that since I was a public voice and subject to this weird kind of worship, that they should know who they were worshipping. I was demanding of myself a deeper and greater honesty, more and more revelation in my work in order to give it back to the people, where it goes into their lives and nourishes them."[2]

As when Dylan went electric, there was a knee-jerk quasi-religious impulse to freeze Joni in time, for her to remain the vulnerable, fragile confessor from *Blue*. Unlike Dylan, who as a prophet needed to keep moving forward on his physical journey, Mitchell as artist was compelled to expand and evolve her musical palette and poetic language, which inevitably revealed deeper aspects of the goddess archetype even as she moved away from the overt themes of the earth mother.

Following the starkly produced and arranged *Blue*, Joni expanded her musical horizons by becoming a band leader and moving boldly in the direction of full-fledged sonic productions. After employing a collection of LA session musicians for the transitional album *For the Roses*, she decided that her complicated chords and structures, along with her increasingly esoteric subject matter, required the support of musicians schooled in jazz—players able to instinctively interpret her deepening musical and emotional vocabulary.

For *Court & Spark*, she stepped in front of Tom Scott and the LA Express, a west coast jazz-fusion quintet with hot, seasoned instrumentalists, and caught commercial lightning in a bottle. Her new image as a strong, confident woman leading a group of men in support positions allowed Joni to transition away from the somewhat hesitant maiden incarnation of her younger years and into the mature and outspoken mother archetype of her mid-period, while still offering a remarkably wide lyrical depth of field. Even still, this commercial "breakthrough" was a misnomer. A pop album only in the sense that it had popular appeal, *Court & Spark*'s polished, accessible presentation masked a radical stylistic transformation in its formative stages, an artist ever willing to move further away from established formulas and the comfort of a predictable marketplace.

In the late '70s, Joni was welcomed into the upper ranks of the jazz world as swiftly as she had been accepted by the male rock stars of the late '60s in Laurel Canyon. Titan players such as Jaco Pastorius, Wayne Shorter, Herbie Hancock, and Pat Metheny were among her core group of musicians on record and in concert until the end of the decade. This unprecedented show of support (for a female folk/pop singer, no less) was a definitive testament to her innovation, and yet it did little to stop what had already become a growing exodus of fans. As she explored the creatively freeing forms of jazz, world music, avant-garde, fusion, scat vocal, and improvisation, her material inevitably became less commercially viable. By the time the eminent bop bassist Charles Mingus called with an offer to collaborate on what would be his final compositions, her commercial fan base had already found an adequate replacement in a beguiling young maiden, Stevie Nicks, who reigned until Madonna stepped in to reinvent the sex/fertility goddess for the age of corporatism, cocaine, and MTV. Mitchell was undaunted, but the following decade was not one to value her gifts—the Reagan/Bush era made the goddess bristle and wither.

Joni cycled into her crone period just as America took a sharp turn to the right and quality music listening was supplanted by the instant gratification of music video. She found she still had much to say but was essentially muzzled due to her marginalized drawing power at the concert hall and record counter. Now a wise woman with a warrior spirit and nothing left to prove, she railed on record against Christian fundamentalism, corporate greed, environmental destruction, abuse toward women, and world hunger. In interviews, she caustically decried her misunderstanding and mistreatment by the culture at large and music industry specifically, attributing these slights to a combination of gender inequality, artistic ignorance, and societal apathy.

Most of all, she longed for her voice to be heard. She sings of her frustration on the 1991 album *Night Ride Home*: "I am not some stone commission, like a statue in a park. I am flesh and blood and vision; I am howling in the dark." A culture that had long looked to Mitchell for guidance and insight was barely listening; those who were got an earful—the earth mother was gravely ill. On 1994's *Turbulent Indigo,* she connects the decay of the planet with the loss of sex as a sacred act, painfully crying, "The ulcerated ozone, these tumors of the skin. This hostile sun beating down, this massive mess we're in. And the gas leaks. And the oil spills. And sex sells everything. And sex kills."

It is noteworthy Mitchell never complained that her material success should have been greater, that she should have sold more records, had more hits, or been more famous. Her lament is more for the artist's diminishing role in our cultural dialog, and, in a more universal sense, for the silencing of the goddess in our spiritual lives. Joni wasn't saying *she* wasn't getting enough from her work; she was saying *we* weren't getting enough from it.

At the turn of the first century, the Roman poet Juvenal wrote: "Nature never says one thing; Wisdom another."[8] Symbolically, women are almost invariably linked to nature, the body, and the physical world, and yet, as is clear in the goddess archetype, they also represent the depths, mystery, and processes of internal reality, which links them fundamentally with the concept of *spirit.*

In Christianity, the Holy Spirit is the "third person" of the Trinity, the point of intersection between transcendence (the "up-in-the-sky" God the Father) and created reality (the "in-the-flesh" God the Son). In a syncretistic sense, it can be compared with the Daoist concept of *qi* and the Yogic notion of *prana,* both representing universal life force. Essentially, it's the aspect of the divine that acts and manifests in the world, the divinity that resides in the human "soul," and the indefinable animating force that sets the universe (and the living human being) in motion. As the Christian Trinity inexplicably ignores the divine feminine in its construct, it seems the goddess was smuggled into the theology somewhat clandestinely. After all, many traditions (including various strains of Hinduism and Buddhism and numerous ancient Greek and Stoic philosophers) identify Woman as the *anima mundi,* which translates as "world soul." Jung considered this feminine symbol as co-equal concept to his notion of a primordial *cosmic man* archetype.[9]

Spirit is not a definition, argument, or equation. It is no thing. Writers in both mystical and scholarly traditions have long noted the ineffable nature of spirit, and therefore, the challenges of describing it through words. The fourteenth century German mystic Meister Eckhart said of the godhead, "Whatever words we use, they are telling lies, and it (the power of the spirit) is far above them. It is free of all names; it is bare of all forms, wholly empty and free."[10] In his book *The Seven Mysteries of Life*, contemporary philosopher Guy Murchie writes that "there is something intangible behind the life in physical bodies—indeed behind all matter—and that this immateriality (energy, if you will) is revealed by the flow of time, which literally makes things into events."[11] Spirit is therefore understood as an indefinable sense of underlying energy and the point of direct experience that is beyond the physical world, the logic of the brain, and, most frustratingly, language. In sum, spirit must be *experienced*; it can't be *explained*.

In London in 1964, an electrified, self-destructive, maximum R&B band with an unparalleled stage show decided they needed a name that better suited their sound and image than "The Detours." After a characteristically heated, nearly-violent band meeting in which they almost settled on calling themselves "The Nothing," they finally chose an unanswered (and possibly unanswerable) question: "The Who."

The literally and metaphorically electrified aspects of the Who's music were vital to their connection with their audience. It was important that their instruments were electric in a way that was much deeper and more fundamental to their purpose than to that of the Beatles, the Stones, or the Beach Boys. The Who were loud—skeleton-rattlingly loud; they were, in fact, widely considered "The World's Loudest Band" and officially named so by the Guinness Book of World Records in 1976. Guitarist and composer Pete Townshend hinted as early as 1966 that their excessive decibels were essential to the very idea of the Who: "Although I can play the guitar as well as most guitarists on the scene I only specialize in big chords played very loud—which has got nothing to do with music. It's more to do with volume and impact."[12] They were also one of the first bands to utilize electronic feedback as a structural part of their music, indeed, the Who's infamous practice of smashing their instruments began when Townshend broke the neck of his guitar while banging it on the ceiling of a club in the attempt to make it feed back.[13]

Quite simply, no one had ever seen a band perform like the Who. Their use of instruments was both counterintuitive and revolutionary: the bass player thumped out melody, the guitarist kept rhythm, and the drumming was almost lyrical. Keith Moon spun like a whirling dervish behind the kit, punctuating, highlighting, and complementing the work of the other three musicians with furious flurries of syncopation, while bassist John Entwistle stood still as a statue, singer Roger Daltrey marched in step with the thunderous rhythms, and Townshend's arm was a wind turbine, sending waves of energy through his electric guitar and into the charged crowd. He would leap around the stage, jumping so extraordinarily high he earned the nickname "The Birdman."[12] Of course, in both Christian scripture and art, the Holy Spirit is often represented by a dove in flight.

For all the power of their live shows, until the late '60s the Who's recordings were received with relative lack of enthusiasm compared to contemporaries at their level. While their reputation as a performing band grew, their singles and albums failed to generate the same excitement, especially in the United States. In fact, despite their success and reputation after years playing in England, it wasn't until they were "discovered" playing live at the Monterey Pop Festival in 1967 that they finally broke through in America. It was the shared energy and vitality of their live act that earned them their most recognition until the themes and scope of Townshend's songwriting moved into more explicitly spiritual, transcendent territory with the rock opera *Tommy*. However, their two most notable pre-*Tommy* singles, "I Can't Explain," and "My Generation," strongly introduced themes of energy and ineffability into the mythos of the Who.

In "I Can't Explain," the earnest, befuddled protagonist expresses frustrations over his inability to express... anything, really. The lyrics of the song revolve around a vague romantic entanglement, and Townshend has said he wrote it about a kid who can't find the words to tell a girl that he loved her.[14] In the ears of listeners, though, the song's meaning widens and deepens considerably. On the surface it is a song about youth, love, and deep emotion, but in a more universal sense it suggests a profound experience that's exasperatingly beyond words.

It's ironic that with the 1964 release of "I Can't Explain" (their first single) the group was designated as a "voice" of the young generation, specifically the "mods." Mod described a teenage subculture in England in the early-to-mid '60s characterized by attention to fashion, social clubs, rock & roll, blues, and jazz music, amphetamine use, and all-night dancing. Mods lived for the moment, spending entire paychecks on the latest fashions that would be passé (or destroyed) in a matter of days or weeks, and dancing through the night when a full day of work waited in the morning. Mod culture was youth culture, and youth is a concept often used interchangeably with vitality and vigor. Even the mods' drug of choice, amphetamine, served to artificially increase and prolong energy.

"My Generation" was a mod anthem and a youth anthem, but, essentially, an ode to energy. The protagonist insouciantly declares himself a spokesperson for the energetic youth, while telling the out-of-touch older generation to "f-f-f-fade away." The stuttering utterances of Daltrey's vocal delivery are integral to the song's message, evoking the tied tongue of a mod kid hopped up on speed, or a person so full of energy that his words can't keep up with him (recalling the inexpressible frustrations of "I Can't Explain"). With the song's most iconic lyric, "Hope I die before I get old," the Who presented the vivacity of youth as diametrically opposed to stagnation and decay; and extended the materially transcendent experience of spirit to its practical, physical expression: self-negation or self-destruction.

For most of the '60s, the Who opened their concerts with "I Can't Explain" and closed them with "My Generation," the final chords of which segued into one of the most powerful and distinctive aspects of the group's early performances: the violent demolition of their instruments. In art school, Townshend had been influenced by the auto-destructive art philosophy of Gustav Metzner, and for years the Who destroyed their instruments onstage at nearly every show. This bombastic act of showmanship not only brought the incomparable power of the band's stage performance to a definite catharsis, it also dramatized self-immolation in pursuit of this elusive and captivating "energy." It was a negation of the ego and a brutal rejection of the material world. Townshend describes the violence perpetrated by the Who in concert as an unconscious act: "When I'm onstage, I'm not in control of myself at all. I don't even know who I am. ... I'm just not there."[15]

The deification of spirit and the abasement of flesh can be viewed as an example of the Gnostic emphasis on inner understanding of the divine—to be truly holy, the initiate must discard *all* external, physical influences, including their own body. Many Christian traditions have endorsed mortification of the flesh (or "dying to this life," to paraphrase St. Paul)[16] as the means to achieve oneness with spirit. Eckhart says, "The man who has annihilated himself ... has taken possession of the lowest place, and God must pour the whole of himself into this man ... who has utterly abandoned himself."[17] The dichotomy of contradictory truths, as well as the materially-transcendent nature of the divine, inevitably leads into many auto-annulling aspects of both contemplative mysticism and charismatic fervor.

These two principal types of human relationship to spirit were embodied by the most dynamic members of the Who. Townshend assumed the role of the contemplative mystic, pondering, theorizing, and seeking the source of spirit through music, art, and poetry. Moon, on the other hand, represented the charismatic who is overtaken by spirit. While Townshend orchestrated self-aware auto-destructive rituals onstage, Moon—with his gunpowder-enhanced finales, compulsive trashing of hotel rooms, biology-defying alcohol and drug regimen, and death-by-overdose at thirty-two—embraced auto-destructive art as *lifestyle.*

Moon may not have had the detached perspective on his role in the Who's mythos that his contemplative bandmate did, but he personified the concept of spirit in a much more direct way than the other three members. He dove headlong into the rush of the music, the rock & roll lifestyle, and his own mythos in a way that has never been attempted quite so excessively and with such abandon. Moon let the energy consume and control him, and it worked through him to ignite the band. Longtime Who manager Chris Stamp explains: "The Who existed from the time Keith joined the band...until Keith died.[18]...They were this incredible, distorted, dysfunctional energy....Pete was cerebral, John was very isolated and shut down, and Roger was Roger—his anger came through in his voice....It moved because of Keith; his energy energized them."[19]

When the Who finally moved away from their literally auto-destructive performances, it was to create material that explored the inner quest of a boy who, lacking the sensory means to connect with the mundane world, embarks on his own spiritual voyage within, even as his body is used and abused by those around him. Though the group no longer smashed their instruments at every show, they brought the same indefinable yet unmistakable energy to their stage performances of this metaphysical rock opera, and indeed it was 1969's *Tommy* that finally made the Who into superstars.

Townshend has said that the crux of *Tommy* was the song "The Amazing Journey," a direct account of spiritual transcendence.[20] The original working title and first piece composed for the project, the song describes Tommy Walker as the "deaf, dumb, and blind boy, he's in a quiet vibration land." Said Townshend of his protagonist, "In Tommy's mind, everything is incredible, meaningless beauty."[21] "Pinball Wizard" was added later when it was decided the album lacked a single, and the addition of this bit of action and whimsy into the ascetic main character's life is significant in that he's able to interact with the world only through vibration, and pinball provided a strong metaphor. Townshend felt that the inclusion "made it more accessible and that allowed me to go deeper. Suddenly there was this sense that pinball was about the universe and [Tommy] could be the key to it all."[20]

Tommy's awakening occurs as he stares vacantly into a mirror, lost in his own self-image (which might be described by Jungians as indulgence in the ego). It's only when he self-immolates ("Smash the Mirror") that he is able to connect with his higher consciousness ("I'm Free") and bring the fruits of his years of isolated contemplation into the world. In the song "Sensation," Tommy's spiritual essence and purpose is revealed: "You'll feel me coming, a new vibration. From afar you'll see me, I'm a sensation." In this context, Tommy *is* vibration. This is punctuated in the moving finale to the opera, where Tommy implores his followers to "See me, feel me, touch me, heal me," and his flock, in direct experience of his vibratory emanation, responds, "Listening to you, I get the music; gazing at you, I get the heat... on you, I see the glory... from you, I get the story."

By 1971, the Who were the most vital rock band in the world. After having released one of the first rock concept albums with *The Who Sell Out* in 1967, the first rock opera with *Tommy* (and subsequent messianic performance at Woodstock) in 1969, and one of the most acclaimed live albums of the era with *Live at Leeds* in 1970, Townshend was compelled to up his own epic ante with the band's next release. His concept for *Lifehouse* was to create an immersive artistic experience that would illustrate and embody the cyclical interpersonal connections created between audience and performer during a live rock concert. Townshend intended to make the conception fully interactive by eventually incorporating songs about repeat members of the audience during a continuing series of *Lifehouse* shows at London's Young Vic club.

Lifehouse envisioned a future in which most of humanity lives in spiritual isolation akin to Tommy Walker's by being plugged into an electronic grid much like today's internet, through which they experience most of their lives in the form of government-funneled entertainment programming. The music was meant to isolate and explore the energy of rock music, specifically, the rock concert and the ego-annihilating effects of that connective experience. However, the project was abandoned, thwarted by the ineffability of its intended theme and because no one, not even the other members of the band, were able to grasp Townshend's explanation of the concept. The songs that survived formed the core of 1971's seminal *Who's Next*; others found their way onto Townshend's first solo album, *Who Came First*; and three—"Let's See Action," "Relay," and "Join Together (With the Band)"—were released as singles circa 1972 during the period the band was creating what would be yet another widely revered rock opera about fractured personality and redemption, *Quadrophenia*.

Beyond the songs themselves, direct remnants of Townshend's creative methods for *Lifehouse* remained in the tracks of *Who's Next*; the synthesizer parts in "Baba O'Riley" and "Won't Get Fooled Again" are said to be based on frequencies modulated from individual human pulses.[22] Townshend described his approach in a 1971 interview with *New World Express*: "Among my plans for the concert and the film of the concert at the Young Vic was to take a person out of the audience and feed information—height, weight, astrological details, beliefs, and behavior, etc.—about the person into the synthesizer. The synthesizer would then select notes from the pattern of that person. It would be like translating a person into music. On ["Baba O'Riley"] I programmed details about the life of Meher Baba and that provides the backing for the number."[23]

The philosophies of various twentieth century mystics directly informed much of Townshend's work during the late '60s and early '70s, most notably Meher Baba, the Indo-Iranian "Avatar" who taught that the temporal world is illusion and espoused an internal spiritual practice he termed "Involution."[24] Famously, Baba maintained silence for most of his life, from 1925 until his death in 1969. He explained in a 1958 discourse titled "The Universal Message" that "because man has been deaf to the principles and precepts laid down by God in the past, in this present Avataric form, I observe silence." His philosophy and life-example are echoed in the senses-deprived character and inward journey of Tommy Walker, and indeed Townshend dedicated *Tommy* to the mystic in the album's gatefold sleeve.

Townshend was also influenced by the Sufi philosopher and musician Hazrat Inayat Khan, whose books *Music of Life* and *The Mysticism of Sound and Music* explore the relationship between spirit and music, recalling the Pythagorean and Platonic notion of the "Music of the Spheres." Khan writes, "The mystery of sound is mysticism; the harmony of life is religion. The knowledge of vibrations is metaphysics, the analysis of atoms is science, and their harmonious grouping is art. The rhythm of form is poetry, and the rhythm of sound is music. This shows that music is the art of arts and the science of all sciences, and it contains the fountain of all knowledge within itself."[25]

We see the notion of sound as the foundation of existence in many ancient attempts to explain reality through the interplay of the classical elements. While most traditions agreed on the common quartet of earth, water, fire, and air (which align with solids, liquids, plasma, and gasses, respectively), many also proposed a more ephemeral fifth element that underlies the actions and keys the subjective experience of the standard four. The ancient Greeks called it *aether*, which they believed to be the pure essence that the gods breathed and the basic substance of the universe existing beyond the terrestrial sphere. In the Vedantic philosophy of the East, *Akasha* was imagined as an "ethereal fluid pervading the cosmos."[26] Though this elusive element has been given many names depending on the mythos—Akasha, aether, quintessence, void, sky, space, emptiness, consciousness—the concept is invariably best described as spirit.

And what is spirit, really, but another name for sound? After all, these five elements align fundamentally to our most essential interactions with the temporal world—our five senses: Earth corresponds to touch; water to taste; fire to sight; and air to smell. Hearing is the internal, vibratory sense that corresponds to what we call spirit. We can also see this logic in Buddhist philosophy: Earth, the basest element, can be perceived by all five senses; water can be felt, seen, tasted, and heard, but has no odor. Fire can be seen, felt, and heard; and air can be felt and heard. The fifth element—Akasha/aether/spirit—can only be perceived through our sense of sound, our ability to hear.[27]

The relationship of spirit and sound has long been implied by religious traditions. One of the most dramatic Christian examples is the telling in Acts of the Holy Spirit descending on Jesus's apostles and followers during the first Pentecost: "And suddenly from heaven there came a sound like the rush of a violent wind, and it filled the entire house where they were sitting. Divided tongues, as of fire, appeared among them, and a tongue rested on each of them. All of them were filled with the Holy Spirit and began to speak in other languages, as the spirit gave them ability."[28] Whereas the notion of spirit in the New Testament is usually communicated through a symbol, such as the dove that descends during Jesus's baptism,[29] this verse is explicit—the Holy Spirit is *sound*.

And lest we forget, in the beginning there was nothing; then there was sound. God said, "Let there be light," and there was light. The God of the Old Testament did not build or fashion his creation, rather, he *commanded* the heavens and earth into being. God said, "Let there be earth," and the sea receded to reveal coastlines and mountains. God said, "Let there be time," and days and nights began their interminable cycle. God said, "Let there be life," and plants and animals grew and spread across the land. In this story, God continued speaking the world into being for six days, each subsequent phase of his creation adding complexity and subtlety to existence, like a composer adding variations to a musical theme. Here, sound, words, and thought are the basis of all existence—the universal energy that came even before light.

Hundreds of years after the penning of Genesis, the writer of the most mystical and poetic Christian gospel to survive Roman biblical canonization began the Gospel According to John with the verse: "In the beginning was the Word, and the Word was with God, and the Word was God."[30] The "Word" to which John refers is the Greek *logos*, which does not denote a "word" in a grammatical sense (which would be *lexis*); instead, it refers to the instance of speaking itself, as well as the intent underlying the act of speech. According to the Greek-English lexicon, its meaning therefore extends to hypothesis, thought, and grounds for belief. In the West, the concept had been associated with the fundamental energy of the universe long before the author of John composed his opening line—Heraclitus first established this *logos* as the ultimate source of existence circa 500 BCE. The term was widely used throughout Greek antiquity to mean the divine animating will, eventually making its way into Hellenistic Judaism and, at last, Christianity.

In the multifaceted Hindu traditions, Brahman is the transcendent, unchanging, eternal energy from which the universe and all of existence extends. The Trimurti—Brahma, the Creator; Vishnu, the Sustainer; and Shiva, the Destroyer—are mere aspects of Brahman, the Supreme One, which, like the God of the Christian mystics, both envelopes and surpasses such quotidian realities as time, space, and matter, making the task of describing this essential One very difficult, if not impossible. Therefore, attempts to explain it in human terms must invariably take another form.

Aum (sometimes written, *Om*) is a sound consisting of three separate sounds (*A, U, M*) that meld to one, much as the Hindu Trimurti are three distinct personalities while also different aspects of Brahman. Chanted in religious rituals and public and private meditative practices, Aum—the eternal, the essence of all—simply *is*. In the Taittiriya Upanishads, Aum is equated with Brahman in striking parallel to the comparison of God and *logos* found in John's Gospel: "Brahman is Aum. This whole world is Aum."[31] The Chandogya Upanishads elaborate on Aum's elementary and transcendent nature, where it is venerated as the "High Chant" born of speech and breath in coitus, symbolizing the satisfaction and fulfillment of these underlying desires and reflecting the demiurge to become real, to create life.[32]

The notion of sound as the foundation and origin of existence can even be seen in modern science. Astrophysicists refer to the explosion that began the universe as "The Big Bang," when "The Big Flash" might have been equally descriptive. They describe the microwave background left over from The Big Bang as a musical note—an extremely low B-flat (fifty-seven octaves below middle-C), even though what we think of as "sound" cannot exist in empty space.

Townshend explained at the time that *Lifehouse* was "basically based on physics, closely linked with the things mystics have been saying for a long time about vibrations in music. ... There's a note, a musical note that builds the basis of existence somehow. ... This note pervades everything; it's an extremely wide note, more of a hiss than a note as we normally know them ... its music, the most beautiful there is to hear."[33] Here, he may be referring to physicist Niels Bohr's theory that the dual nature of the universe's fundamental subatomic particles—the fact that a quantum dot is simultaneously, somehow, a particle *and* a wave—must correspond to the dual nature of experienced reality: matter and spirit. In this construction, the particle function corresponds to matter (the atoms that make up the body), and the wave function corresponds to spirit (the force that moves it). The natural extrapolation, certainly for a musician and composer, is that sound (being a pure wave) is a direct communicator and/or conduit of spirit.

Both Hinduism and Buddhism recognize an archetype, the *Ātman*, which is a symbol for "the God within" that emerges when the state of *Sunyata* (emptiness or voidness) is achieved and spirit enters and fills the individual. This "true self" is separate from and beyond the confines of the material world—a fully detached "feeler of sensations."[34] As philosopher Ken Wilbur describes in his *A Brief History of Everything:* "This observing Self is usually called the Self with a capital *S*, or the Witness, or pure Presence, or pure Awareness, or Consciousness as such, and this Self as transparent

Witness is a direct ray of the living Divine. The ultimate "I AM" is Christ, is Buddha, is Emptiness itself."[35]

The attainment of this "Christos" or "Buddha-Consciousness" (to once again force language to describe that which is beyond human definition), is, according to Pete Townshend, the primary function of music, and consequently, the modern rock concert: "When live rock is at its best, which often means the Who ... it's an interaction which goes beyond performance. We aren't like super-stars, we're only reflective surfaces. We might catch energy and transmit it, but the audience doesn't take more from us than we take from them.[36] ...You don't go on stage to *find* something; you go on stage to *lose* something. You don't go to a concert in order to be *given* something; you go to a concert in order to become abandoned, to lose yourself."[37]

At the dusk of the classic rock era, the Who, representing spirit and seeking to define its qualities to yet a new generation, condensed it to a vibration from which *everything* emerges and ultimately resounds back to its source. While *Tommy* described the internal transformation through which one opens to the Christ, the Buddha, or whatever face we give to the pure energy available to a freed consciousness, *Lifehouse* sought to demonstrate this process in action. Townshend said that "Pure and Easy" was the "pivotal song ... reflecting creation musically, i.e. there being one infinite consciousness, everything in infinity being one note."[38] Fittingly, its opening verse graces the coda of the powerful and eloquent "The Song is Over" from *Who's Next*, which had originally been intended as the denouement to the *Lifehouse* song cycle, narrative, concert, and film.[39] It attempts to describe and conjure, as have so many of our myths, the essence of spirit and experience of its ineffable yet eternal nature: "There once was a note, pure and easy, playing so free, like a breath rippling by ..."

In a world of peace and love, music would be the universal language.
–Henry David Thoreau

CONCLUSION

❧ ❧ ❧

All You Need is Myth

The rock star is Joseph Campbell's "Hero" as a constellation in Marshall McLuhan's "Gutenberg Galaxy." The deep resonance the Beatles and other rock gods share with characters, symbols, and stories common to mythologies across many times and cultures suggests that the 1960s musical renaissance generated a modern spiritual tradition, rooted not in folklore or sacred scripture, but in the new language of recorded sound and image, commercial entertainment, and mass media. The brightest star of this archetypal techno-firmament is quite clearly the Beatles, who represent the core monomyth within the larger context of the mythology. Like all savior gods, they are the principal "stars" in their mythic pantheon because, as metaphors of inclusion, transformation, and transcendence, they facilitate our evolution towards an integrated consciousness, which is essentially the goal and modus operandi of myth itself.

Jung understood that what he termed the *Self*—the highest manifestation of the fully actualized personality—is the psychological analog of the savior archetype of mythology: "Psychologically, Christ means unity.[1] ... In Christian countries, the Self is projected onto the second Adam: Christ. In the East, the relevant figures are those of Krishna and Buddha.[2] ... The Self refers neither to Christ nor to the Buddha but to the totality of the figures that are its equivalent, and each of these figures is a symbol of the Self."[3]

The "individuation process," as Jung called it, is a universal striving in every person to fully integrate the unconscious aspects of the psyche with the conscious elements, the goal being ever-increasing self-awareness. The archetype of the self/savior exists to light this path of personal spiritual evolution, ultimately harmonizing and incorporating the other archetypes of the psyche. He writes, "Empirically it can be established, with a sufficient degree of probability, that there is in the unconscious an archetype of wholeness which manifests itself spontaneously in dreams, etc., and a tendency, independent of the conscious will, to relate other archetypes to this center."[4]

The Beatles are a powerful symbol for these concepts, both within the context of the rock mythology and for the culture of their time. Their story is one of a group of individuals who band together with harmonic purpose, and—through their ability to transform themselves and continually transcend to higher levels—fully integrate their various personae, influences, talents, and creative visions into a meta-personality expressing profundity and spiritual significance to millions of individuals. Accordingly, the Beatles' story exists as the central narrative within the larger framework of rock mythology, just as the ancient savior gods were the primary protagonists in their respective traditions, just as the Self harmonizes and ultimately completes the other archetypes of the unconscious.

Of critical significance is the fact that the rock mythology isn't fictional. Unlike the spiritual writings, literature, and poetry of antiquity or the film and television drama of today, which purposefully employ symbolic tropes in story and character, the rock mythos sprang from real human lives and events, signaling a momentous shift in how myth can now be created and experienced. Further, the grand narrative of rock unfolded in a proper mythic *structure*, the archetypes of the herald, prophet, and child pre-figuring and informing the savior, whose emergence and promise was quickly challenged by his great adversary, the devil. The drama then in full bloom and exhibiting age-old dualities, the shamans and mediums surfaced to provide equilibrium before the story reached its inevitable conclusion—an illumination of inner experience through the cyclical wisdom of the goddess and the edifying purity of the spirit. This distinctly mythic formation suggests a phenomenon imagined and fueled by the collective unconscious, our need for a new mythology to reflect the modern world now projected onto the artists and celebrities of mass media.

Let's not forget, when John Lennon (sort of) recanted his popularity observation in 1966, he incisively commented, "If I had said television was more popular than Jesus I might have got away with it." There is much truth to this statement, not in the sense that he might have been spared the cultural backlash, but because television, representing the new language of mass media, was indeed supplanting the increasingly antiquated delivery systems through which mythology had formerly been shared. It also suggests a useful and telling metaphor. Many of us, when considering what television *is*, might respond that it is mere entertainment, as though what is *on* television—*Seinfeld, Downton Abbey, Game of Thrones*, etc.— somehow defines its very nature. Television, like radio before it, and the printed word before that, and word-of-mouth before that, are simply channels of communication through which we "broadcast" and exchange information. As we see from centuries of clear example, mythology will adapt to and reconfigure within any new culture, language, or form of communication. In this sense, if a modern-day Matthew, Mark, Luke, or John attempted to deify the phenomenon of rock & roll, we could imagine them beginning the "Gospel According to the Beatles" with the verse, "On February 9, 1964, on *The Ed Sullivan Show*, the Word made Flesh made Music made Television."

To be sure, the '60s rock icons were not gods in a literal sense, any more or less than the gods of mythologies past. They were archetypal symbols, absorbed in cultural consciousness through the communication mediums of their time. How they were able and came to embody those symbols—the historical synchronicities that made way for them, the previous music that inspired them, even the personal creative processes they employed to receive and refashion archetypal information—is ultimately of less importance than the *meaning of the symbols* they represented. Such is the same for the saviors and gods of antiquity; they were the symbols that activated the archetypal unconscious for their times and places, and they persist as exemplary characters in the classic arts—literature, poetry, song, drama, dance, sculpture, painting. For the mythic archetypes of rock & roll we simply see more communicative arrows in their quiver—recorded sound and image technology and an ever-expanding and evolving mass media through which their art, philosophy, and narrative is disseminated.

The rock icons of focus in the current study were certainly not the only ones to display distinct archetypal characteristics and narratives. Many others come quickly to mind: Frank Zappa, musical and intellectual *trickster*, his ridicule of commercial entertainment and societal hypocrisy scathingly cogent in his mockery of the Beatles with *We're Only in it for the Money* as riposte to *Sgt. Pepper*; David Bowie, the *alien* archetype, offering detached perspective and cultural redefinition in the cosmic, genderless, futuristic guise of Ziggy Stardust; the Grateful Dead, evangelizing the Summer of Love ethos and inspiring their flock to seek collective rebirth through a shared psychedelic vision-quest; Led Zeppelin, musical sorcery and occultic symbolism suggesting secret and perhaps sinister knowledge and methods; and Pink Floyd, post-modern musical mystery school, their consciousness-expanding *Dark Side of the Moon* and other seminal works functioning as contemplative sonic initiation rituals.

The artists discussed in this book were chosen for the fullness with which they communicate the symbolism associated with their archetypes; essential characteristics now prototypal in the modern media landscape and emanating through countless succeeding musical entities. Emanation (as a mythic concept most identified with the Hindu deities) describes the manner through which all things/ideas/memes derive from a first principle, often (but not necessarily) diffusing with each incarnation removed from point of origin, as a stone thrown into water produces a series of ringed ripples that become increasingly faint as they separate from source.

From this perspective, we can see the "Elvis principle" flowing through artists as seemingly disparate as Michael Jackson and Eminem. Likewise, Dylan, through interpreters the Byrds and the Band, troubadours Donovan and Gordon Lightfoot, poetic lyricists Paul Simon and Jackson Browne, and voices of the common man John Fogerty and Bruce Springsteen; Brian Wilson through playful, idiosyncratic studio-marvels Harry Nilsson, Lindsey Buckingham, and Prince; the Rolling Stones through the dark art of Black Sabbath, sex-obsessed swagger of Aerosmith, and debauchery of Mötley Crüe; Jimi Hendrix through guitar magi Jeff Beck, Eddie Van Halen, and Stevie Ray Vaughn; Jim Morrison through the seemingly inevitable, art-statement suicide of Kurt Cobain; Joni Mitchell through the introspective maidens of Lilith Fair; and the Who through punk music, its roaring, unrestrained, auto-destructive elevation of spirit superseding the need for even melody, harmony, or arrangement. For these rock prototypes, the imitators are legion, whereas their direct emanations reverberate through the entire classic rock era, and continue now into the new millennium in various, ever evolving forms.

As for the Beatles, they have been emulated, to some degree, by nearly every musician and composer in their wake, and they remain the modern musical and cultural template for ultimate creativity, broad appeal, ubiquitous fame, and enduring influence. Significantly, they defined the very concept of "band," i.e. *inclusion*, and not just once, but twice. With their appearance on *Ed Sullivan*, they indelibly exemplified the very nature of a self-contained rock group; with *Sgt. Pepper's Lonely Hearts Club Band*, they expanded into the realm of pure vibration, associating that concept with a transformed image of themselves and an all-embracing invitation to realize the redemptive power of love. In these ways, the Beatles, as a mythic allegory singing the music of love, incarnated, transfigured, resurrected, and ultimately ascended in the 1960s through archetypal sound and symbol.

Certainly, the mythic implication of their own phenomenon was not lost on the Beatles themselves. In a deeply telling interview in May 1968, Lennon and McCartney spoke with radio host Mitchell Krauss on his public television program *Newsfront*, where they waxed insightfully about their mythic status, reminding listeners that they too were searching for answers and truth. Concerning their recent pilgrimage to India, John offered, "We had a false impression of Maharishi, the way people do of us.... We were looking for it and superimposed it on him...waiting for a guru." When asked about the responsibility they feel regarding the Beatles' influence, Paul explained that the ethical challenges they face are universal: "You know, you've got your life and you're faced with choices in it...we've got a choice of doing what either most people do, which is just making more and more money, and getting more and more rich and famous...or trying to DO something which will help." He then speculated, "Everyone needs someone to say 'this is how you do it'...it would be great if we knew how you do it. We make guesses, but they're not always right. They're often wrong, in fact. It would be great if we knew, because we're in a good position to say to all the people, 'This is how you do it.' Because there's so many phony institutions saying, 'And this is how you do it!' Nobody can believe them anymore." To which John quipped, "Well, it would have to be Jesus, or Buddha, or something. But they don't seem to be around at the moment."[5]

To the end of his life, John freely discussed his unique societal role with candor. In his and Yoko's *Playboy* interview shortly before his passing, he clarified, "I'm not claiming divinity. I've never claimed purity of soul. I've never claimed to have the answers to life. I only put out songs and answer questions as honestly as I can.... But I still believe in peace, love and understanding."[6] On the day of his death, in his last interview, he explained, "My role in society, or any artist's or poet's role, is to try and express what we all feel. Not to tell people *how* to feel. Not as a preacher, not as a leader, but as a reflection of us all."[7]

The creative process, according to Jung, consists of the "unconscious activation of an archetypal image and in elaborating and shaping this image into the finished work … the artist transforms it into the language of the present … educating the spirit of the age, conjuring up the forms in which the age is most lacking."[8] In 1958, soon after the big bang of rock & roll and yet before its mythic expression noticeably cohered, he sensed, "We are living in what the Greeks called the right time for a 'metamorphosis of the gods,' i.e. of the fundamental principles and symbols. This peculiarity of our time, which is certainly not of our conscious choosing, is the expression of the unconscious man within us who is changing."[9] Jung died in 1961; it is regretful he didn't live long enough to experience the emergence of the Beatles, as he may have recognized a mythic incarnation precisely in line with this perception.

According to Campbell, a valid mythology must fulfill four functions. It must (1) inspire a realization of a metaphysical, unifying energy behind the surface phenomena of the world; (2) mark the scientific evolution of its society, reflecting its knowledge and understanding of the universe; (3) maintain the values and moral code of its culture; and (4) guide the individual through the significant stages of life, from childhood to maturity to old age to death.[10]

Upon its arrival, the rock mythology promised fulfillment of all four of Campbell's functions. It (1) inspired a sense of transcendent energy and connectedness in its followers; (2) was a product of the technological and scientific evolution of its time; (3) maintained the moral code of the '60s counter-culture and broadcast that value system; and (4) marked the stages of life through song, story, and the real-life narratives of the artists.

Many communal mythologies (including Christianity as widely practiced in the United States) fail Campbell's second function. To be clear, the popular Christian idea of God and religion was fated to be irreconcilable with reason and scientific progress because it wasn't understood as metaphor, but instead as a factual account of the physical world. Its sense of validity therefore hinged on an ancient cosmology, and with every new scientific discovery the Western God's power was further weakened.

Art rises above this tendency to freeze the archetypal in time; it is a participation in the eternal without the attachment that its fruits remain so. Art allows for the evolving expression of the time-less without an accompanying demand that it be the only such definition accepted. It therefore avoids the human inclination to incarcerate truth in the existential prison of a petrified past or pre-destined future. Art may echo the past while intuiting the future, but in its very essence is always an expression of the present, align-ing it functionally with archetypal mythology as an evolutionary agent of transformation in the now.

Religious scholar Karen Armstrong draws a parallel between art and religious meaning: "A lot of the arguments about religion going on at the moment spring from a rather inept understanding of religious truth.... Our notion changed during the early modern period when we became convinced that the only path to any kind of truth was reason. That works beautifully for science but doesn't work so well for the humanities. Religion is really an art form."[11]

The religious fundamentalist may insist on the historical sup-position, and the skeptic may reject all that cannot be subject to or proven or negated by the scientific method; in the end they both share, along with all humanity, a far greater and deeper archetypal reality. Ignoring its existence only serves to separate us further from the message and meaning of the archetypes, usurping the individuation process through which we become ever-aligned with the potential of life as transcendent experience.

It is very difficult to look at the past with a vision uncolored by the lens of the present. Worshiping, as we often do now, a notion of scientific truth (which many laypeople hold on to despite the unsettlingly relativistic discoveries of the last hundred years of physics), we picture Egyptians, Greeks, Hebrews, and Indians of antiquity constructing their myths as we build our models of the universe. That is, we tend to imagine these ancient people creating myths to explain their place in the cosmos, rather than to assign a sense of purpose, beauty, and depth to something that is essentially mysterious.

Whether or not these myths were "real" is moot. They offer the underlying metaphors that provide the psychic infrastructure of our everyday reality, created out of human need for meaning and direction. Myth is more important precisely because it isn't "true." The malleability of mythic symbolism to meet the needs of every age and culture deems temporal occurrence as secondary at best, and often completely at odds with the fundamental message of the myth itself. In other words, temporal mythology is ephemeral, archetypal mythology eternal, and communal mythology always in danger of misinterpreting the meaning as it strives to constrain the archetypal in temporal terms.

Although communal mythologies fulfill a human need for community, positive recognition, and a reminder of truths—sometimes ageless, sometimes not—expressed by earlier cultures, the practice invariably becomes one of ritual rather than an active individuation process in accord with the spirit of one's own age. And, if this is true for the great religions, the logic also applies to the rock mythology. In fact, we can already see its psychic deflation in effect; the rock gods of the '60s, once the invigorating spiritual life-blood of their generation, now mere objects of worship to millions attempting to relive the past rather than welcome the archetypal present to spring and nourish once more.

Philosopher and religious scholar Jacob Needleman suggests: "What has been lost everywhere in the life of man is the confrontation within oneself of the two fundamental forces of the cosmic order: the movement of creation and the movement of return, the outer and the inner. The whole of what is known as 'progress' in the modern world may be broadly characterized as an imbalanced attention to the outward-directed force of life, combined with a false identification of the 'inner' as the realm of thought and emotion. The thoughts and emotions that are given the name of 'inwardness' actually serve, as has been shown, the movement outward and degradation of psychic energy. In Christian terms, this is 'flesh.' "[12]

If vibration (energy) can be understood as the channel for spirit, we are both receptor and reflector according to and through our experience of it, a process the Greeks referred to as *qualia*. Thus, the more open and expanded our personal vibration, the more receptive we become, the clearer our conductivity. As we've seen, the seemingly diametric approaches in the meditative practices of contemplative mystics and auto-annulling rituals of charismatics share the same ultimate objective: to empty oneself of material attachment and thought processes to clear the way for immersion within pure vibration.

The universal path to this spiritual destination, illuminated by savior gods from Krishna to Buddha to Jesus to the Beatles, is paved with *love*. A definition we employ in countless ways to describe various qualities of intimate experience, we often reduce our idea of love to an emotional response when it is really the allowance of vibratory expansion to witness one's connectivity with everything that is. In the Bhagavad-Gita, Krishna says, "Actions do not affect Me, and a reward for actions does not attract Me.... Only love can behold Me thus."[13]

Thaddeus Golas, in his *Lazy Man's Guide to Enlightenment*, provides this simple explanation: "Enlightenment is any experience of expanding our consciousness beyond its present limits. We could say that perfect enlightenment is realizing that we have no limits at all, and that the entire universe is alive.... Love is the highest and holiest action, because it always contains that which is not love within itself, it always and ever moves to include the unloving.... The higher the ratio of expansion to contraction in yourself, the more expanded and loving you are, the faster you vibrate."[14]

Vibration doesn't just tell the story. Vibration *is* the story. Everything is vibration—music is vibration, archetypal symbols are vibration, *we* are vibration. And beyond the vibratory physical realm in which we are all immersed, with its demonstrable or perceived contradictions and oppositions, there appears to be a universally accessible vibratory psychic realm consisting of symbols unrestrained by the duality—even, perhaps, the *physical laws*—of the temporal world. Mythology, by bringing this symbolic mindscape into the wake-a-day realm, provides a potential pathway to at least *imagining* the resolution of dualism in our physical reality. This is the primary function of both artistic and religious allegory: the manipulation of symbolic vibration until it approximates or suggests the transcendent energy of the archetypal unconscious.

Artists mirror us, but we, each and every one of us, contain the universal energy that the artist merely appropriates for our edification. The archetypes are already present within us; indeed, they *are* us. Further, we possess the ability to love, and are therefore pure potentiality incarnate. This is not an abstraction. Love is how we resolve both the duality of the temporal world and our own psychic discordance. Love is how we transcend all that is, including evil, suffering, division, judgment, even death. Love is the harmony of all existence available within human consciousness.

Could this be the revelation St. Paul experienced on the road to Damascus? Was this the understanding that led to his coherence of Christian philosophy and emphasis on gnosis? As Jung reminds, "St. Paul, for instance, was not converted to Christianity by intellectual or philosophical endeavor or by a belief, but by the force of his immediate inner experience."[15] Is it possible that he wasn't talking about a physical, historical event, that what he was expressing is ultimately too vast, too deep, and too eternal to be confined by temporal reality? That the revealed "Christ" is really the all-inclusive, ever-resurrecting, always present spirit of love available to us all? That everything—including the bottomless archetypal wellspring within our psychic purview—is ultimately resolved through love? If so, we are "saved," not by something outside or beyond ourselves, but by our ability to love.

Along with the original Christians, St. Paul's glimpse of this eternal truth manifested one of the most evocative and healing symbols in world history, and it reflected our highest ideals for centuries, offering hope, comfort, and inspiration. Dozens of generations have lived and died viewing Jesus Christ as their savior, either literally or symbolically, but like Demeter's wheat fields, most things on Earth run in cycles. Humanity will evolve, and its gods must evolve along with it, coming back around again in a new form relevant for each new age. As the human race's view of the universe changes, new incarnations of the savior god are needed.

The Beatles as a ubiquitous symbol of love may not last two thousand years—no mythology may ever again persist for the duration Jesus Christ has enthralled mass-consciousness (at least in recent history; Inanna/Ishtar/Astarte and Osiris would certainly be formidable contenders in the longevity sweepstakes)—but this isn't really applicable, because communication technology is rapidly evolving. It only took the Beatles a few years to create and inspire a global mythology with the depth and reach of a major religion. The faster and wider our communication capability, the more immediate, and perhaps short-lived as a result, the mythic imprint. In the end, given the mercurial nature of myth itself, it doesn't matter which "goes" first, Christianity or rock & roll, likewise who is more popular, Jesus or the Beatles. Mythology will still evolve.

Mythology exists not to define a god of the physical world, but rather to bring about our own cultural and personal transformation and growth, again and again. Therefore, the mythic gods (the only gods we can prove exist, and only then in an abstract state of conception) will always be in flux. As our scientific and philosophical understanding of the universe matures, as our ability to communicate expands, as our interaction with the physical world changes, as our cultural trends mark time, as our social agreements shift, as our old memes are replaced with new memes, so will our symbolic and conceptual representations of ourselves continue to reinvent, reflecting ancient mysteries through modern mirrors.

Our mythic archetypes are perpetually primed to illuminate our human experience, present the answers we ache for, and point our way forward—and they do this, like the good celebrities they are, by staying current. Remaining constant at their core, the archetypes adorn themselves with whatever costumes help them best fit into a given time and place. They can thereby continue to lead us down the evolutionary path while still connecting us with generations of the past, always reminding that love is all we need.

ACKNOWLEDGMENTS

All You Need is Myth: The Beatles and the Gods of Rock represents for me both a labor of love and a life's work, clichés perhaps, but in this case accurate ones. It was a labor of love because at its core love is what this book is about. The writing process demanded a decade of labor, requiring an immense amount of research and personal education. I may never again have the singular opportunity to delve so deeply into such a multi-layered topic of historical and contemporary import, one so dear to my heart for most of my life.

In the end, it took a village to manifest *All You Need is Myth*, and I was merely the midwife. The ideas and perspective contained here rely upon the work and insight of many writers and philosophers who precede this study, and the support, encouragement, and direct creative assistance of many more I am honored to call family, friends, and colleagues.

First, I thank my late father Bill, mother Jane, and sister Julia for showing me how love and family provide the basis for personal growth and that success and failure are concepts with little meaning when understanding and acceptance are the gifts from those closest to you. I thank Jack, my son, and Malinna, his mother, for their love and support in everything I do. Jack, you are the light of my life. I dedicate this book to you.

There are several individuals without whom this book, as it is, would not exist. I offer my deepest gratitude to those listed below for their support, hard work, and invaluable assistance:

Jade Sylvan—During a chance meeting at the San Francisco Art Exchange, I learned Jade was a writer and poet. I told them about the book I was writing, and they offered immediately to help with any aspect I needed, explaining that they had also been obsessed with the premise since their college years majoring in religious studies at Indiana University. We quickly developed a close creative connection and forged an early collaboration on what eventually became *All You Need is Myth.* Jade worked with me in various capacities for several years, bringing valuable insight and perspective in numerous areas. Their efforts and singular vision permeate this study. Thank you, Jade, for everything you've done to help manifest this work.

Dennis Willis—The ups and downs of a long creative partnership (like co-hosting and producing a television show, which we did for many years) can either inspire deep connection or challenge a friendship, and the former always prevailed for Dennis and me. He remains a champion of my work and has supported *All You Need is Myth* from the beginning, offering valuable editorial critique and producing and editing video that accompanies my lectures on the topic. Dennis, thanks for your diligent work on behalf of this project.

David Friedland—When looking at the careers of "successful" artists, one nearly always finds a benefactor behind the scenes, without whom the work would never come to fruition, much less find an audience. I have been blessed in my life with just such a friend and patron. It would be impossible to recount the many times David came to my rescue personally and financially. His belief in me carried me through many of my most difficult challenges, and his personal integrity and steadfast support has been vital to my life and work. David, you have my eternal gratitude. You are my superhero. You are my true brother.

Michael Gosney—San Francisco culture-shaper that he is, Michael has worked conscientiously on behalf of so many creative projects and high-minded initiatives in so many fields that his accomplishments cannot be summarized on this page. I have certainly been the beneficiary of his generosity; his support of my creative endeavors in general and this book particularly—both

194

philosophically and professionally—has been crucial to my work and career. I can recall so many evenings spent (mostly in his kitchen) discussing the theories explored in this book. Michael, your insights abound in these pages and I am grateful for your friendship, representation, and efforts to bring *All You Need is Myth* to the public.

Dave Randall—My closest friend and creative partner, and editor and illustrator of *All You Need is Myth*. From our early musical collaboration to our cross-country adventures to our continual dialog on, yes, the meaning of life, I can only say that Dave made the music come alive for me. A titan talent who seeks no recognition, true intellectual who judges no person, and man who gives tirelessly to everyone around him with no thought of reward, Dave is a beacon in this world, and angel to me. When I finished the manuscript, I turned to him for editing, structural analysis, and accuracy of content. The edit he provided polished many rough edges and deepened elements throughout, while his illustrations perfectly capture the book's archetypal content. Dave, thank you for everything but mostly for just being you, a friend like no other and a collaborator with whom I am humbled to share pen, paper, and piano.

Dr. Jonathan Young—As former assistant to Joseph Campbell and founding curator of the Joseph Campbell archives, Jonathan's encouragement fueled my commitment to the work and set a high academic bar. Thank you, Jonathan, for your foreword to *All You Need is Myth*. I am honored to share these pages with you.

Bill Gladstone—After its completion, Michael Gosney sent *All You Need is Myth* to Bill, and his Waterside Press in San Diego is now the book's publisher. After a decade of toil, it is exhilarating to have found such a sympathetic and enthusiastic home for the work. To Bill and everyone at Waterside, I offer my heartfelt thanks for your belief in this book.

I thank the following friends, teachers, and colleagues for their encouragement, support, and inspiration over the years: Kelly Mooney, Keith Mackie, Jeff LaBarge, Lisa Hannah, James Baggett,

Natalie Pelafos, Tony Schraut, Dr. Patrick Berger, Karin Scholz Grace, Dr. Harry James Cargas, Colleen Joern, Dallas Petersen, Kris & Lillian Lonborg, Pat Jones, Vince Atwell, The Backsliders (Dave Randall, Tod Hunter, Terry Burford, Ricky Wilson, Rob Wilpur, Pat Quinn, Steve Ozark, Keith Snyder, Steven D. Hunt, & Nick Kounas), Jeff Shibley, Ray Velasquez, Chuck Mead, Tony Combs, Joe Unger, Amy Bowyer McComb, Vadim Nemirovsky, Magenta Crow, Amy Miller, Josh Rosen, Kristy Simpson, Bob Haya, D'Este du Plessis, Laura Green, Amy Coffman, Jim Hartley, Theron Kabrich, the staff of the San Francisco Art Exchange (Cheryl, Marcie, Melissa, Elizabeth, Shannon, Ron, & Ed), Roger Dean, Storm Thorgerson, Jon Anderson, Esther Vela, Niels Mortenson, Stanford Lee, John LaBarber, Steve & Trudy Bhaerman, Alex Theory, Debra Michelle, Janice Pieroni, Caroluna Michelson, Eric Johnson, Marc Kasky, Dixie Gillaspie, Philip Penrose, Chris Winfield, Diana Maxwell, Jody Weiner, Kevin Renick, and Chet Helms.

Given the content of *All You Need is Myth*, I would be sorely remiss to not acknowledge the many writers and philosophers who provided its contextual foundation. The most difficult aspect of this book's creation was structural—how does one best tell this story? After toying with many potential ways of communicating the book's various ideas, I decided to let the true innovators in these fields speak for themselves. Indeed, my recognition that they seemed to be, in so many cases, pointing toward the same phenomenon from different academic viewpoints, gave me confidence that this was a book I could, and indeed must, take seriously. The names are too numerous to thank them all, but certainly include Carl Jung, Joseph Campbell, Mircea Eliade, Marshall McLuhan, Northrup Frye, Emile Durkheim, Marie-Louis von Franz, Guy Murchie, Elaine Pagels, Susan J. Douglas, Gerald Messadié, Hazrat Inayat Khan, Ken Wilbur, Karen Armstrong, Jacob Needleman, and Thaddeus Golas. Also, to the many outstanding Beatles and rock music biographers—Jonathan Gould, Bob Spitz, Hunter Davies, Barry Miles, Michael Frontani, Barney Hoskins, David Leaf, Dominic Priore, Peter Ames Carlin, Mark Wilkerson, and Philip Norman, among many others—and stalwart rock journalists—Anthony DeCurtis, Lester Bangs, Greil Marcus, Robert Christgau, Jonathan Lethem, and Jules Seigel, to name but a few—I offer thanks for your writings and perspectives.

There are three authors I would like to recognize for their direct influence—*All You Need is Myth* is unequivocally in their debt:

Ian MacDonald, whose book *Revolution in the Head: The Beatles' Records and the Sixties* sits atop the Beatles literary genre as its most essential tome, an acutely thought-provoking work that employs the Beatles' music and story as a springboard for razor-sharp social and historical commentary.

Elijah Wald, whose book *How the Beatles Destroyed Rock & Roll* provides the most incisive history and deconstruction to date of twentieth century popular music, uniquely insightful and written with impressive depth and style.

Dr. Richard Carrier, whose book *On the Historicity of Jesus: Why We May Have Reason for Doubt* is perhaps the most significant peer-reviewed study yet on the birth and growth of Christianity, an impeccably researched work offering vital perspective on the figure of Jesus Christ.

Finally, I would like to thank the musicians without whom our collective experience, much less this book, would lack a considerable substance. Indeed, for millions of people all over the world, our lives would be impossible to imagine without them.

It is important to note that our "rock gods" gave us much more than their music—they gave us their lives, in many cases literally. While we can relax in our lounge chairs and passively envy their fame, wealth, and talent, a merely cursory study of their personal stories reveals men and women of singular strength and fortitude willing to sacrifice everything for their art and vision. This has, of course, been the paradox for artists and philosophers for millennia, however, as I hope this book shows, the personal and emotional toll increased exponentially during the era of these artists particularly. Their various pitfalls, addictions, and in many cases physical deaths should remind us that they were human beings—uniquely gifted, soaring to tremendous commercial and artistic heights, and achieving rare recognition, yes—but in the end simply people laboring under immense social expectations and pressures. I imagine the air is very thin up there at such elevations. Their ability to maintain relevance to the greater community, mirror the experience of the commoner while living such uncommon lives, create meaningful art under such weight and distraction, and persist (even for a short time) as individuals—searching for truth and personal meaning just like the rest of us—is truly awe-inspiring.

And so, to (among many others) the Beatles, Elvis Presley, Bob Dylan, Brian Wilson, the Beach Boys, the Rolling Stones, Jim Morrison, the Doors, Jimi Hendrix, Grace Slick, Janis Joplin, Yoko Ono, Joni Mitchell, and the Who, I offer my endless respect and undying affection. Your efforts mattered more than perhaps you, and certainly we, have yet to fully grasp. It is my hope that *All You Need is Myth* will help us further understand the depth and breadth of your accomplishment.

SOURCES AND WORKS CITED

❧ ❧ ❧

Preface: More Popular Than Jesus.

1) McLuhan, Marshall. *The Book of Probes*. Gingko Press. 2001. p. 21.
2) Campbell, Joseph. *Thou Art That: Transforming Religious Metaphor*. New World Library. 2001. p. 8.
3) Jung, Carl. *Jung on Mythology*. Princeton University Press. 1998. p. 40.
4) Jung, Carl. *Collected Works: Archetypes and the Collective Unconscious*. Vol. 9. Princeton University Press. Tenth edition. 1990. pp. 42-43.
5) Frye, Northrup. *Notebooks: Lectures on the Bible and Other Religious Texts – 1912–1991*. Collected Works, vol. 13. University of Toronto Press. 2003.
6) Jung, Carl. *Collected Works: Psychological Types – Vol. 6*. Princeton University Press. 1976. para. 80.
7) Frye, Northrop. *Late Notebooks: Architecture of the Spiritual World – 1982–1990*. Collected Works, Vol. 2. University of Toronto Press. 2002. p. 716.
8) *Beatles Anthology*. DVD. Liner notes.
9) Campbell, Joseph. *The Hero with 1,000 Faces*. Princeton University Press. Second edition. 1968. p, 382.
10) Campbell, Joseph. *The Hero with 1,000 Faces*. Princeton University Press. Second edition. 1968. p. 3.
11) "The Beatles 'bigger than Jesus' on Google." *The Telegraph*. September 21, 2009.
12) "Vatican forgives The Beatles for 'bigger than Jesus' comment." *The Telegraph*. April 11, 2010.

Chapter 1: Roll Over, Jehovah

1) "Early Humans lived in PNG highlands 50,000 years ago." *Reuters*. September 30, 2010.
2) "Cargo Cult lives on in South Pacific." *BBC News*. February 17, 2007.

3) Robbins, Joel. "Becoming Sinners: Christianity and Desire among the Urapmin of Papua New Guinea." Journal of Ethnology, Vol. 37, No. 4. Autumn 1998. University of Pittsburgh. p. 299-316.

4) Carrier, Richard. *On the Historicity of Jesus: Why We May Have Reason for Doubt.* Sheffield Phoenix Press. 2014. p. 159-163.

5) Haile Selassie Denies Divinity. 1967. https://www.youtube.com/watch?v= TZ4cvQlXMzg

6) "Rastafari at a Glance." *BBC News.* October 2, 2009.

7) 2 Esdras 7:28. KJV Bible.

8) Barnett, Michael. "The Many Faces of Rasta: Doctrinal Diversity within the Rastafari Movement." Caribbean Quarterly, Number 51. June 2005. p. 67–78.

9) Jung, Carl. *Collected Works: Archetypes of the Collective Unconscious,* Princeton University Press. Tenth printing. 1990. p. 153.

10) Dubois, Julie. "Peron Strives to Perpetuate Spirit of Eva." *Chicago Daily Tribune.* August 1, 1952.

11) Crassweller, Robert D. *Peron and the Enigmas of Argentina.* W.W. Norton & Co. 1987. p. 209-210.

12) Martínez, Tomás Eloy. "The Woman Behind the Fantasy: Prostitute, Fascist, Profligate—Eva Peron Was Much Maligned, Mostly Unfairly." *Time.* January 20, 1997.

13) McManners, John. "Latin America." *The Oxford Illustrated History of Christianity.* Oxford University Press. 2001. p. 440.

14) Jung, Carl. *Psychology of the Unconscious.* Princeton University Press. 1991.

15) Jung, Carl. *Memories, Dreams and Reflections.* Vintage Books. 1965. p. 210.

16) Vahanian, Gabriel. 1966. *The Death of God: The Culture of Our Post-Christian Era.* George Braziller, Inc: Third printing. 1966. p. 7.

17) *Time.* Friday, Oct. 22, 1965.

18) MacDonald, Ian. *Revolution in the Head: The Beatles' Records and the Sixties.* Chicago Review Press. Third edition. 2007. p. 29-30.

19) Jones, Landon Y. "Swinging 60s?" *Smithsonian Magazine.* January 2006.

20) MacDonald, Ian. *Revolution in the Head: The Beatles' Records and the Sixties.* Chicago Review Press. Third edition. 2007. p. 14.

Chapter 2: We'll Follow the Sun

1) Trust, Gary. "April 4, 1964: The Beatles make Hot 100 History." *Billboard.* April 4, 2012.

2) Frontani, Michael R. *The Beatles: Image and the Media.* University Press of Mississippi. 2007. p. 54.

3) Southall, Brian; Perry, Rupert. *Northern Songs: The True Story of the Beatles Song Publishing Empire.* Omnibus Press. 2006. p. 204.

4) Richards, Kevin. "The Beatles Smash Global Sales Records." *American Songwriter.* September 22, 2009.

5) Christman, Ed. "Beatles being paid directly in iTunes deal." *Reuters.* January 5, 2011.

6) "The Beatles' Songs are Played 50 Million Times." *The Daily Mail.* December 28, 2015.

7) Griggs, Brandon; Leopold, Todd. *CNN Business.* April 26, 2013.

8) Frontani, Michael R. *The Beatles: Image and the Media.* University Press of Mississippi. 2007. p. 14.

9) *Washington Post-Times Herald.* February 8, 1964.

10) *Los Angeles Times.* February 10, 1964.

11) *New York Times.* February 13, 1964.

12) "The Beatles are Coming." *Newsweek.* Feb 3, 1964.

13) "Bugs About Beatles." *Newsweek.* February 24, 1964.

14) "The Unbarbershopped Quartet." *Time.* February 21, 1964.

15) "Britons Succumb to Beatlemania." *New York Times Magazine.* December 1, 1963.

16) "Why the Girls Scream, Weep, Flip." *New York Times Magazine.* Feb 23, 1964.

17) "Beatlemania – The Most or the Worst?" *Senior Scholastic.* February 4, 1965.

18) "The Return of The Beatles." *Saturday Evening Post.* August 8, 1964.

19) *The Beatles Anthology.* San Francisco: Chronicle Books. 2000. p. 142-143.

20) John Lennon Interviews. https://www.youtube.com/watch?v=_JLOtvikKXc

21) *The Rolling Stone Illustrated History of Rock & Roll.* Random House. 1992. p. 212.

22) *How the Beatles Changed the World.* Documentary film. 2017.

23) "Introduction to the Beatles." *The Beatles Literary Anthology.* Plexus. 2004. p. 333.

24) Bangs, Lester. "Dandelions in the Air: The Withering Away of the Beatles." The Real Paper, number 23. April 1975.

25) Marcus, Greil. "Another Version of the Chair." *Read the Beatles.* Penguin. 2006. p. 78.

26) Sonneck, Oscar George Theodore. "Henrick Heine's Musical Feuilletons." The Musical Quarterly, Vol. 8. 1922. p. 457–58.

27) McLuhan, Marshall. 1967. "The Invisible Environment: The Future of an Erosion." Perspecta, Vol. 11. MIT Press. 1967. pp. 162-167.

28) McLuhan, Marshall; Powers, Bruce. *The Global Village*. Oxford University Press. 1989. p. 143.

29) McLuhan, Marshall; with McLuhan, Eric. *Laws of Media: The New Science*. University of Toronto Press. 1988. p. 48.

30) "Interview: Marshall McLuhan." *Playboy*. March 1969.

31) McLuhan, Marshall. *The Gutenberg Galaxy*. University of Toronto Press. 1962. p. 269.

32) Hall, Calvin S.; Nordby, Vernon J. *A Primer of Jungian Psychology*. New American Library. 1973. p. 117.

33) Smith, Huston. *Forgotten Truth*. Harper One. 1992. p. 40.

34) Eliade, Mircea. *The Sacred and the Profane*. Harcourt. 1959. p. 72.

35) Durkheim, Emile. *The Elementary Forms of Religious Life*. Free Press, Reprint edition. 1995. Ch. 1.

36) Durkheim, Emile. *The Division of Labor in Society*. Free Press, First edition. 2014. p. 79-80.

37) Durkheim, Emile. *On Suicide: A Study in Sociology*. Free Press, Reissue edition. 1997.

38) Jung, Carl. *Collected Works of C. G. Jung, Vol. 7: Two Essays in Analytical Psychology*. Princeton University Press. 2014. para. 234.

39) Stein, Murray. *Jungian Psychoanalyisis: Working in the Spirit of C. G. Jung*. Open Court. 2010. p. 25.

40) Eliade, Mircea. *The Sacred and the Profane*. Harcourt. 1959. p. 11.

41) Marchessault, Janine. *Marshall McLuhan*. Sage. 2005. p. 184.

42) "The 100 Greatest Entertainers." *Entertainment Weekly*. Special Edition: 10. September 2000.

43) Marshand, Philip. *Marshal McLuhan: The Medium and the Messenger*. MIT Press. 1998. p. 216.

Chapter 3: Sgt. Pepper's Magical Mystery School

1) George Lucas on the mythology of "Star Wars." http://billmoyers.com/content/mythology-of-star-wars-george-lucas/

2) Carrier, Richard. *On the Historicity of Jesus: Why We May Have Reason for Doubt*. Sheffield Phoenix Press. 2014. p. 58, 169-173

3) Mark 4:9-11. NIV Bible.

4) Cleave, Maureen. "How Does a Beatle Live?" *London Evening Standard*. March 4, 1966.

5) Matthew 26:64. NIV Bible.

6) Matthew 17:1-3. NIV Bible.

7) Andreopoulos, Andrea. *Metamorphosis: The Transfiguration in Byzantine Theology and Iconography.* St Vladimir's Seminary Press. 2005. p. 60-65.
8) John 20:26. NIV Bible.
9) Luke 24:31. NIV Bible.
10) Mark 16:12. NIV Bible.
11) John 20:17. NIV Bible.
12) MacDonald, Ian. *Revolution in the Head: The Beatles' Records and the Sixties.* Chicago Review Press: Third edition. 2007. p. 249.
13) Spitz, Bob. *The Beatles.* Little, Brown & Co. 2005. p. 697.
14) Gould, Jonathan. *Can't Buy Me Love.* Three Rivers Press. 2007. p. 420.
15) *The New Yorker.* June 24, 1967.
16) Wald, Elijah. *How the Beatles Destroyed Rock & Roll.* Oxford University Press. 2009. p. 236.
17) John 3:16. NIV Bible.
18) 1 John 4:8. NIV Bible.
19) MacDonald, Ian. *Revolution in the Head: The Beatles' Records and the Sixties.* Chicago Review Press, Third edition. 2007. p. 106.

Chapter 4: The Ballad of Yin and Yang

1) "Interview: John Lennon and Yoko Ono." *Playboy.* January 1981.
2) Shotton, Pete; Schaffner, Nicholas. *John Lennon: In My Life.* Stein & Day. 1983.
3) Spitz, Bob. *The Beatles.* Little, Brown & Co. 2005. p. 764.
4) Spitz, Bob. *The Beatles.* Little, Brown & Co. 2005. p. 834.
5) Yorke, Ritchie. "John, Yoko & Year One." *Rolling Stone.* February 7, 1969. # 21.
6) McLuhan, Marshall; McLuhan, Eric; Zingrone, Frank. *Essential McLuhan.* Basic Books. 1995. p. 237.
7) McLuhan, Marshall; McLuhan, Eric; Zingrone, Frank. "Letter to Harold Adam Innis. March 14, 1951." *Essential McLuhan.* Basic Books. 1995.
8) "John Lennon Squabbles with Church on Acorns." *New York Times.* July 17, 1968.
9) "John Lennon & Yoko Ono Launch Art Exhibition You Are Here." *The Beatles' Bible.* July 1, 1968. https://www.beatlesbible.com/1968/07/01/john-lennon-yoko-ono-launch-art-exhibition-you-are-here/
10) "Frost on Saturday." *London Weekend Television.* August 24, 1968.
11) John Lennon & Yoko Ono: Bagism Press Conference. March 31, 1969. http://www.beatlesinterviews.org/db1969.0331.beatles.html

12) "Plastic Ono Band live at Lyceum Ballroom, London." *The Beatles' Bible*. December 15, 1969. https://www.beatlesbible.com/1969/12/15/plastic-ono-band-live-lyceum- ballroom-london/

13) "John Lennon & Yoko Ono's 'War is Over' Campaign is Launched." *The Beatles' Bible*. December 15, 1969. https://www.beatlesbible.com/1969/12/15/john-lennon-yoko-ono-war-is-over-poster-campaign-launched/

14) *Beatles Anthology*. San Francisco: Chronicle Books. 2000. p. 263.

15) Unidentified newspaper clipping reproduced in "The Press" pamphlet included in Yoko Ono and John Lennon's boxed Wedding Album. Apple SMAX- 3361.

16) John Lennon radio interview with Tom Campbell and Bill Holley. KYA radio. 1969.

17) Kovarick, Bill. *Revolution in Communication: History from Guttenberg to the Digital Age*. Bloomsbury. Second Edition. 2015. Ch 6.

18) *Rolling Stone*. June 28, 1969.

19) Genesis 2:25. KJV Bible.

20) *Melody Maker*. September 20, 1969.

21) Christgau, Robert. "Double Fantasy: A Portrait of a Relationship." *The Ballad of John and Yoko*. Rolling Stone Press: Dolphin-Doubleday. First edition. 1982. p. 293.

22) Herrmann-Pfandt, Adelheid. "Yab Yum Iconography and the Role of Women in Tibetan Tantric Buddhism." The Tibet Journal. Vol. XXII, No. 1. Spring 1997. p. 12-34.

23) Gross, Rita. *A Garland of Feminist Reflections: Forty Years of Religious Reflection*. University of California Press: Berkeley. 2009. p. 207.

24) "Hieros gamos." *Encyclopedia Brittanica*. https://www.britannica.com/topic/hieros-gamos

25) Jung, Carl. *Memories, Dreams and Reflections*. Vintage Books. 1965. p. 395.

26) Devi, Kamala. *The Eastern Way of Love*. Simon & Schuster. April 1975. p. 19-27.

27) Gospel of Thomas. vs. 114. Pokomi, Petr. *A Commentary on the Gospel of Thomas: From Interpretations to the Interpreted*. A & C Black. 2009. p. 154.

28) "Pistis Sophia. First Book, Ch. 36." Meade, G.R. S. *Pistis Sophia: A Gnostic Gospel*. Book Tree. 2006. p. 47.

29) Gospel of Philip. *The Other Bible: Ancient Scriptures*. Harper San Francisco. 2005. p. 92.

30) Mark 16:5-10. NIV Bible.

31) Matthew 28:9-10. NIV Bible.

32) John 20:16-17. NIV Bible.

33) Haberman, Clyde. "Silent Tribute to Lennon's Memory is Observed." *The Ballad of John and Yoko*. Rolling Stone press. Dolphin/Doubleday. First edition. 1982. p. 207.

34) "Throughout the World." *The New York Times*. December 15, 1980.

35) John Lennon Archives 1968-69. DVD. Apple Films, Ltd., 2004.

36) "Interview: John Lennon and Yoko Ono." *Playboy*. January 1981.

37) *Yorkshire Evening Post*. August 22, 1968.

38) McCarry, Charles. *Esquire*. December 1970.

39) *People*. August 22, 1988.

40) *Mother Jones*. June 1984.

41) *Larry King Live*. December 4, 1999.

42) DiLello, Richard. *The Longest Cocktail Party*. Mojo Books: Edinburgh, Scotland. 1972. p. 38.

43) Fricke, David. *Rolling Stone*. August 10, 2016.

44) Spitz, Bob. *The Beatles*. Little, Brown & Co. 2005. p. 777.

45) Toy, Vivian S. "A Brush with a Beatle." *New York Times*. March 7, 2010.

Chapter 5: The Long and Winding Myth

1) Miles, Barry. *Many Years from Now*. Henry Holt & Co. 1997. pp. 286-287.

2) MacDonald, Ian. *Revolution in the Head: The Beatles' Records and the Sixties*. Chicago Review Press: Third edition. 2007. p. 157.

3) MacDonald, Ian. *Revolution in the Head: The Beatles' Records and the Sixties*. Chicago Review Press: Third edition. 2007. p. 206.

4) Richards, Keith. *Life*. New York: Little, Brown and Company. 2010. p. 176.

5) Stewart, Jez. "The lesser-spotted British animated feature." *Film Forever*. February 12, 1982. https://www.bfi.org.uk/news-opinion/ bfi-news/lesserspotted-british-animated-feature-film

6) Hieronymus, Robert R. "Hidden Meanings in the Yellow Submarine." *Octopus's Garden*. February 12, 1982. http://21stcenturyradio.com/yellowsub/articles/secret.htm

7) Hieronymus, Robert R. "Symbolic and Mythological Interpretations of Yellow Submarine." 2001. http://www.21stcenturyradio.com/YS/ symbolmythointerp.html

8) "100 Greatest Beatles Songs." *Rolling Stone*. September 19, 2011.

9) *Yellow Submarine*. Special feature: "The Mod Odyssey." MGM Home Entertainment. DVD. 1999.

10) Adler, Renata. *New York Times*. November 14, 1968.

11) *Beatles Book Monthly.* February 1967.

12) Womack, Kenneth. *The Beatles Encyclopedia: Everything Fab Four.* ABC-CLIO. 2016. p. 387.

13) *Life.* November 7, 1969.

14) "The 'Paul is Dead' Myth." *The Beatles' Bible.* https://www.beatlesbible.com/features/paul-is-dead/

15) Carrier, Richard. *On the Historicity of Jesus; Why We May Have Reasons for Doubt.* Sheffield Phoenix Press. 2014. pp. 81-88; 137-141; 200-2005.

16) Romans 15:4; Romans 16: 25-26; Galatians 1:11-12. NRSV Bible.

17) Reeve, Andru J. *Turn Me on Dead Man: The Beatles and the "Paul is Dead" Hoax.* AuthorHouse. 2004. pp. 277-278.

18) Bordia, Preshant; Difonzo, Nicholas. "Problem Solving in Social Interactions on the Internet: Rumor as Social Cognition." Research Article. March 1, 2004.

19) Noymer, Andrew. "The Transmission and Persistence of Urban Legends." Research Article. April 26, 2001.

20) Hornung, Erik. *The Ancient Egyptian Books of the Afterlife.* Cornell University Press. 1999. pp. 38, 77-78.

21) Jung, Carl. *Collected Works of C. G. Jung: Mysterium Coiunctonis.* Vol. 14. Routledge. 2014. para. 513.

22) Buckley, Peter. *The Rough Guide to Rock.* Rough Guides Illustrated. 2003. p. 83.

23) "Abbey Road." *The Beatles' Bible.* https://www.beatlesbible.com/albums/abbey-road/4/

24) Cocks, Jay. *Time.* December 22, 1980.

Chapter 6: The Fab Four Elements

1) Koestler, Arthur. *The Act of Creation.* MacMillan. 1969. p. 342.

2) Danesi, Marcel. *The Quest for Meaning: A Guide to Semiotic Theory and Practice.* University of Toronto Press. 2007. pp. 123-127.

3) Frontani, Michael R. *The Beatles: Image and the Media.* University Press of Mississippi. 2007. p. 7.

4) Berg, Charles. "The Unconscious Significance of Hair." Essay. Allen & Unwin. 1951.

5) Leach, Edmund. "Magical Hair." Essay. 1958.

6) Judges. 13-16. NIV Bible.

7) Jung, Carl. *Collected Works, Vol. 9. Part 1: The Archetypes and the Collective Unconscious.* Princeton University Press: Tenth printing. 1990. p. 364.

8) Revelation. 1:3. NIV Bible.

9) Davies, Evan. Journal of the History of Ideas, Vol. 30, No. 2. April – June 1968. p. 273-280.

10) Douglas, Susan J. *Where the Girls Are: Growing up Female with the Mass Media.* Three Rivers Press. Reprint edition. 1995. pp. 116-119.

11) Douglas, Susan J. *Where the Girls Are: Growing up Female with the Mass Media.* Three Rivers Press. Reprint edition. 1995. p. 149.

12) Campbell, Duncan. "Jesus 'healed using cannabis.'" *The Guardian.* January 6, 2003.

13) "Jesus used cannabis oil to perform healing miracles, claims controversial expert." *Deccan Chronicle.* July 3, 2018. https://www.deccan-chronicle.com/lifestyle/viral-and-trending/030718/jesus-used-cannabis-oil-to-perform-healing-miracles-claims-controvers.html

14) Monier-Williams, Monier. *A Sanskrit-English Dictionary.* Oxford University Press. 2001. p. 1137.

15) Rig Veda. 8.43.3

16) "Rites & Ceremonies." *Encyclopedia Britannica.* 1991. p. 789.

17) Simha, Rakesh Krishnan. "How Russian scientists cracked the secret of a Vedic ritual drink." *Russia Beyond.* January 9, 2017.

18) Burket, Walter. *Greek Religion.* Harvard University Press. 1985. p. 285.

19) Brusco, Robert. "Tripping Through Time: The Fascinating History of the Magic Mushroom." *Ancient Origins.* February 1, 2017. https://www.ancient-origins.net/history-ancient-traditions/tripping-through-time-fascinating-history-magic-mushroom-007474

20) Wasson, R. Gordon; Hoffman, Albert; Ruck, Carl. *The Road to Eleusis: Unveiling the Secret of the Mysteries.* Harcourt, Brace, Jovanovich. 1978.

21) Ruck, Carl; Staples, Blaise Daniel; Heinrich, Clark. *The Apples of Apollo: Pagan and Christian Mysteries of the Eucharist.* Carolina Academic Press. 2001.

22) Pinch, Geraldine. *Egyptian Mythology: A Guide to the Gods, Goddesses, and Traditions of Ancient Egypt.* Oxford University Press. 2004. pp. 131-132.

23) Berlant, SR. "The entheomycological origin of Egyptian crowns and the esoteric underpinnings of Egyptian religion." Journal of Ethnopharmacology, Number 102. 2005. p. 275-288.

24) Budge, E.A. Wallis. *The Gods of the Egyptians.* Dover Publications. 1969. p. 164.

25) Hadith. Book 23, #5084.

26) Numbers 11:9. NRSV Bible.

27) Exodus 16:35. NRSV Bible.

28) John 6:51. AKJV Bible

29) Matthew 6:22 AKJV Bible.

30) Matthew 6:22 NRSV Bible

31) Harrison, George. *I, Me, Mine*. Simon & Shuster. 1980. p. 118.

32) MacDonald, Ian. "The Psychedelic Experience." *MOJO*. Special Limited Edition. March 2002.

33) MacDonald, Ian. *Revolution in the Head: The Beatles' Records and the Sixties*. Chicago Review Press. Third edition. 2007. p. 150.

34) Brown, Peter; Gaines, Steven. *The Love You Make: An Insider's Story of The Beatles*. New York: New American Library. 2002. pp. 171-172.

35) Fonda, Peter. *Don't Tell Dad: A Memoir*. New York: Hyperion. 1998. pp. 207-209.

36) "The New Far-Out Beatles." *Life*. June 16, 1967.

37) *Beatles Anthology*. San Francisco: Chronicle Books. 2000. pp. 177-179.

38) Giuliano, Geoffrey. *The Lost Beatle Interviews*. Copper Square Press. 2002. p. 106.

39) Allison, Dale Jr. *The Love There That's Sleeping: The Art and Spirituality of George Harrison*. Continuum. 2006. p. 144.

40) "Interview: John Lennon and Yoko Ono" *Playboy*. January 1981.

41) Luke 1:31. NRSV Bible.

42) Matthew 1:21. NRSV Bible.

43) "The British Are Coming! The British Are Coming!" *Pop Chronicles*. Episode 27. 1969-1976.

44) Guthrie, Kenneth Sylvan. *Pythagorean Sourcebook*. Planes Press. 1987. p. 94.

45) Plato. *Republic*. VII.XII.

46) Jones, Marie D.; Flaxman, Larry. *11:11 The Time Prompt Phenomenon: The Meaning Behind Mysterious Signs, Sequences and Synchronicities*. Red Wheel. 2009. p. 132.

47) Lao-Tzu. *Tao Te Ching*. Ch. 42.

48) Lennon, John. *Skywriting by Word of Mouth*. Harper and Rowe. 1986. p. 18.

49) Wenner, Jan.; Lennon, John. *Lennon Remembers*. Verso. 2001. p. 133.

50) *Beatles Anthology*. San Francisco: Chronicle Books. 2000. p. 72.

51) *The Beatles Biggest Secrets*. Documentary film. 2007.

52) Jung, Carl. *Psychology and Religion*. Yale University Press. 1938. p. 71.

53) Jung, Carl. *Man and His Symbols*. Doubleday. 1964. p. 214.

54) Jung, Carl. "The Structure and Dynamics of the Self." *Collected Works of C. G. Jung*. Volume 9, Part 2. Princeton University Press. 2014. p. 224.

Chapter 7: The Inner Grooves

1) "Elvis is Everywhere." *The New York Times*. August 16, 2007.

2) von Franz, Marie-Louise. *Creation Myths*. Shambhala, Revised edition. 1995. p. 5.

3) Campbell, Joseph. *Thou Art That: Transforming Religious Metaphor*. Novato, California: New World Library. 2001. p. 50.

4) 1 Corinthians 15:45. NRSV Bible.

5) Quotes on Elvis Presley. https://en.wikiquote.org/wiki/Elvis_Presley

6) Whitmer, Peter O. *The Inner Elvis: A Psychological Biography of Elvis Aaron Presley*. Hyperion. 1996. pp. 67, 101.

7) Mark 1:1-3. NRSV Bible.

8) Matthew 3: 18-25. NRSV Bible.

9) Luke 1: 26-38. NRSV Bible.

10) Luke 2: 8-14. NRSV Bible.

11) Luke 1: 5-20, 39-45. NRSV Bible.

12) Luke 3:16. NRSV Bible.

13) *Beatles Anthology*. DVD. 2003.

14) Davies, Hunter. *The Beatles Authorized Biography*. McGraw-Hill. 1968. p. 19.

15) Dylan, Bob. *Chronicles*. Simon & Schuster. 2004. p. 236.

16) Dylan, Bob. *Chronicles*. Simon & Schuster. 2004. p. 116.

17) Dylan, Bob. *Chronicles*. Simon & Schuster. 2004. p. 219.

18) Dylan, Bob. *Chronicles*. Simon & Schuster. 2004. p. 118.

19) Gates, David. "Dylan Revisited" *Newsweek*. Oct 6, 1997.

20) Lethem, Jonathan. "The Genius of Bob Dylan." *Rolling Stone*. Aug 21, 2006.

21) List of Beach Boys Top-40 singles. https://en.wikipedia.org/wiki/The_Beach_Boys_discography

22) Jung, Carl. *The Archetypes of the Collective Unconscious*. Princeton University Press: Paperback printing. 1990. pp. 161, 178.

23) Eliot, Samuel. *Journals and Other Documents on the Life and Voyages of Christopher Columbus*. Morison, Heritage Press.1963. p. 291.

24) Description of Shambhala in ancient texts. http://en.wikipedia.org/wiki/Zhang_Zhung

25) Fic, Victor M. *The Tantra*. Abhinav Publications. 2003. p. 49.

26) Description of Shambhala in ancient texts. http://en.wikipedia.org/wiki/Shambhala

27) Revelation 21. NRSV Bible.

28) Description of Beach Boys harmonies. https://www.allmusic.com/artist/the-beach-boys-mn0000041874/biography

29) Quotes about the Beach Boys. http://www.brianwilson.com/quotes/

30) Hoskins, Barney. *Waiting for the Sun*. Backbeat Books. 2009. p. 65.

31) Desowitz, Bill. *IndieWire*. December 28, 2015.' "

32) Surah 47:12; Quran.

33) Surah 47:15; Quran.

34) John 5:1-18. NRSV Bible.

35) John: 4:14. NRSV Bible.

36) Uebel, Michael. *Ecstatic Transformation: On the Uses of Alterity in the Middle Ages*. Palgrave/Macmillan. 2005. pp. 119-120.

37) Revelation 21:18 NRSV Bible.

38) *Brian Wilson: Songwriter*. Documentary film. 2010.

39) Wald, Elijah. *How the Beatles Destroyed Rock & Roll*. Oxford University Press. 2009. p. 229.

40) Priore, Domenic. *The Story of Brian Wilson's Lost Masterpiece Smile*. Sanctuary. 2005. p. 62.

41) Jung, Carl. *Answer to Job*. Meridian. Ninth printing. 1970. p. 83.

42) Carlin, Peter Ames. *Catch a Wave: The Rise, Fall & Redemption of the Beach Boys' Brian Wilson*. Rodale. 2006. pp. 10-11.

43) Luke 2:46-47. NKJV Bible.

44) Infancy Gospel of Thomas: 19:1-12. *The Other Bible: Ancient Scriptures*. Harper San Francisco. 2005. p. 400.

45) Jung, Carl. *Answer to Job*. Meridian. Ninth printing. 1970. p. 92.

46) Carlin, Peter Ames. *Catch a Wave: The Rise, Fall & Redemption of the Beach Boys' Brian Wilson*. Rodale. 2006. p. 43.

47) *Pet Sounds*. Box Set booklet. p. 61.

48) *Beautiful Dreamer: Brian Wilson and the Story of Smile*. Documentary film. 2004.

49) Gould, Jonathan. *Can't Buy Me Love*. Three Rivers Press. 2007. pp. 371, 377.

50) Seigel, Jules. "Goodbye Surfing, Hello God." *Cheetah*. October 1967.

51) Jung, Carl. *The Archetypes of the Collective Unconscious*. Princeton University press. 1990. P. 170.

52) Dillon, Mark. *Fifty Sides of the Beach Boys: The Songs That Tell Their Story*. ECW Press. 2012. p. 73.

53) MacDonald, Ian. *Revolution in the Head: The Beatles' Records and the Sixties*. Chicago Review Press. Third edition. 2007. p. 215.

54) Granata, Charles L. *I Just Wasn't Made for These Times: Brian Wilson and the Making of the Beach Boys' Pet Sounds*. London: Unanimous. 2003. p. 17.

Chapter 8: Standing in the Shadow

1) Job 1:7-12. NRSV Bible
2) 1 Samuel 16:14 NRSV Bible
3) Jubilees 10:8-9; 17:15-16; 18:9. Box, George Herbert. *The Book of Jubilees: Or the Little Genesis*. Society for Promoting Christian Knowledge. 1917. pp. 80, 108-110.
4) Vedidad: Fargard 19.1-8. *The Zend-Avesta, Volume 4*. Clarendon Press. 1880. pp. 204-206.
5) Massadie, Gerald. *A History of the Devil*. Kodansha International. 1996. p. 77.
6) Coleman, Ray. *Melody Maker*. March 14, 1964.
7) Fornatale, Peter. *50 Licks: Myths and Stories from Half a Century of the Rolling Stones*. Bloomsbury. 2013. p. 45.
8) McMillian, John. "Beatles or Stones?" *Believer*. Issue 45. June 1, 2007. https://believermag.com/beatles-or-stones/
9) *Crossfire Hurricane*. Documentary film. 2012.
10) Kern, Edward. "The People's War." *Life*. Vol. 67, Number 18. October 17, 1969. p. 77.
11) "On Luther's Love for and Knowledge of Music." *The Musical World*. Vol VII, No. 83. Oct 13, 1837.
12) Norman, Phillip. *Sympathy for the Devil: The Rolling Stones Story*. Simon & Shuster. 1984. p. 227.
13) *San Francisco Chronicle*. June 9, 1972.
14) *San Francisco Examiner*. June 7, 1972.
15) *Billboard*. June 24, 1972.
16) *Grapevine*. August 1972.
17) *Washington Post*. July 5, 1972.
18) Norman, Phillip. *Sympathy for the Devil: The Rolling Stones Story*. Simon & Schuster. 1984. p. 91.
19) Coscacorelli, Joe. "The Art of the Rolling Stones: Behind That Zipper and That Tongue." *New York Times*. June 7, 2015.
20) Luke 10:18. NRSV Bible
21) Rev 12: 7-10 NRSV Bible
22) Isaiah 14: 12. KJV Bible.
23) Pagels, Elaine. *The Origin of Satan*, XVII. Vintage Books: Paperback edition. 1995.
24) Jung, Carl. "The Philosophical Tree." *Collected Works of C. G. Jung, Vol. 13: Alchemical Studies*. Princeton University Press. 2014. para. 464.
25) Jung, Carl. *Memories, Dreams, Reflections*. Chapter XII: Late Thoughts. Vintage Books. 1965. p. 329.

26) Gospel of Thomas. Saying 70. *The Other Bible: Ancient Scriptures.* Harper San Francisco. 2005. p. 305.

27) Matthew 4:8-9; Luke 10:17-18; James 4:4; Romans 8:7; 1 John 5:19; Ephesians 2:2. NRSV Bible.

28) *The Story of the Guitar: Complete Three-Part Documentary.* Pete Townshend. http://www.openculture.com/2012/08/story_of_the_guitar.html

29) Inuit Shaman image. https://commons.wikimedia.org/wiki/File:Yupik_shaman_Nushagak.jpg

30) Demonstration of the tri-tone, known as the "Devil's Interval." https://www.youtube.com/watch?v=j7zrS0Y-JMA

31) McDermott, John; Kramer, Eddie. *Hendrix: Setting the Record Straight.* Warner Books. 1992. p. 2.

32) Shapiro, Harry; Glebbeek, Caesar. *Jimi Hendrix: Electric Gypsy.* St. Martin's Press. 1991. p. 366.

33) Elidae, Mircea. *The Sacred and the Profane.* Harcourt: Harvest. 1959. pp. 53, 54, 149.

34) George, Gordon N; Byron; *Don Juan, Cantos iii, iv, and v, by Lord Byron.* Canto IV, Stanza 12. Ulan Press. 2012. p. 131.

35) Frank Lisciandro on Jim Morrison's fascination with death: https://www.youtube.com/watch?v=cf0WtrvYd9Q

36) Revelation 6:7-8 NRSV Bible.

37) The Doors interviewed by Mike Lazar & Steve Flesser at Pierce College, Oswego, New York, September 11, 1967. https://www.youtube.com/watch?v=OlICbl26ZGU

38) James, Lizzie. "Jim Morrison: Ten Years Gone." *Creem.* Special edition. 1981.

39) Jim Morrison interviewed by Salli Stevenson for *Circus*, October 13, 1970. https://archives.waiting-forthe-sun.net/Pages/Interviews/JimInterviews/circus.html

40) Roby, Steven; Schreiber, Brad. *Becoming Jimi Hendrix: From Southern Crossroads to Psychedelic London, the Untold Story of a Musical Genius.* Da Capo. 2010. p. 184.

41) *Rolling Stone.* September 17, 1981.

42) Warner, Jay. *Notable Moments of Women in Rock.* Hal Leonard Publishing. 2008. p. 164.

43) Slick, Grace. *Somebody to Love? A Rock-and-Roll Memoir.* Warner Books. 1998. p. 192.

44) Grace Slick on *The Donny and Marie Show.* October 22, 1998. https://www.youtube.com/watch?v=5Gr2jryiqOM

45) Eliade, Mircea. *Shamanism: Archaic Techniques of Ecstasy*. Pantheon Books. 1964. pp. 3-7.

46) Guiley, Rosemary. *The Encyclopedia of Witches, Witchcraft, and Wicca*. Checkmark Books. 2008. p. 223.

47) Godwin, William. *Lives of the Necromancers*. Harvard Collection. 1876. p. 12.

48) Plutarch. "The Obsolescence of Oracles." *Moralia, Vol. 5*. Loeb Classical Library: Harvard University Press. 1936. pp. 347-501.

49) Broad, William. *The Oracle: Ancient Delphi and the Science Behind Its Lost Secrets*. Penguin. 2007. pp. 194-195.

50) H.V. Harissis. "A Bittersweet Story: The True Nature of the Laurel of the Oracle of Delphi." Perspectives in Biology and Medicine. Vol. 57, Number 3. Summer 2014. 295-298.

51) Stone, Merlin. *When God was a Woman*. Mariner Books. 1978.

52) Janis Joplin quotes. http://www.janisjoplin.net/life/quotes/

53) Hendrickson, Paul. "Janis Joplin: A Cry Cutting Through Time." *Washington Post*. May 5, 1998.

54) *Hit Parader*. September 1, 1970.

55) Heraclitus (of Ephesus). *Fragments*. # 92. University of Toronto Press. 1991.

56) Comfort, David. *The Rock and Roll Book of the Dead*. Citadel Press. 2009. pp. 2, 94.

Chapter 9: Pure and Easy

1) Bego, Mark. *Joni Mitchell*. Taylor Trade. 2005. p. 82.

2) "Joni Mitchell: A Life Story—Woman of Heart and Mind." Documentary film. *American Masters*. Season 17, episode 5. 2003.

3) Weller, Sheila. *Girls Like Us*. Atria Books: First edition. 2008. pp. 282-283.

4) Weller, Sheila. *Girls Like Us*. Atria Books: First edition. 2008. p. 274.

5) Weller, Sheila. *Girls Like Us*. Atria Books: First edition. 2008. p. 280.

6) *Rolling Stone*. February 4, 1971.

7) *Rolling Stone*. February 3, 1972.

8) Juvenal. Satires, XIV. 321.

9) Jung, Carl. "Answer to Job." translated by R.F.C. Hull. *Collected Works*. Volume 11. London: Routledge and Kegan Paul. 1954. pp. 153-163.

10) Wendlinder, Anastasia. *Speaking of God in Thomas Aquinas and Meister Eckhart: Beyond Analogy*. Ashgate. 2014. pp. 5-6.

11) Murchie, Guy. *The Seven Mysteries of Life*. Mariner Books. 1999. p. 6.

12) "Who's Birdman Pecks Beach Boy." *Disc and Music*. September 17, 1966.

13) *Amazing Journey: The Story of the Who*. Documentary film. 2007.

14) Green, Andy. "Who's Done? Pete Townshend's Ambivalent Farwell." *Rolling Stone*. May 7, 2015.

15) *The Kids Are Alright*. Documentary film. 1979.

16) Romans: 8:13. NRSV Bible.

17) Egan, Harvey D. *An Anthology of Christian Mysticism*. Meister Eckhart Texts. Pueblo Books: Second edition. 1991. p. 300.

18) *The Real Keith Moon*. Documentary film. Biography 6.

19) Blake, Mark. *Pretend You're in a War. The Who and the Sixties*. Aurum Press. 2015.

20) Pete Townshend discusses *Tommy*. https://www.thestar.com/entertainment/stage/2013/05/17/pete_townshend_talks_about_the_whos_tommy.html

21) Sanders, Rick; Dalton, David. "Pete and Tommy, Among Others." *Rolling Stone*. July 12, 1969.

22) Wilkerson, Mark. *Amazing Journey: The Life of Pete Townshend*. Bad News Press. 2006. pp. 162-163.

23) *New Musical Express*. August 21, 1971.

24) Townshend, Pete. "In Love with Meher Baba." *Rolling Stone*. November 26, 1970.

25) Khan, Hazrat Inayat. *The Music of Life*. Shambhala. 1996.

26) Iannone, E. Pablo. *Dictionary of World Philosophy*. Taylor and Francis. 2001. p. 30.

27) *Encyclopedic Dictionary of Buddhism*. Sarup & Sons. p. 653.

28) Acts 2:2. NRSV Bible.

29) Luke 3:22 NRSV Bible.

30) John 1:1. NRSV Bible.

31) Taittiriya Upanishads. Ch. 8.

32) Chandogya Upanishads. Ch. 1.

33) Wilkerson, Mark. *Amazing Journey: The Life of Pete Townshend*. Bad News Press. 2006. pp. 156-157.

34) Collins, Steven. *Selfless Persons: Imagery and Thought in Theravada Buddhism*. Cambridge University Press. 1990. p. 4.

35) Wilber, Ken. *A Brief History of Everything*. Shambhala: Second edition. 2000. p. 179.

36) Wilkerson, Mark. *Amazing Journey: The Life of Pete Townshend*. Bad News Press. 2006. p. 164.

37) Wilkerson, Mark. *Who Are You: The Life of Pete Townshend.* Omnibus. 2009. p. 154.

38) Wilkerson, Mark. *Amazing Journey: The Life of Pete Townshend.* Bad News Press. 2006. p. 181.

39) Swenson, John. "The Who Puts the Bomp." *Crawdaddy.* December 5, 1971.

Chapter 10: Conclusion

1) Jung, Carl. *Collected Works – Vol 9: Archetypes of the Collective Unconscious.* Princeton University Press: Tenth printing. 1990. p. 367.

2) Jung, Carl. *Man and His Symbols.* Doubleday. 1969. p. 224.

3) Jung, Carl. *Jung on Christianity.* Princeton University Press. 2012. p. 194.

4) Jung, Carl. *Answer to Job: The Problem of Evil: Psychological and Religious Origin.* Meridian. Ninth printing. 1970. p. 199.

5) John Lennon and Paul McCartney interviewed by Mitchell Krauss on *Newsfront.* http://www.beatlesinterviews.org/db1968.0514.beatles.html

6) "Interview: John Lennon and Yoko Ono." *Playboy.* January 1981.

7) John Lennon interviewed by Dave Sholin for KFRC Radio, San Francisco. December 8, 1980.

8) Jung, Carl. "On the Relation of analytical Psychology to Poetry." *Collected Works 15: Spirit in Man, Art and Literature.* Princeton University Press. 1966. pp. 82-83.

9) Jung, Carl. *The Undiscovered Self.* New American Library. 2014. p. 123.

10) Joseph Campbell Lectures II.1.1: The Function of Myth. Given at the Esalen Institute in August 1969.

11) Armstrong, Karen; Brunton, Michael. "The Reason of Faith." *Ode.* September – October 2009.

12) Needleman, Jacob. *Lost Christianity: A Journey of Rediscovery to the Centre of Christian Experience.* Doubleday. 1980. p. 222.

13) Bhagavad-Gita. 4:14; 11:54.

14) Golas, Thaddeus. *The Lazy Man's Guide to Enlightenment.* Bantam. 1972. pp. 24, 25, 55.

15) Jung, Carl, *Selected Letters of C. G. Jung: 1909-1961.* Princeton University Press. 2014. p. 128.

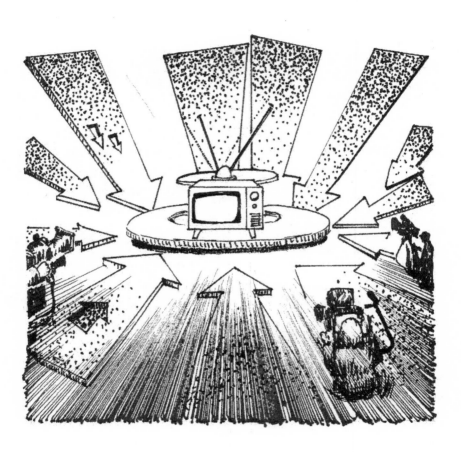

AUTHOR BIOGRAPHY

A veteran San Francisco media personality, Steve Wagner is a member of the San Francisco Film Critic's Circle and was co-host, writer, and executive producer of the Bay Area television programs *Reel Life* and *Filmtrip*. He was the featured weekly film critic on KFRC Classic Rock FM 99.7 and KKSF Talk AM 910 in San Francisco, and broadcast host for the California Music Awards (Bammies). In all, he has reviewed over one thousand films and interviewed over three hundred actors, directors, writers, and musicians.

Throughout his twenties, Steve was lead vocalist and guitarist of the Backsliders, a touring rock band that performed over eight hundred shows and opened for many national acts, including: Cheap Trick, Three Dog Night, REO Speedwagon, Ozark Mountain Daredevils, Bad English, and Mick Taylor.

For a decade, Steve was a director of the San Francisco Art Exchange, a gallery specializing in rock & roll photography, collectables, and original album cover art. He has brokered sales of many of the world's most famous album cover original artworks, including: Hipgnosis's Pink Floyd album covers (*Dark Side of the Moon; Wish You Were Here; Animals; Ummagumma*); Iain Macmillan's *Abbey Road* photography; Michael Cooper's *Sgt. Pepper* photography; Robert Freeman's Beatles' album cover photography (*With the Beatles; Beatles for Sale; Rubber Soul*); Jerry Schatzberg's *Blonde on Blonde* photography; and numerous Yes album cover paintings and drawings by Roger Dean.

Made in the USA
Coppell, TX
25 January 2020

14981706R00146